THE YEARS OF LIVING
DANGEROUSLY

For all the partners and staff of The Sandwich Club
in Hong Kong, one of the real 'Asian Miracles'

THE YEARS OF LIVING
DANGEROUSLY

*Asia – From Financial Crisis
to the New Millennium*

STEPHEN VINES

ORION BUSINESS
BOOKS

First published in Great Britain in 1999 by
Orion Business
An imprint of The Orion Publishing Group Ltd
Orion House, 5 Upper St Martin's Lane, London WC2H 9EA

A CIP catalogue record for this book is available
from the British Library.

ISBN 0 75282 072 9

Designed by Staziker Jones, Cardiff
Typeset at The Spartan Press Ltd, Lymington, Hants
Printed and bound in Great Britain by
MPG Books Ltd, Bodmin, Cornwall

CONTENTS

PREFACE

Well-meaning friends urged me to hurry up and complete this book. They were worried that, if I did not, the Asian financial crisis might sink into quickly forgotten history. I did not share their concerns. For a start it was far too big a crisis to sink without trace. Moreover, there was so much about this crisis that remained to be written about and could come to light only after a decent period of time had elapsed.

Perhaps more importantly, it was clear to me that the financial crisis was a reflection of a more fundamental crisis of Asian business which remains unresolved.

This book, therefore, is about something more than history: it deals with a present that is, perhaps, as ominous as what happened when the financial markets ran riot in 1997 and 1998.

When they did so governments were brought down, companies collapsed, millions of people were forced out of work, while others were sent into penury as the crisis spread like wildfire across the Asian region and beyond. By the time the crisis had run its course some $1,000 billion in incomes had been lost, according to Joseph Stiglitz, the chief economist at the World Bank.[1]

I set out, maybe with excessive ambition, to write a book that would answer all the questions likely to be lingering in an intelligent reader's mind when contemplating the Asian crisis and what comes next.

Statistics tell one part of the story; the debate about ideas tells another; a look at Asian business practices provides yet another part of the picture. Trying to put the whole picture into a historical context also helps answer questions.

The advantage of waiting a little before bursting into print is that it took time for vital data about the crisis to come trundling out. It is now easier to look back on what happened since the decision to devalue the Thai baht was taken on 2 July 1997, setting in motion the events that turned the 'Asian Miracle' into the 'Asian Nightmare'.

This book tries to make sense about what happened, to explain how the crisis occurred, why it was so devastating, but, more importantly what were and are the underlying forces that gave birth to the crisis and remain in place ready to cause more chaos, or at least more problems.

I also hope to give some flavour of the crisis times and of what it is like doing business in Asia. A dish without flavouring is inevitably dull. Some of the flavour is derived from my personal involvement in this region, which has been my home for almost a decade and a half.

Because of my personal experience, I approach some of the issues from an angle that is somewhat different from that chosen by other writers who, as journalists, are covering business matters in Asia. I lead a curious and hybrid existence as a journalist and businessman. 'You better bloody well decide whether you are a businessman or a journalist', one angry company executive shouted at me after I had written some uncomplimentary things about the management of his company. I thought about this and decided that it was a decision I need not take because it seems to me that you actually get a better perspective on business management by getting your hands dirty and being involved in business rather than merely writing about it.

My businesses are in the food and catering industry, not a sector for making a quick buck, especially in the highly competitive environment of Hong Kong where they are located. However, it is a business I think I understand and a business that constantly teaches me new lessons. It also provides an important reality check. Every time I hear about grand plans for economic reform, fiscal reform and the like, it does no harm to consider how this can possibly pan out at ground level.

This is why so much of this book is taken up with the problems of corporate management in Asia. Economies do not emerge from the ether: they are made up of component parts, such as businesses, which determine the direction they take. Looking at component parts is often more rewarding than looking at the whole if you want to understand what is really happening.

So, I cannot claim to be a clinical, neutral observer, I live here in Hong Kong by choice, not force of circumstance. Like all people who have formed strong attachments to where they live, I get angry when the things I have become attached to are undermined by bureaucrats, politicians and businessmen. You will find hints of this anger in these pages, alongside hints of the admiration I have for the people whom I live among and work with. By all means make allowance for this lack of objectivity but do not expect me to apologise for it.

Some authors are faced with the problem of a paucity of data about their subject – this was not the problem here. There is a great mountain of data. The trick is to make sense of this data and to get some of the figures to yield the information required to put all these facts into some kind of perspective.

The more you read, the more you talk to Asian businessmen, the more you discover that much that has been written about the so-called 'Asian Miracle' is way off the mark; moreover, there is statistical data to demonstrate that this is so.

In looking at this data I often started with a hunch and then followed up on the hunch in the hope that it would shed some light on what was happening. In some cases the hunch proved wrong. In others it proved right. I had, for example, always suspected that not only were Asian financial markets becoming increasingly detached from Asia's real economy but that they were not contributing much to the development of these economies. Chapter 5 considers the evidence that shows how little these markets have contributed to corporate development. Elsewhere, in Chapter 8, one of the great crisis myths is examined, namely that foreigners were mainly responsible for the big capital movements that characterised the crisis. It is more than likely that the reverse is true and that the bulk of the capital outflow from Asia came from domestic sources.

The central thesis of this book is that underlying the financial crisis is a more profound and unresolved corporate crisis in Asia. East Asia, where the crisis began, is stuffed full of badly run companies which grew in the asset bubble that developed before the crisis broke. When it burst some companies disappeared, but others survived, albeit in poor shape.

Once, not so long ago, books and articles were being written about the coming of the Pacific Century. It was confidently predicted that the economies of Asia and the companies of Asia would soon be assuming world leadership. These assertions were derived from an extraordinary paucity of analysis. The crisis helped expose some of the myths, but they still linger.

I have tried to explain why most of these predictions are no more than illusion. The blunt fact of the matter is that Asia is severely deficient in world-class companies. Without the presence of globally competitive companies Asia (outside Japan) is struggling to maintain globally competitive economies. There is no reason why this situation will not change sometime in the future but the very structure of corporate Asia as presently constituted represents a severe restraint on the development of the kind of companies that can assume global leadership. Chapters 4, 5 and 6 look at this issue in some detail – they may be considered to be the heart of this book.

The simple proposition I have advanced is that financial crises do not kill off good companies or seriously weaken sound economies, even though they may be battered by forces well beyond their control. It does not require a Masters in Business Administration to grasp this obvious point, but it was *not* grasped for the simple reason that so many people were and remain in denial. Instead of acknowledging the shambles that characterises Asian corporate structures, they have lavished praise on the entrepreneurship and agility of these companies. This is a dangerous illusion.

It is even more dangerous because it demonstrates a stubborn refusal to learn from history and to see that the crisis had the effect it had precisely because it swept down on badly run companies and economies suffering from serious structural weaknesses.

Chapter 7 examines some of the governmental and private-sector responses to the crisis; only a determined optimist would garner much comfort from this. Chapter 8 considers why the problems identified earlier are laying the ground for a new crisis.

Others have written at length about great global plans for a new financial architecture. I am not very impressed with all this and give the matter less space than this debate has been given elsewhere – the reason being is that I am confident that these ideas will quickly fade and be replaced by more incremental, less ambitious solutions.

Chapter 1 looks at what the pundits said before the crisis. It will, no doubt, win few friends in influential places. Chapter 3, which looks at the great Asian-values debate, will probably serve to knock my name off even more invitation lists. So be it – there are worse things in life.

Although the general tenor of the book may be seen as highly critical of conventional wisdom about Asian businesses and even more critical of the assumptions that underpinned the 'Asian Miracle', it is not the intention to throw the baby out with the bathwater. There have been some phenomenal achievements in Asian economies, achievements that will survive the crisis. Chapters 2 and 9 consider these matters.

The focus of this book is the eight Asian Miracle economies. That is to say the four tiger economies of Hong Kong, South Korea, Singapore and

Taiwan, alongside the four tiger cubs: Indonesia, Malaysia, the Philippines and Thailand. They were collectively known as Asia's high-growth economies and formed the heart of the Miracle and the heart of the crisis.

Of course it is hard to talk about Asia without paying some attention to Japan, which plays such a dominant role in the region and has problems of its own, which impacted on the Crisis Eight. However, Japan's role in the region has been well documented by others and is given only passing treatment here. I have paid even less attention to China, which casts a big shadow, but, as the crisis showed, it was not big enough really to affect what was happening in the rest of Asia. If China sneezes there is no doubt that Hong Kong will catch the flu, but elsewhere in the region the contagion is likely to be limited. Therefore, China looms in the background but I have left it to others to elaborate on this matter.

So much, then, for what this book is about. I would now like to mention a few details which should be helpful to readers. All monetary figures are given in United States dollars, to facilitate comparisons.

There is no standard way of rendering many Asian names in English: for example, the Chinese of China, Hong Kong and Taiwan, all use different systems for transliteration. Therefore I have opted for the pragmatic solution of rendering the names of people and companies in the manner that they are likely to be best known to English-language readers. I realise that this gives rise to inconsistencies but I hope that is compensated for by greater accessibility.

As far as endnotes are concerned, I have followed the practice of referring only to written sources. Information gathered by oral means or from sources (such as speeches) that are hard to trace is, generally speaking, indicated in the text.

I would like to acknowledge the tremendous amount of help I have received in writing this book. It has come from many people, some of whom are not mentioned here but all of whom have been generous in contributing to this work. I am extremely grateful for their assistance. I can think of no more imaginative or satisfactory way of listing those who have helped, other than in alphabetical order. So here we go:

Thanks are due to Graham Barrett, the external adviser to the World Bank for the East Asia and Pacific Region, for help with supplying valuable World Bank data; to Jean Chen in Taipei, who knows a great deal about business and the economy of Taiwan and is always helpful in sharing her knowledge; to Peter Churchouse, the managing director of Morgan Stanley Dean Witter in Hong Kong, who kept me supplied with a constant flow of incisive economic and market-related research reports; to Chad

Hansen, who holds the chair of Chinese Philosophy at Hong Kong University, for clearing up some of my confusion about Confucius and generally contributing a great deal to Chapter 3; to Jeremy Kidner, the managing director of Intelligence Asia, who, at an early stage, helped me develop some ideas on Asian management practices and offered sound advice; to Martin Liu from Orion Books, who has supported and provided enormous enthusiasm for this project from day one; to Catherine Ong and other colleagues at *Business Times* in Singapore, who were, as ever, both extremely knowledgeable and helpful on Singapore-related matters; to Stephen Proctor, at Morgan Stanley Dean Witter in Hong Kong, who found bits of data that I could not unearth; to Philip Segal, the Hong Kong correspondent of the *International Herald Tribune*, who has a special interest in corruption in Asia and gave me valuable advice for Chapter 6; to Dianne Stormont, who knows a lot about computers and helped me out a great deal in this department, not to mention finding bits of information that were elusive. Last, but not at all least, I wish to put on record that a great deal of the research for this book was undertaken at the library of the Hong Kong University of Science and Technology, an extraordinarily good library whose staff routinely went well beyond the call of duty in providing all manner of help.

Despite all this assistance, no doubt errors remain and oversights have been made. I bear full responsibility

Stephen Vines
Hong Kong, November 1999

INTRODUCTION

There is a moment when abstract knowledge becomes uncomfortably real. Such a moment came to me in the summer of 1998, a full year after the Asian financial crisis had begun its sweep across the continent.

As a journalist I had been writing about the steady erosion of the so-called 'Asian Miracle' since 2 July 1997, the day the Thai government took the fateful decision to devalue the local currency and set in motion the bursting of the great Asian bubble. But it was in my other capacity, as a businessman, that I came to understand what was really happening when I had to interview some candidates for a management post in my company. I will describe what happened shortly, but first we need to step back a moment and look very briefly at the period before the crisis broke.

In the years before 1997 I was among those who took the view that the East Asian economies were overheating and would need to cool down. I claim no prescience here: this view was common. Some of us thought that there would be a short sharp period of adjustment and that the wheel of fortune would bounce back up, carrying the Asian economies to greater heights.

However, my eye was off the ball in early 1997 because, being based in Hong Kong, I was heavily focused on that other big historical event: the end of British colonial rule and the reversion of the colony to China. I cannot honestly say that if I had been watching more closely I would have been able to see the sheer scale of disaster that was looming.

Anyway, I did not, and like many others watched in some amazement as the cards began to tumble, first in Thailand, then Indonesia, then Malaysia, followed by the always shaky Philippines. By October South

Korea joined the collapse with some vigour. Even prosperous Singapore found it was affected by the virus and, perhaps more surprising, although not known at the time, ludicrously rich Brunei, awash with cash from oil and gas, started to feel the strain. Hong Kong, which thought it was somehow immune, witnessed a wipe-out in the share market at the end of October, knocking nearly a quarter off the market's capitalisation.

The financial crisis galvanised the International Monetary Fund (IMF) into what may be described as the biggest collective corporate bail-out in history. By the time it had finished $17.2 billion had been handed over to Thailand, Indonesia was promised $43 billion and South Korea negotiated the IMF's biggest ever loan package of $57 billion. Later we shall see how the IMF's actions became a part of the problem, albeit not to the extent claimed by some critics.

As I followed this implosion I felt myself to be drowning in a sea of figures. The figures gave way to charts which showed the familiar curve of the roller coaster but not quite, because those drawing the charts had to readjust the parameters to allow the line going down to travel further than was previously thought possible.

Although this mass of data was pretty alarming it was somehow unreal. To some extent I was sheltered by living in Hong Kong, where the state of denial was much stronger than elsewhere in the region. Sir Donald Tsang, Hong Kong's Financial Secretary, was among the more forceful performers in the Great Denial Show. He would regularly trot out in front of the microphones to assure anyone prepared to listen that 'Hong Kong's fundamentals remain sound'. He even believed that the whole crisis would blow over by Christmas 1997. As things turned out, not only did the crisis not blow over but, especially for Hong Kong, it turned far more nasty.

Hiring a manager

Even at the time Sir Donald's predictions seemed little short of daft but little else was clear. I knew, or thought I knew, all about the theory of what was happening but as 1997 gave way to 1998 my business, which is mainly involved in contract catering, was in the happy position of being able to expand. So I did not feel beleaguered. Of course I was worried, but the worry was somewhat intellectual.

Concern moved from the intellectual plane to a more gut feeling when, in the summer of 1998, I started interviewing candidates for a manager's job. Staff shortages and lack of skills have plagued the Hong Kong catering industry ever since I became involved in it. An advertisement for a manager usually produced a meagre crop of responses. Not on this occasion. We were flooded by applications. Moreover, they came from very well-qualified people. The overwhelming majority were facing both a pay cut and a loss of status by coming to work for my company.

It is always awkward to offer jobs to overqualified people but I thought that the least I could do was to see some of them. A number had been laid off by joint-venture hotel projects in China (where, so we were told, economic growth remained buoyant); others were victims of what is euphemistically called downsizing in large corporations; a few had had their own smaller businesses, which went under. Without exception these candidates were willing to take the job on offer and – here's the crucial point – stick with it because they were digging in for a long recession and saw any form of employment as better than none at all.

In other words these job candidates were clear-headed, hard-working people, quite prepared to do whatever it took to keep afloat. There is not much of a social-security safety net in Hong Kong and even if there were, these were the sorts of people who would be reluctant to use it. Before meeting them I had shared the lingering illusion that all this bad economic news was about to dissolve or, at worst, maybe linger for not too much longer.

They, on the other hand, knew that this was not the case. Speaking to them I got a real sense of people who had formulated survival tactics. This was all the more impressive because most of the would-be managers had spent their working lives in an environment where growth was taken for granted and where unemployment was barely a feature. Having left Britain over a decade ago, where unemployment cast a constant shadow over large parts of the country, I could not help but marvel that this threat was of so little consequence in my new home.

In Hong Kong I was living among people who are mainly either immigrants or from families who have emigrated to Hong Kong within recent memory. This has created an unusual community, one that is particularly focused on self-improvement and the achievement of economic security. Coming from an immigrant background myself, I notice that people who have shifted themselves from one place to another, either to escape some form of persecution or in search of a more prosperous life, have an uncanny sense of vulnerability. There must be something of a folk memory which flashes alert signals and equips these hard-working people with the means to cope with the worst.

I cannot be sure to what extent this spirit of determination is at work elsewhere in Asia but there is enough anecdotal and concrete evidence to show that this is not a region where people will passively accept a slide into recession without fighting back. I can think of no East Asian country devoid of examples of people who are making short-term sacrifices to secure the longer-term goal of economic prosperity.

One of the best-publicised and most interesting examples comes from Thailand in the shape of Sirivat Voravetvuthikun, who became something of a media star for his determination to claw back the massive losses he made when the Thai financial system started sinking. Mr Sirivat is interesting because his story also reflects a career in the kind of bubble-economy world that produced the Asian financial crisis. He first shot to fame after the 1987 Black Monday global stock-market collapse. Mr Sirivat was then the chief executive of Asia Securities Trading plc, a prominent Bangkok stockbroking company. While others were fleeing the stock market he shrewdly jumped in and bought shares. He was one of the bright, youngish men in shiny suits making easy money and not at all embarrassed to tell everyone how well he was doing. 'I helped Asia Securities make about two hundred million baht [then over $5 million] profit from its portfolio investment that year,' Mr Sirivat recalled.

After parting company with Asia Securities he decided to jump aboard the bandwagon that was taking the property market into the outer stratosphere. In 1994, alongside his brother, he launched a multimillion-pound luxury-condominium project at Khao Yai, northeast of Bangkok. The two brothers borrowed heavily from banks who were all too anxious to fund projects aimed at Thailand's nouveau riche. However, the project never took off. After four years of hard selling over 70 per cent of the units remained without takers.

By 1996 the fizz had gone out of the property market. Corporate debt was rising everywhere and, after the July 1997 decision to devalue the local currency, the government went further and started tackling the debt problem. Mr Sirivat said, 'I knew I was irrevocably broke the day the central bank closed down fifty-six finance companies.' He was right. The banks quickly shut down his business and he was left with a mountain of debt.

He paused for breath, considered his options and decided he just had to get back into business. He decided to do so by starting an enterprise selling sandwiches, a low-capital-investment option (I am prejudiced in favour of

Mr Sirivat because my first business involved selling sandwiches but, unlike him, I did not need literally to stand in the street flogging my wares).

He does not think that the sandwich business will take him back to where he was before the crisis erupted but hopes that some of his creditors will roll over the sums he owes, providing a breathing space to prepare for a return to the financial markets ready for what he, and all the other Asian optimists, view as the inevitable market upturn.

'My ambition', he said, 'is to be known as Mr Sandwich, the same way you go to McDonald's for hamburgers and visit KFC when you crave for fried chicken. One day when you think of sandwich, you would think of Sirivat.' That's Asian optimism for you.

Mr Sirivat could be viewed as a typical example of Asian hubris or, more accurately in my eyes, as one of the many people whose sheer hard work and dogged determination to succeed will ensure that Asia gets back on its feet. The cause of the crisis was not a lack of people prepared to work, nor a lack of markets for their goods (although overproduction played a part). No, it was much more a problem of bad, voracious management which squandered the efforts of these hard-working people and diverted investment that could have been devoted to productive use. Moreover, as I will argue later in this book, there is a fundamental problem of structurally bad management which is limiting the growth of Asian companies and, at times of crisis, is poorly equipped to offer solutions.

Counting the cost

There are many ways of looking at the crash of '97. Most are quantifiable and readily so when it comes to examining the carnage in the financial markets themselves. Twelve months after the June devaluation of the Thai baht it had lost 42 per cent of its value. The Malaysian ringgit fell by 37 per cent. This was nothing compared with the 84 per cent fall in the value of the Indonesian rupiah, which brought its largely foreign-denominated national debt up to a level where it accounted for 192 per cent of gross domestic product (GDP). According to Dr Mahathir Mohamad, the Prime Minister of Malaysia, the depreciations wiped some $200 billion off the wealth of Southeast Asian nations.[1] He saw the currency falls as part of a large, ill-defined foreign plot, but Dr Mahathir has tended to view the entire crisis in these terms. As we shall see later, this explanation of how the crisis occurred was well received in some circles, even though it was wide of the mark.

In the regional stock markets, where the wipe-out was quickest to take effect, market capitalisation fell even more rapidly than the value of currencies. A year after the crisis broke out (i.e. by the end of June 1998) most regional markets had lost well over half their value. In Indonesia the Jakarta stock exchange saw capitalisation tumble by 88 per cent, leaving the entire stock market capitalised at just $12.44 billion. In other words the combined value of all shares in the Indonesian market were worth around a sixth of capitalisation of a company such as HSBC Holdings, the previously Hong Kong-based banking group that now has a primary listing in London and owns banks on four continents.

The picture was not much brighter in Malaysia where market capitalisation plummeted by over 74 per cent, ending up at $75.28 billion, just about enough to buy out the stock of HSBC but leaving no small change.

In Seoul the market's value was down almost 71 per cent, leaving the entire stock exchange capitalised at just $45.64 billion. The Korean exchange is the only one of the 'Tiger' stock markets that hosts a clutch of domestically nurtured international conglomerates or *chaebols*, such as Daewoo, Hyundai and Goldstar. In 1994 the top ten *chaebols*, had net assets and additional investments valued at around $37 billion, which meant that alone they were valued at the level at which the entire stock exchange could have been bought some four years later.[2] Individual companies found their share prices plunge to an extent that made a total nonsense of the value of the assets they owned. Korean Air, for example, saw its share price drop to a level where the capitalisation of the entire company equalled the price of some three jumbo jets. This was at a time when the airline had around sixty jumbo jets in its fleet.

In Thailand, where the troubles started, the market fell less dramatically but still ended the twelve-month period with a loss of over 63 per cent.[3]

According to the World Bank $400 billion was wiped off equity values in East Asia during the first twelve months of the crisis.[4] To put that figure in some kind of global perspective, it is equivalent to almost twice the level of all private-capital flows to developing countries in 1996 ($265 billion).[5]

Taking a twelve-month view of what happened in the markets rather disguises the even greater volatility that took place on a micro level. On single days markets moved by over 10 per cent. Considering that in Europe and the United States single-day movements of 1–2 per cent are regarded as significant, this level of volatility is enormous. Individual shares gyrated even more violently, some lurching so wildly out of control that they quickly found themselves on the suspended list. And, as the level of volatility deepened and big-league foreign investors were scared off, volumes in the stock markets started to tumble, which in turn made the markets even more volatile because quite small purchases of stocks had the ability to change prices significantly.

Meanwhile, out in the real economy where products and services are bought and sold, the effect on economic growth was slower to register. However, the dread word 'recession' quickly became a reality. In pre-crisis East Asia economic growth was taken as a given – indeed it was at levels far higher than had been seen at any period of history. Between 1965 and 1990 the twenty-three East Asian economies were growing by an average of over 5 per cent per year. Japan started the ball rolling, but most of the growth was focused among just eight countries – the four tigers of Hong Kong, South Korea, Singapore and Taiwan, and the tiger cubs: Indonesia, Malaysia, Thailand and the Philippines. These countries saw annual growth rates soaring into double digits, even in the late to middle 1990s and were still well above the 5 per cent level by 1997. By 1998 every one of these eight countries (with the exception of Taiwan) was showing negative economic growth and had fulfilled the normally accepted definition of recession by registering negative growth records in two successive quarters.

Looked at in US dollar terms the crisis had an even more severe impact on per-capita GDP. Estimates prepared by the US-based investment house Goldman, Sachs & Co. show that, from 1997 to 1998, per-capita GDP in, for example, Indonesia fell by a massive two-thirds to $391. This was the level it stood at three decades ago. In Thailand per-capita GDP was down by over a quarter and even in Singapore it slumped by over 15 per cent, albeit to a still respectable level of $26,377.

The social and political costs

Aside from the obvious economic consequences of East Asia's abrupt reversal of economic fortune, the social and political consequences were arguably even greater. The International Labour Organisation (ILO) produced a report in April 1998 which argued that two decades of poverty reduction in Asia was about to be reversed by the financial crisis.[7] The report stated that 'in the absence of unemployment benefits and social assistance this inflicts severe economic hardship, way above that suggested by the fall in GDP, on job losses and new job seekers'.

Unemployment, which had already been high in some of these countries – notably Indonesia, owing to the uneven spread of economic development – soared to new heights. In September 1998 the ILO forecast that some 10 million East Asian workers would loose their jobs as a result of the crisis.[8] Worst affected was Indonesia, where unemployment rose quickly into double-digit figures. Even in relatively prosperous places such as Hong Kong unemployment shot up to over 5 per cent. In some countries, notably Thailand, this coincided with sharp rises in inflation, making the poor even more poverty-stricken.

I have travelled around the region fairly extensively since the outbreak of the crisis and been struck by the impact of the malaise, which started in the banking systems of the capital cities, and, although they are far removed from the rural areas, it quickly reached into these areas, too. Despite all the talk of industrialisation and export-led growth, the bulk of the people in the region remain rurally based and dependent on agriculture and natural resources for their livelihood.

In September 1997 I went to the island of Mindanao, in the southern Philippines, which, in addition to extreme poverty, is plagued by separatist conflicts. In small villages people were talking about how the credit squeeze emanating from Manila was crippling their ability to obtain cash for basic amenities, such as a fresh water supply and, even more exotic, in their eyes, electricity, which would have provided the means to lift them out of the survival-level mode of agriculture and up to a more comfortable standard.

When the East Asian economies were roaring there was a consistent and accelerating drift from the rural areas to the towns offering employment in the new export-generating industries. As many of these companies went under, the drift reversed, but those returning to the rural areas were faced with exactly the same levels of poverty they had sought to escape, and so the towns increasingly became filled with a jobless, dispossessed stratum of people desperate to make a living and willing to turn to nonlegitimate means to achieve this end.

No one emerged unscathed from the economic meltdown. In the traditions of gallows humour people throughout the region sought to make light of their troubles and deal with the uncomfortable reality by joking about it. In Korea, for example, many retailers and food outlets began offering 'IMF Specials', in other words cheap deals named in honour of the IMF bail-out. In Thailand I found that a surprising number of people who barely spoke English had learned the word 'recession' and were making jokes about recessionary times.

Understandably the malaise in the economy had a rapid impact on politics. Since the start of the crisis three of the eight countries (Japan, Korea and Thailand) have had a change of government inspired by economic pressures but undertaken by constitutional means. The new governments all swept to office on promises of taking firm action to curb the economic decline. In Thailand the voters unambiguously punished the outgoing Chavalit government for what was widely seen as the corruption and cronyism that exacerbated the crisis.

Far more severe punishment for corrupt practices was to be seen in Indonesia and Malaysia, which experienced tremendous political unrest resulting, in the case of Indonesia, in the downfall of the three-decade-long dictatorship of President Suharto in 1998. In Malaysia the unrest has provided the most serious challenge since independence to the ruling party UMNO but, at the time of writing, has not resulted in a change of government.

In Hong Kong there was also a change of government, brought about by the resumption of Chinese sovereignty, but this was unrelated to the crisis.

On the other hand the ruling parties in Taiwan and Singapore have, if anything, been strengthened by the crisis. They have achieved this by asserting that they are a force for stability in uncertain times. In Taiwan the ruling Kuomintang has nevertheless been forced into a more reformist position than it might otherwise have planned. The same can be said of the authoritarian People's Action Party in Singapore, which has initiated a slew of economic reforms while keeping the mechanisms of political control unchanged.

It is still too early to say whether the meltdown of 1997 started a real political and social revolution in East Asia but a clearer picture of how the meltdown came about is now emerging and it seems that understanding the causes provides considerable help in identifying the remedies.

The debt problem turns nasty

The trigger that sent the markets tumbling was a panic about loans to commercial companies whose ability to repay them was questionable. The global investment community had previously thought in terms of shaky sovereign debt triggering financial crises, the most recent example being the Mexican crisis of 1995. In East Asia sovereign debt was relatively low, whereas reckless lending to commercial entities produced a mountain of bad or potentially bad debt. At the beginning of 1999 the Deutsche Bank estimated that the collective bad debts for Indonesia, Malaysia, Philippines, South Korea and Thailand amounted to $250 billion. If China and Taiwan were added in, the figure rose to $600 billion. In Japan alone banks were holding bad debts of $600 billion.

According to the American economist Jeffrey Sachs of Harvard University, commercial banks had poured $65 billion into emerging Asian markets in 1996 and withdrawn $25 billion the following year and $35 billion in 1998.[6] In other words, in the space of just two years the banks had withdrawn almost all the money they had funnelled into these markets in the year prior to the crash.

Who's to blame?

It is only slightly exaggerated to say that a mini-industry has emerged devoted to the business of identifying the causes of the Asian financial crisis. I will attempt to identify some of the main arguments made and positions adopted by this new industry and then offer what seems to me to be a realistic explanation for what happened.

Paul Krugman, an American academic at the Massachusetts Institute of Technology who has extensively studied Asian economies, has developed an explanation which has found considerable favour in the West and rather less favour in Asia.[9] Dr Krugman believes that the roots of the crisis are to be found internally as a result of bad local investments and a concentration of funds flowing into areas such as property and the stock market, which yielded little in foreign-exchange earnings. The misdirection of investment, in his view, was compounded by problems of corruption, crony capitalism, low levels of regulation and inadequate professional supervision over businesses.

The other major American 'guru' of Asian economic studies is Jeffrey Sachs, cited above. He also acts as an adviser to many companies and governments, particularly in East Asia. Unsurprisingly, he is less prone to blame the victims of the crisis for being its cause, and, equally unsurprisingly, has offered explanations that find a more receptive audience in Asia. Dr Sachs's attention is directed towards the ruthless behaviour of the international fund managers who invested in East Asian markets. He sees them as having succumbed to the herd instinct that caused mass panic and an irresponsible flight from investments that were fundamentally sound.[10]

Let's all blame the ghastly foreigners

The Sachs view, in a more exaggerated form, has been enthusiastically adopted by Dr Mahathir Mohamad, the Malaysian premier and leading advocate of the theory of a conspiracy against East Asia. In a barnstorming speech to a World Bank seminar, held at the Bank's annual meeting in Hong Kong on 20 September 1997, Dr Mahathir set out the basis of a theory which he later developed as a trademark view of the crisis.[11]

'There may be no conspiracy as such,' he said, 'but it is quite obvious that a few at least, media, as well as fund managers, have their own agenda, which they are determined to carry out.'

Plunging into irony, Dr Mahathir explained how the East Asian economies grew by 'toil and sweat'. 'Disobedient, recalcitrant and at times impudent, these upstarts, Malaysia in particular, had the temerity to aim higher than the developed countries, the powerful, the movers and shakers of the world. All along,' he said, 'we had tried to comply with the wishes of the rich and mighty. We have opened up our market, including our share and capital markets. On the other hand, most foreign companies operating in our country do not allow foreign participation. They are not open, but we have not complained.'

According to Dr Mahathir the East Asian economies were being punished for being too successful and too ambitious. Moreover, they had become pawns in the global money game where 'the trade in currency is actually twenty times bigger than real trade in goods and services . . .

Unfortunately their profits come from impoverishing others, including very poor countries and poor people. Southeast Asian countries have become their target simply because we have the money but not enough to defend ourselves.'

I watched Dr Mahathir make this speech to a large assembly of bankers, fund managers and the like – the very people he was attacking. They listened attentively, applauded loudly. Had they gone quite mad? Not quite, because when the Prime Minister later moved from words to actions and froze international trading in the Malaysian ringgit – curtailing the ability of foreign investors to trade on the local stock market and severely restricting the movement of capital – they rushed for the exit. But back in September 1997 the crisis had only started gathering steam and many of those paying homage to Dr Mahathir thought the problems would soon blow over.

It was as if they had all been to obedience lessons teaching them to sit quietly while being lectured by all manner of tinpot dictators, dubious politicians and even more dubious businessmen who either held the keys to the doors of political power or, at least, were perceived as being the keyholders. They believed that these people could throw open the doors and reveal untold economic riches. The smartly attired assembly that day suspended the belief they held in democratic institutions back home. They believed that water flowed in another direction once they got to Asia and so they had to go with the flow. What I witnessed in that hall of the Hong Kong Convention Centre was probably the last of the mass homage making to one of those at the centre of the crisis. It was a stupid affair yet typical of the last days in which belief was suspended while the Asian miracle show played its sunset performances to dwindling audiences.

Among those sitting listening to Dr Mahathir's rant were some high-ranking hedge-fund managers, the people who became the *bête noire* of the crisis. It was said by many, including the Malaysian premier, but also by supposedly less excitable people, such as Joseph Yam, the head of the Hong Kong Monetary Authority, the territory's central bank, that the hedge funds had run riot across Asia making hay out of the region's misfortunes and accelerating them by placing large bets on currency and stock-market falls, bets that became self-fulfilling prophecies. 'The essence of the problem', said Mr Yam, 'is in the highly leveraged and very large hedge-fund flows that move around the world rapidly and without any regulation. They are subject to no disclosure rules. They dart from market to market, seizing on weaknesses and contradictions, particularly in the smaller, more malleable markets that are frequently carried away by euphoria or panic. By distorting or manipulating markets in search of profits they are capable of throwing many smaller, vulnerable economies into chaos.'[12]

The idea of blaming the crisis on shadowy fund managers, mainly operating out of the United States, was attractive. For a start it appealed to the latent feelings of xenophobia that easily come to the surface at times of crisis. Secondly, it is always attractive to have a sinister enemy who can be depicted as lurking in the shadows ready to pounce on the defenseless. Thirdly, it is helpful to depict the enemy as being mega-rich and somehow cold and clinical in the way it operates. Who better than hedge-fund managers to be the bogeymen? The problem is that there is no empirical evidence to support this theory. On the contrary, such empirical evidence as exists rather suggests that the role of hedge funds was minimal.

A group of American academics looked at the positions the ten largest international currency funds held in the Malaysian ringgit and a basket of other Asian currencies and found that those positions fluctuated dramatically over the preceding four years but were not associated with changes in exchange rates. During the crash period, the positions of the funds were similar to those in the preceding period. Therefore the study concludes that it is impossible to find evidence that these large funds were responsible for the crisis.[13]

Let's all blame the awful people in Washington

It seems therefore that the so-called evidence about hedge funds causing the crisis is lacking foundation. But what about another attractive bogeyman, which appeared in the shape of the very institution that was supposed to be coming to the rescue of the failing economies: the International Monetary Fund? This subject will be discussed more thoroughly later. For the time being we will merely outline the case made for the fund's role in causing the crisis. It was argued that the remedies it applied were actually causing the patient's state of health to deteriorate. Influential critics lined up to castigate the fund for its mismanagement of the crisis. Among the most influential was Henry Kissinger, the former US Secretary of State, who accused the IMF of blundering into action and promoting political instability. In October 1998 he wrote that, 'in the name of free market orthodoxy it usually attempts to remove all at once every economic weakness in the economic system of the affected country, regardless of whether these caused the crisis or not'.[14]

The fund was charged with applying remedies that were not suited to the problems and with insisting on fiscal belt-tightening measures that came close to strangling the patient. However, no one went so far as actually to accuse the IMF of causing the crisis: it merely stood charged with having exacerbated it.

Why not blame the Japanese?

Another tempting target for attributing blame was Asia's largest economy. There is a widely held notion that the Japanese government was responsible for both causing the crisis and lacking the resolve to tackle the consequences of its actions, which in turn exacerbated the problem.

The Nobel economics laureate Merton Miller, from Chicago University, for example, stated that Japan was responsible for the underlying cause of the crisis by allowing its currency to devalue rapidly against the US dollar after the domestic economy's downturn stated in the early 1990s. Japan, it is alleged, tried to export its way out of a half-decade-long recession.[16] Not only was the yen declining in value but it had become a highly volatile currency. In 1995 it was trading at around 80 yen to the US dollar; by the end of 1997 it had risen to a level of 130 yen. Some observers believe that this is an unprecedented movement for a major currency within this kind of time frame.

Japan was the main investor in the region – it was also one of the main consumers of the region's products and one of the biggest exporters to East Asia – so it played a disproportionate role in the economics of the area. As the crisis spread there was a chorus of calls for Japan to do more to reflate its economy and reform its financial system so that it would again be an engine of demand for the region and its fiscal sector would contribute to financial restructuring by shaking some of the mountain of bad debt out of the market.

Not only was the value of the Japanese yen sliding but Japanese interest rates, especially in the early to mid-1990s, were very low. In part rates were low because the G-7 states prevailed on the Japanese to lower them as a means of reducing Japan's massive trade surplus with the West. At a famous meeting in New York's Plaza Hotel in 1985, the leaders of the world's biggest economies decided that the best way of ensuring economic stability was to engineer a weakening of the American dollar and thus shrink Japan's trade surplus with the US, which was then standing at $40 billion, a figure that looked high then but was easily overtaken in the years that followed. The so-called Plaza Accord was a failure, but instead of taking lessons from this failure, two years later, Japan was persuaded that what it needed to do was to reduce its interest rates. This pledge was incorporated in the Louvre Accord of 1987. The effect of this was to make the yen an attractive source of international borrowing, which resulted in the Japanese currency steadily gaining value. In theory it should have discouraged Japanese exports and made imports more attractively priced, but this was not what happened.

The funds start flowing

The whole approach was muddle-headed and it resulted in both an enormous export of capital by Japanese companies and a mass of yen borrowing by foreign money managers who promptly invested the proceeds in US-dollar-denominated instruments where yields were far higher. Attractive yields were most easily found in emerging markets and US corporate debt. Borrowing cheaply and investing in high-yielding instruments proved to be pretty much a no brainier way of making money but was also a classic form of bubble investment waiting to burst as soon as yields dropped – or worse, as happened, the borrowers defaulted. Once the defaults and threatened defaults started it had an immediate effect on those providing the loans. First, the value of the loaner's assets plunged; second, they had to cover their positions in Japanese yen to prevent themselves defaulting and so there was a big sell-down of assets, which gathered avalanche force as even those with relatively strong positions in the markets started to fear that the sell-off would damage their invest-ments; and so they clamoured to sell, fearing that if they did not do so they would be left at the bottom of the market.

Usually, big-scale sellers face the problem of finding a satisfactory new home for their money. However, in the pre-crash period this problem was diminished by the extraordinary strength of the American financial markets, which both had the capacity to absorb funds flowing out of

Asia and were in a position to offer growth for investments heading their way. Some funds, however, were designated as dealing only in Asian equities and were constitutionally not allowed to have the majority of their assets outside the region. This proved to be a real problem and led, in extreme cases, to the merging or winding up of certain funds and in others to a flight to cash which might have breached their mandates but kept their performance records from dissolving.

So, *that's* what globalisation entailed

When the foreign fund managers started pouring money into Asia in the late 1980s and early 1990s they were welcomed with open arms as canny investors, but when they poured money out they were depicted as being ruthless speculators. Asian markets desperately wanted to attract foreign funds, which was why they were welcome in the first place. The Malaysians, who emerged as the most vocal critics of foreign speculation, went so far as to create an offshore centre precisely for this purpose in the tiny island of Labuan, off the Borneo coast. Incidentally, Malaysia's central bank was a very active participant in highly leveraged currency plays in the early part of the 1990s. The problem was that it usually blundered in its investments and lost impressive sums of money. 'Oh, how we miss them,' a money manager in a Hong Kong fund said to me. 'To make money you have to have a fellow on the other side who's willing to take your bets.'

Hong Kong and Singapore went much further than Malaysia and put out their stalls as regional financial centres. When the going got tough Singapore, to the government's credit, rode the waves without complaining about the consequences of globalisation, which it had sought to encourage. Over in Hong Kong the administration let out a wail of complaint about how it was subject to international speculative pressures. The panicky people who run that administration went further than merely whingeing: in August 1998 they ordered the most audacious raid on the stock and futures markets ever undertaken by a government anywhere and bought up something like 7 per cent of the market in a single day's trading. Their aim was to give a 'bloody nose' to the speculators who had gone short in the market – in other words were gambling on the market going down. Sure enough the speculators were forced into retreat but, as we shall see later, at a cost that left a permanent scar on Hong Kong's reputation for running free markets.

Although moaning about the unfairness of globalisation became the crutch for governments devoid of real ideas as to how to tackle the financial crisis, their complaints were not without foundation. The power of the vast pension funds, money-management companies and, yes, the hedge funds is indeed awesome and governments need to have some means of, at least, monitoring the flows of their investments.

One of the most articulate advocates of some form of control on foreign funds is George Soros, the American-based financier who was depicted as the devil incarnate by Dr Mahathir for his hedge-fund operations. In Malaysia and elsewhere the name Soros became shorthand for reckless speculation. As for Mr Soros himself, he said, 'the laissez-faire idea that markets should be left to their own devices remains very influential. I consider it a dangerous idea. The instability of financial markets can cause serious economic and social dislocations.' He also admitted that 'foreign capital is notoriously fickle'.[17]

Maybe it's not so easy to blame the foreigners

However, in East Asia domestic capital is also notoriously fickle, and, as we shall see later, much of the selling pressure in Asian markets was generated internally. There is no need to make value judgements about this because many of the domestic investors who were busy moving out of their own stock markets and their own currencies did so for perfectly sound business reasons. Many had high levels of liabilities denominated in foreign currencies, mainly US dollars, and so to service loans and pay for imported services and products they needed big reserves of foreign currencies. Others were engaged in straightforward speculation but the line is thinly drawn where hedging goes out and speculation comes in.

No one has produced satisfactory evidence that large foreign fund movements triggered the crisis. In December 1997 the IMF reported on its examination of this question and concluded that hedge funds may have exercised some pressure which led to the devaluation of the Thai baht but that the 'driving force' behind the big sell-off came from domestic investors.[18]

Blame the herd instinct

Whether it was foreign or domestic investors who caused the panic can be debated endlessly, but what cannot be questioned is that one of the main reasons for the rapid fall of the dominos that caused the crisis was the power of the herd instinct. The famous British economist John Maynard Keynes was also a successful fund manager who attributed his success in share dealing more to an understanding of psychology than a knowledge of financial markets. He argued that understanding the psychology of the herd was the key to predicting what markets were likely to do.

In his intriguing book *Against the Gods – The Remarkable Story of Risk*, Peter Bernstein recalls taking part in a discussion on paper entitled 'Does the Stockmarket Overreact?'. He writes, 'At long last, the academic world has caught up with what investors have known all along. Their answer to the question posed by the title was an unqualified "Yes".' Mr Bernstein proceeds to discuss Prospect Theory, which suggests that, 'when new information arrives, investors revise their beliefs, not according to objective methods . . . but by over weighting the new information and underweighting prior and longer term information . . . As a consequence stock prices systematically overshoot so far in either direction that their reversal is predictable regardless of what happens to earnings or dividends or any other objective factor.'[19]

In the heady atmosphere that surrounded the East Asian markets in 1997 the bevy of new information was flowing thick and fast and the herd instinct was notably acute. It is sometimes hard for people who have not experienced the atmosphere of trading rooms and investment managers' offices to appreciate the extent of twitchiness among those who populate these establishments. Reputations, fortunes, status and all that comes with them jostle for space as the people who make markets wrestle with ever-increasing demands for better performance. They are the custodians of the old adage about 'buying on rumour, selling on facts'.

Working in Asian financial markets in the mid- to late 1990s meant working in an artificial world of easy money, made easier as big bonus payments were handed out when markets rose. In reality, however, the money was not easily made because those sitting hunched in front of their computer terminals spewing out charts and figures worked very long hours in a state of almost hypertension. The worst offence they could possibly commit was to miss out on the action. The phones glued to their ears conveyed the latest market gossip and spurred them to action.

Everyone knew in their heart of hearts that the party would have to end and they wanted to be sure not to get caught in the rush for the exit. It was only human nature to want the party to carry on and for those busy partying to assure each other that it could last just a little longer as there was still plenty of upside.

Well-known doomsters such as the Hong Kong-based fund manager Marc Faber, known as Dr Doom, were regarded as amusing sideshows, and with reason: those following some of Mr Faber's advice would have missed out on a number of prime buying opportunities. And no one wanted to be accused of missing out. How could the traders or analysts or their managers have faced their clients to explain their failure? They were truly at the sharp end and lived in perpetual fear of misreading the market.

Thus when, on 2 July 1997, the news flashed up on their screens saying that the Thai government had given up the unequal battle of protecting the value of the local currency, a cold shiver ran down many spines. Was this the beginning of the end? Maybe not, but what if it were? Surely the only safe thing to do was to start offloading investments, first in Thailand itself, then in the other emerging markets, which at times like these were uncritically lumped together as a single entity.

The very mechanism of offloading is in itself enough to cause alarm. The computer monitors that show every movement in the market are suddenly filled with a mass of electronic activity. By a click on the keyboard those playing the market can summon up individual share prices, and charts showing principal market indexes appear on the screen and look pretty alarming when a line dipping downwards refuses to move in any other way. Unsure, individual traders are almost certain to get on the phone to their colleagues. They tend to talk in hyperbole. Snap judgements are the common currency of their exchanges. They work themselves into something just short of a frenzy. In the middle of this frenzy what is known as 'market sentiment' is created. It is sometimes spoken of as though it were the product of mature reflection, but this is rarely the case. For a start many of those creating market sentiment are far from mature in years and often extremely immature in their level of excitability.

Lurking behind the frenzy is the fact that so many of those trading on behalf of their clients were also trading on behalf of themselves. The phenomenon of 'own-account' trading is particularly prevalent in Asia, where controls are more lax than in, for example, US markets. In some places the analysts and traders are openly playing the market alongside their clients; in others they do so in a covert fashion either because company policy prevents or limits this kind of trading or because it is based on insider information. In all events anecdotal evidence suggests that own-account trading was very substantial during the height of the market boom in the mid-1990s. It is therefore curious that it is so little mentioned, particularly because when so-called market professionals become market participants on their own behalf they lose a degree of objectivity that might otherwise make their behaviour more rational. However much it is denied, there is no doubting that having a direct stake in market movements introduces an element of subjectivity which, during the rise of Asian markets, added considerably to the lack of clear thinking about which way they were heading.

When I was investigating the Hong Kong government's 1998 stock-market intervention I went to see some of the senior officials from the Hong Kong Monetary Authority who was trying to convince me that the territory was facing a conspiracy by big foreign funds determined to profit from the fall of the equity market and the local currency. Show me the evidence of the conspiracy, I demanded. 'They were all talking to each other', said one of the officials. Oh dear, I thought. Are these regulators really so removed from the market that they really think that chatting among fund managers and traders amounts to a conspiracy?

This is the way they do their business, not just in Hong Kong but everywhere where financial markets exist. Considering the level of supposed sophistication surrounding these markets, it may be thought that shouted telephone conversations lack a certain degree of subtlety, but human nature cannot be ignored. Remember, these are marketplaces. They can be dressed up as something more but at the end of the day they are bear pits filled with people living on their wits trading like mad to stay afloat. Looked at in this way the only difference between the floor of say, a futures exchange and a cattle market is that cattle sales tend to be conducted a little more slowly. The atmosphere and the outcome are otherwise remarkably similar. If a bull somehow gets loose at a cattle auction there is likely to be something of a panic. If, in the frenzied atmosphere of an overheated financial market, one of its key components – in this case the Thai baht – goes walkabout, there is also something of a panic.

It is a panic induced by the fear of being caught short and it is the panic of market players who play across a whole spectrum of markets and know full well that the integration of markets is far more advanced than the integration of economies. That is why, for example, when the Russian currency went into free fall in the summer of 1998, the already battered

Asian markets were hit. Investors who had taken short positions in Russia needed cash to cover these positions and many obtained it by pulling money out of Asia, particularly the very liquid Hong Kong market.

This is global contagion writ large. And this is why the impact of the herd instinct is so important to understanding the Asian financial crisis.

Making too much – earning too little

However, the phenomenon of the herd instinct explains only *how* things happened, not why. This is a far more complex matter and one that occupies much of this book.

One explanation of the underlying cause is offered by the Indian New Zealand-based academic Ravi Arvind Palat. His views are far from mainstream but very interesting. Dr Palat argues that East Asia got caught up in a spiral of overproduction, mainly fuelled by Japanese companies investing in the region with the proceeds of cheap loans. When interest rates began to rise in the early 1990s the Japanese bubble started to collapse. The companies who were caught with high borrowings which became hard to repay turned increasingly to their East Asian production centres in an attempt to recoup profitability. This fuelled the race for ever greater levels of production. However, the rise in demand did not meet this massive rise in output, thus prices were forced down and inventories grew to ridiculous levels and the seeds of the collapse were sown.[20]

More villains than heroes

Dr Palat's views on overproduction as a cause form one part of the underlying explanation of the crisis. More generally I would tend rather towards the Krugman school of thought, which stresses the internal weakness of Asian governance as creating the conditions for the collapse. However, I would add to that a need to look at the management of Asian companies, which, as I shall argue later, explains why they moved from positions of strength to weakness with such ease.

Although exaggerated, the views of Dr Mahathir also have some foundation. Clearly globalisation has made individual financial markets vulnerable to the whims of big fund managers and clearly they tend not to be angels. It is also true that there has been an enormous overreaction to Asia's woes.

Lamentably in these circumstances, there are more villains than heroes and few simple explanations of what happened. As we shall see in the following chapter, this is hardly surprising given the enormous myth-making machine that developed before the bubble burst and created the notion of an 'Asian Economic Miracle', giving rise to false expectations of its worth.

1

WHAT THEY SAID BEFORE

The mystery of 'the Orient'

To understand some of the extraordinary myth-making which was commonplace before the crisis broke, requires an appreciation of the Western fascination with 'the Orient' and Orientals. It was this fascination that obscured the common sense which should have led to a wider appreciation of the dangers of the Asian Miracle. The myth making is not of recent origin, nor are the high expectations of the riches to be gained from this part of the world. Marco Polo, arguably the most famous European traveller to China, could also be said to have started the trend. At the end of the thirteenth century he returned to Europe with marvellous stories of the ancient and sophisticated civilisation he had found. As a trader he was convinced that fortunes were to be made in the Orient. Partly in awe and partly in affectionate mocking, the Italians called Marco Polo *Il Milione*, because when he talked about China he always talked in thousands and millions. In the years that followed many more travellers have followed in his footsteps and returned in a state of awe. What changed over the years was that their stories were filled with talk of billions, rather than humble millions.

It might be thought that the passage of time and the benefit of experience would have tempered some of the mysticism and expectations of the Orient. However, if anything, the myths and expectations have grown and become far more elaborate, or, it may be argued, more absurd.

As a result the strange idea came about that business relations with the countries of Asia were not supposed to be conducted in the same way as with other regions. The bottom line of doing business with Asia often becomes submersed in all sorts of fanciful and allegedly 'culturally sensitive' nonsense which tends to amuse and embarrass business people from the region.

One of the most amusing stories about foreign businessmen travelling to this part of the world comes from an event in November 1986 when Deng Xiaoping, China's paramount leader, welcomed a high-level delegation of bankers, financiers, lawyers and executives from the United States. John Phelan, who was then the chairman of the New York Stock Exchange, was clearly overawed by the occasion. 'I would hope', he said, 'the US business community would win a gold medal in terms of investment in China in the future.'[1] Mr Deng asked Mr Phelan whether he knew why they had been invited. He groped for a reply. The Chinese leader enlightened him: 'The main purpose is to exploit you,' he said. 'Well,' said Mr Phelan, 'it's a great honour to be exploited'.[2]

China's 'open-door' economic policies were only just starting to creak open at this point. Foreign investors dreamed about the extraordinary market which lay behind the door and the fabulous investment possibilities that beckoned. As things turned out, for every American company that rushed into the China market with high hopes, at least another ten were retreating bruised, disillusioned and somewhat poorer. Even those who succeeded found it was a long, uphill struggle. Coca-Cola, the world's soft-drinks market leader, spent eleven years in China without making a cent.[3] It has now established its brand in the Chinese market but is an exception among American companies because it actually makes money in the country.

The cheerleaders

The fact that many foreign businesses are making nothing at all in China has not prevented the assembly of a band of foreign cheerleaders who have chosen to promote the Chinese cause and become apologists for the Chinese Communist Party (which, interestingly, is rarely mentioned as such in their writings). As a result of the efforts made by the Chinese cheerleaders, China has become the centre of the Asian myth making absurdity. It is absurd because it distorts both expectations and clear-headed thinking about what is going on in Asia.

Few of the Chinese myth makers are more avid than the American banker William Overholt: 'contemporary China is not another Soviet Union, nor the totalitarian state that China was in 1966,' he wrote, 'but rather a gigantic, vintage 1972 South Korea.'[4]

Mr Overholt's date stamping is interesting because he locates China at the height of the era in which the notorious Korean dictator Park Chung Hee ruled. He was assassinated seven years later. It was also a time when tight labour controls created a vast, disciplined and ultimately very militant labour force. The Park regime had virtually nationalised the banking system and imposed a policy of strict industrial licensing, hardly policies of economic liberalism which Mr Overholt maintains were holding sway in China. This heavy hand of government placed inordinate economic power in the hands of the big *chaebols*, or conglomerates, which were later found to be riddled with the weaknesses which helped drag Korea under in 1997. In addition it was an era noted for corruption and the sort of dubious practices which are prevalent in China today giving rise to what Mr Overholt delightfully calls some 'very messy intermediate phases'.[5]

However, he notes that China has 'a potentially decisive advantage' because no one accuses the top leadership of being motivated by financial greed.[6] This in itself is a dubious proposition, given widespread concern about the corruption of senior Communist Party cadres. Indeed, it was concerns about corruption that were at least as high on the list of priorities as democracy for those involved in the widespread 1989 protests ending with the Tiananmen Square massacre (known to the apologists as the 'Tiananmen Incident').

As for democracy, we are reliably informed by Mr Overholt that most of those pressing for democracy in China 'are infinitely more concerned about enlarging the scope of personal freedom than about electoral democracy'. That sounds plausible enough but the 'old friend' of China cannot help himself. He continues, 'most are willing to tolerate the regime in practice while noisily opposing it, so long as steady progress is made in economic growth and suppressing the worst of the evils'.[7] So here we have it, the hoary old myth that Chinese people (and, others would argue, Asians in general) do not need democracy as long as they are given economic growth.

Let them eat cake – Asian style

This is nothing more than a patronising update of Marie Antoinette's 'let them eat cake' philosophy. It may make sense in the banking circles in which Mr Overholt moves but is entirely contrary to my experience gained at a less elevated level of Asian societies where I have constantly found people wanting a say in government, perhaps not on the Westminster model, but in ways that are meaningful – in other words in ways that involve elections.

The Overholt argument is taken further by the journalist Jim Rohwer, author of the book *Asia Rising*. He maintains that what most of us know of as democracy is really something he calls 'lobby-based democracy' in which 'the link between the broad wishes the voters express when they elect their rulers and the forces that actually shape the decisions of the rulers once they are in office has been stretched to a point where it has almost snapped'.[8]

This terrible state of affairs has, Mr Rohwer argues, imposed a terrible restraint on economic development. He maintains that 'the reason why Asia has so far escaped the special interest trap is that successful authoritarian governments – in the forefront of which are South Korea, Taiwan, Hong Kong and Singapore – had the laserlike aim of modernising their countries by getting their economies to grow fast. In practice this meant that they outlawed the dollar-bill game. They refused to accommodate the claims of special interests over those of the economy as a whole.'[9]

I read these sentences a couple of times to make sure my eyes were not deceiving me but, no, not only were they there on the page, but unwittingly they provided an insight into much of the muddled thinking that led to such impressive misunderstandings about what was happening at the political end of the Asian Miracle. Mr Rohwer says that 'special interests' have been pushed aside by single-minded governments in pursuit of noble economic goals. This is breathtaking because the reality is that the 'special interests' of the general public may well have been ignored by authoritarian governments but the special interests of the big tycoons in the countries he mentions were unequivocally given special attention.

That is why, for example, the big bosses of the *chaebols* in Korea had state backing to squeeze out competition, why in supposedly laissez-faire Hong Kong, monopolies flourished in all sorts of areas where they had been swept aside in democracies and that is why in Taiwan, the financial sector became hopelessly uncompetitive as the cronies of the ruling Kuomintang party successfully persuaded the government to avoid competition.

The failure to understand that authoritarian governments, heavily influenced by small coteries of reactionary businessmen, were actually preventing the development of free markets and balanced economic development is at the heart of the failure to understand what caused the crisis of the late 1990s, a crisis triggered in the financial markets but nurtured by years of misgovernment.

What is most notable about the cheerleaders for the Asian Miracle is their contempt for the people who were behind the alleged miracle, the *hoi polloi* who needed firm government to keep them in line and prevent the miracle running off the tracks. As we shall shortly see the argument that 'authoritarian government equals economic success' became a guiding principle for some Asian leaders when the Miracle was doing its stuff and producing the goods. The Korean President Park Chung Hee reduced the argument to the simple motto: 'Economics before politics'.

The democracy versus economic growth myth

It was argued, by people like President Park and Lee Kwan Yew, the former Prime Minister of Singapore, that the Asian Miracle occurred because the countries of the region had thrown off the restraining ropes of Western hegemony and were focused on economic growth. Economic growth could be achieved, they said, only if Western ideas about human rights, representative government and the like could be put to one side and governments got on with the job of governing unhindered by these restraints. 'I would say that democracy is not conducive to rapid economic growth,' Mr Lee remarked in 1991.[10] He added that 'without military rule or dictatorship or authoritarian government in Korea and Taiwan, I doubt whether they could have transformed themselves so quickly'. Looking at the Philippines, India and Sri Lanka (described by Mr Lee as 'Ceylon', its former colonial name), he says that their 'lack of discipline made growth slow and sluggish'.

Mr Lee performed the classic trick of taking one indicator, in this case democratic development, and extrapolating from it an entire theory, or apologia, for a view of economic development. In the case of Taiwan, for example, it is quite correct to say that it achieved a high level of growth in the 1980s (annually averaging around 8 per cent) but it is also the case that when the strictures of authoritarian government were relaxed, it still managed, from a higher base level, to sustain economic growth throughout the 1990s (annually averaging around 6 per cent), whereas Korea, still experiencing authoritarian government into the late 1990s, maintained a more or less constant rate of annual economic growth of some 7.5 per cent until the collapse in 1997.[11] The difference was that Taiwan continued to grow economically after 1997 whereas Korea fell into recession. The reasons for the disparities and similarities between the two states cannot be explained by a simple application of the argument about democratic versus authoritarian government. Other examples also demonstrate the problematic nature of trying to produce a direct equation between economic development and representative government. For example, Hong Kong and Singapore share very similar levels of prosperity yet one was founded on a more or less laissez-faire government, allowing considerable liberty but little democracy, while the other was built on the basis of heavy-handed state controls combined with severely curtailed civil liberties and a notionally democratic system. In economic development terms they both arrived at similar destinations although their social and political systems were heading in entirely different directions. Because economic growth patterns obstinately refuse to fit neatly into the argument over whether authoritarian government is necessary to achieve economic development, those maintaining this position are left struggling to find evidence that substantiates their case.

Asian values – Asian myths

Before the crash, the crux of the Asian values debate was supposed to be that, whatever bleating may be heard from the faint hearts criticising Asian values, they could not deny that this value system created the basis for the economic miracle.

This line of argument was bought hook, line and sinker in some parts of the West. It was then thrown into the cauldron of misunderstanding about what was happening in Asia when the economies started to boom and ended up compounding the general state of confusion.

Look on the shelves of any library with a big collection of Asian books and you will see an array of titles, such as *Asia Rising, Megatrends Asia, Hyper-growth in Asian Economies, The Asian Century, The ASEAN Success Story, The Eastasia Edge* and, of course, the highly influential World Bank report called *'The East Asian Miracle'*. (This publication is not in fact part of the cheerleading school. On the contrary, it is a very useful and well-researched attempt to identify the roots of Asian economic success. However, the publication's title led to excitement that went far beyond the measured judgements it contained.)

The audience for these books was nowhere more responsive than in Asia itself. They provided assurance where doubt existed and gave a certain intellectual credibility to the bubbly feeling of economic wellbeing.

Self promoters and myth makers

Once the idea of the Asian Miracle took hold there was no shortage of Asian self-promoters and myth makers, some of them aggressive and chauvinistic. The groundbreaking book by Akio Morita and Shintaro Ishihara, called *The Japan that can say 'No' – The new US–Japan relations card*, is a good example of the assertive 'Asia-is-best-and-will-no-longer-be-subjugated' literature that found an enthusiastic readership in its home country. A Chinese book on the same theme followed the Morita – Ishihara work.

Interestingly, however, the trailblazing books on the ascendancy of Asia came from Western authors. Once their works appeared in Asian language translations they started the ball rolling. In Japan, for example, there was an enormous response to the Japanese version of Ezra Vogel's book called *Japan as Number One*, published in 1979. In marketing terms it can be said that Dr Vogel was giving 'third-party endorsement' to something that many Japanese wanted to believe.

Towards the end of the 1980s the theme of Eastern supremacy and the growing bankruptcy of the West was taken up with vigour by Asian leaders such as Singapore's Lee Kwan Yew. His warm-up act at domestic big rallies was to reel off statistics of economic growth for Asian economies and then compare them with the declining or static levels of growth being achieved in the West. He particularly liked to take snipes at Singapore's former sovereign state, Britain. In Mr Lee's speeches Britain was depicted as a class-ridden, union-controlled, arrogant and impotent nation – 'so if you tell me the British are less hard working, less patriotic than the Japanese, I say, yes, it tallies with my observation,' he said at the National Day Rally in August 1981. The none-too-subtle point he was making was that Singapore had thrown off the colonial shackles, spurned what Australians call 'the colonial cringe' and roared off into a better future anchored by Asian values and Asian ways of doing things.

Mr Lee was the first proponent of the 'Look East' policy which boiled down to the view that there was more to be learned from Japan than the West. This view was taken up with even more enthusiasm by Dr Mahathir Mohamad, the Malaysian prime minister. 'In the past,' he said, 'we looked to the West to get new knowledge, to learn about technology, about the methods of production, even systems.' However, according to Dr Mahathir, things started to change: 'We see the Japanese made headway while the West has not only not made headway, but appears to be regressing. So in order for Malaysia to progress, we have to learn from a better example, and the better example is the Japanese example. That is why we now want to look East where before we were looking West'.[12]

A certain degree of disillusionment with Japan set in after Singapore and Malaysia declared themselves to be looking East. There was frustration over the Japanese reluctance to transfer technology. There was also irritation over investment not coming in at what was considered to be an appropriate rate. Like the more aggressively complaining Americans, Asian countries soon discovered that the Japanese domestic market was hard to penetrate. For these reasons and others 'Look East' was subtly replaced by a wider concept of 'Asian values', which were said to form the basis on which the 'Asian Miracle' would flourish.

The subject of Asian values will be more closely examined in Chapter 3.

Some saw things more clearly than others

Contrary views and questioning about the fundamentals of the alleged Miracle were not well received. Yet there were a number of observers who saw something of what was coming. Paul Krugman was an early sceptic and made his views clear in an influential essay, 'The Myth of the Asian Miracle', published in *Foreign Affairs* some four years before the crash. It is also true that some publications, notably *The Economist* magazine in London, consistently flashed up warnings about the so-called Asian

Miracle. However these warnings were easily dismissed by the cheerleaders as typical *Economist*-type iconoclastic behaviour. Yet *The Economist* was also ahead of the pack in cautioning against an over-reaction to the crisis as the first signs of the Miracle coming to an end emerged in the early part of 1997. 'In truth,' said a leader published before the bubble burst,

> it is as foolish to exaggerate the region's recent troubles as it was to react hysterically to its success. One lesson to draw from its current problems is that, contrary to all the talk about East Asia's growth being founded on cultural advantages, its various economies are in fact 'normal' after all. They are no more immune to the ups and downs of the economic cycle than are developed economies.[13]

Another pre-July 1997 prophecy of what was to come came from the well known Canadian trader Andrew Sarlos and Patricia Best, who published a book called *Fear, Greed and the End of the Rainbow.* It argued that the big bull run was coming to an end and that investors had better be prepared for a bear run lasting into the early years of the twenty-first century. The book had reasonable reviews but the authors were accused of living in the past and not acknowledging how times had changed.

Using a number of electronic databases I set out to see what had been written about the Asian Miracle in the three years before the 1997 crash. The result was that no more than 20 per cent of the articles, brokers' reports and the like, could be described as critical of the underlying assumptions about why Asian economies were roaring away. Indeed it was alarming how many of these articles repeated the same old clichéd formulas. Even less of the material reviewed contained forecasts of a messy ending in the near future.

Of the hundreds of articles, one stood out in particular. It was head-lined: *No More Prospects Of Easy Fortunes*[14] and appeared in the *San Francisco Chronicle* on 24 September 1996. Up towards the top of this long piece by Jonathan Marshall, the paper's economics editor, was a quote from Robert Oxnam, a senior research fellow at Columbia University. He said,

> For the last twenty years, it was hard not to make money in Asia. You could go in blindfolded and make money, the region was growing so fast. In the next twenty years you can still make money but it's going to be much harder. The political risks are greater and growth rates can't keep going at their current pace.

This seems like a rather unremarkable statement in the post-crash period but it was far more striking in late 1996. The article was impressive because it focused on nearly all the big trouble spots that were soon to trigger the crisis. It covered high levels of corporate debt, the corruption of the Suharto regime in Indonesia and the stalemate in Japanese politics which was paralysing the government, rendering it incapable of taking decisive action on the economic front.

However, those wanting to make good money by jumping on a lecture circuit visiting Asian countries were well advised not to be writing this kind of stuff, or, of course, saying it out loud. These audiences wanted to be told that happy days were here to stay. In part this was based on reality, because the days were indeed happy. Asian audiences (including those containing Westerners working in Asia) liked to hear confirmation that they were doing better than their erstwhile colonial masters. In addition the feel-good effect and the morale boosting was simply good business. While the boom was under way and people believed it would continue, there was easy money to be made in the financial and real estate markets. There was less easy money to be made in the real economy, which produced goods and services, but if you were in the real economy you could always supplement income by speculative investments. Anyone questioning the prudence of these investments was undermining the income they were producing. In other words the doomsters were as welcome as a slab of pork at a Muslim wedding.

And so the party rolled and generated an impressive array of cheerleading and confidence-building publications. They make for interesting reading in the post-1997 period. It is hard to resist the temptation to point out where they went wrong, albeit with the caveat that hindsight is often more clear than foresight. Yet, as we shall see, there was much to see before the crash happened, even though it was hard to do so when so many people were wearing rose-tinted glasses.

Let's learn nothing from history

As ever when excitement mounts, history is quickly forgotten. For that reason few of those who got so excited about the Asian Miracle seem to have noticed that a couple of decades earlier, in the 1960s and 1970s, there was similar excitement about the three giants of Latin America: Argentina, Brazil and Mexico. At the time it was thought that they were about to go out and conquer the rest of the world. When they did not, those suggesting that they were poised to do so slipped quietly into the night to be replaced by a new band of prophets focused on the other side of the Pacific Ocean.

Perhaps the worst offender in the Asian cheerleading stakes was John Naisbitt's *Megatrends Asia*, first published in 1996. He is a brave man, not given to reserved predictions. Here is a flavour of the enthusiasm that made this book so popular in some of the big business houses and government offices in Asia: 'As we move to the year 2000, Asia will become the dominant region of the world: economically, politically and culturally.'[15] In the new world depicted by Mr Naisbitt, sitting in the United States, Asian countries are all busy working together, embracing free markets and 'increasingly irritated by the West's lecturing and hectoring them about freedom and human rights'.[16] And there is plenty more of this.

'It is becoming apparent to the East and to some in the West that we are moving towards Easternisation of the world,' Mr Naisbitt wrote in one of his typically enthusiastic ramblings, 'in the global context, the West is still important, but no longer dominant. The global axis of influence has shifted from West to East.'[17]

A year earlier Jim Rohwer correctly predicted that 'Asia's trajectory over the next twenty-five years is unlikely to be a smooth continuation of the curve it has traced over the past twenty-five'.[18] He also acknowledged some of the region's institutional weaknesses, ranging from the 'opacity of company governance to lack of political accountability to paucity of infrastructure'. However, he then went and spoilt it by writing:

These weaknesses have done little damage so far – so little, indeed, it could be argued they have been strengths. Modern Asia has been a lot smarter than other parts of the poor world: Asia let its societies and economies run away with themselves at first rather than smothering them under government directives.[19]

The sticky hand of the state

It was popular at the time Mr Rohwer was writing to imagine that what were seen as weaknesses everywhere else in the world could be viewed as 'strengths' in Asia. There was a school of thought that argued, for example, that corruption was not such a bad thing because it was a means of getting things done. Having encountered a small degree of corruption in my Asian business career, I remain to be convinced of how the payment of hard-earned money for nonproductive services is somehow a plus. This, of course, is not the argument. The apologists for corruption say that, if the payment of sums of money to, for example, government officials, short-circuits a cumbersome bureaucracy, surely it is nothing to worry about. To my mind this is much the same as arguing in favour of a non-lethal cancer on the grounds that it is far better than a cancer attacking a vital organ. The problem of corruption is dealt with in some detail in Chapter Six.

For the time being it is sufficient to note that it was this kind of muddled thinking, severely deficient in elementary morality, which was much in vogue in the go-go years of the Asian Miracle. People who really under-stood how to do business in Asia, we were told, were not afraid of a bit of rough and tumble – it was all part of the marvellous game. Morality was for wimps.

Moreover it suited the people who ran big businesses not to have the government on their backs as they shovelled shareholder's money into dubious investments. These investments, in turn, were made on the backs of loans that could be repaid only if the asset bubble kept growing. Meanwhile, on the sidelines they were insider trading like mad. How nice for them to be told that what they were doing was actually positive.

What is more, it is an extraordinary myth to believe that the Asian tigers and the Asian tiger cubs ran streamlined governments free of bloated bureaucracies. Even in Hong Kong, portrayed as the bastion of free enterprise, there is a vast civil service which employs more people than any other entity in the territory.

As someone who does business in Hong Kong I can supply countless examples of bureaucratic obstruction that has hampered the development of my enterprise. I fear that those who speak only to the leaders of big corporations have no idea what it is like at the coal face, dealing with sullen bureaucrats who see rule books as the Holy Grail and understand very little about how business is actually conducted. I have swapped bureaucracy horror stories with business acquaintances in other Asian countries; it is easy to fill an entire evening with this kind of talk. When I told a friend in Thailand that Asia was being written about as a place where government kept its nose out of business, he rubbed his eyes in amazement and volunteered to give the authors of this calumny a guided tour of bureaucratic meddling. The meddling occurs most significantly at the lower end of the business food chain. Yet small and medium-sized businesses are the backbone of the 'Miracle' economies. The power of the big businessmen is the power to override the bureaucracy, but this hardly creates the kind of level playing field in which entrepreneurship thrives.

In an interesting article published in 1987, Hans Dieter Evers argued that the Southeast Asian 'Miracle' economies experienced 'runway bureaucratisation' in the 1970s and 1980s leading to ever-increasing bureaucratic control over business and the blurring of lines between the state and private enterprise in the running of business. He described this as 'bureaucratic capitalism'.[20]

The tendency for increased state intervention is seen in a more positive light by the World Bank in its famous 'Asian Miracle' study: 'Our judgment is that in a few economies, mainly in Northeast Asia, in some instances, government interventions resulted in higher and more equal growth than otherwise would have occurred.'[21] The Bank, however, agrees with Mr Evers that 'in the newly industrialising economies of Southeast Asia, government interventions played a much less prominent and frequently less constructive role in economic success.'[22]

However the myth of nonintervention exercised a strong fascination over the peddlers of the Asian Miracle story. At its most absurd level it ignored the even more direct and pernicious intervention of the corrupt regimes, notably the venal Suharto government in Indonesia and the Marcos regime in the Philippines, which made it difficult to do any serious business without the involvement of the first families. One estimate suggests that the Suharto family owned no fewer than 1,251 companies, running or taking stakes in everything from toll roads to airlines to condom manufacture and mineral water bottling. According to Michael Backman, author of *Asian Eclipse*, 'the Suharto empire was the biggest "kleptocracy" the world has ever seen. Its tentacles worked their way into every crevice of the Indonesian economy'.[23]

Cronyism and state-led corruption constituted a form of interventionism which was at least as thoroughgoing as that seen in the command economies where the state owns most of the economy.

Ersatz capitalism

Before the crash, the mantra of government noninterventionism was chanted by those who believed that the key to development was a laissez-faire system, protected by authoritarian government that would not have to bow to the kind of political pressures that exercised restraint on unbridled capitalism. Asia thus became the kind of place where a person could get seriously rich with few questions asked. The reality was that those who got seriously rich did so precisely because of the ties they forged with the ruling elites. In a book published in 1988 called *The Rise of Ersatz Capitalism in Southeast Asia* the Japanese scholar Yoshihara Kunio exposed many of the myths about how businesses were growing in the region. The book had a less than welcome reception in the countries he reviewed and earned him a ban from entering Indonesia. Another scholar, Frank Tipton, later described 'ersatz capitalism' as a way of doing business in which

> rather than seeking excellence, ersatz capitalists have been content to exploit their political connections to enrich themselves and their families. Their profits go to spending consumption, and when they do invest, their money goes overseas or into urban real estate. In effect they have remained the compradors of foreign firms.[24]

It is interesting that Mr Kumio, a decade before the crash, and Mr Tipton, just before the crash, could have seen this so clearly while the cheerleaders had their view obscured by the mountains of cash the ersatz capitalists were generating from their quickie investments.

Visiting Western politicians join the myth makers

But it was not only cheerleading Asia 'experts' whose vision was obscured; the Asian Miracle also became a subject of fascination among Western politicians. Perhaps they were hoping for some of the success to rub off on their shoulders. The problem is that politicians, especially those in search of the 'vision thing', can usually be regarded as lagging indicators. In their pursuit of new ideas for implementation in the West many politicians piled on to jet planes to discover what could be learned from the East. Among them was Peter Mandelson, who in 1996 was the leading star of the British Labour Party's modernising crusade which turned this once social democratic party into a far less ideological organisation, promoting what the Prime Minister, Tony Blair, called the 'third way'.

After returning from a whirlwind Asian tour, Mr Mandelson wrote a somewhat breathless article for the *Times*. 'What were the lessons I came home with?' he asked. The answer, in his words:

> Eclipsing all others is the Asian achievement of sustaining local cohesion alongside rapid economic change. Outside the region, some have the impression that the success of the 'tiger' economies is based on sweatshop labour producing cheap, bargain-basement goods, with huge profits and vast wealth for a few, being earned through exploitation of the many. This is a false picture.
>
> Of course, profits are substantial and there are some very rich entrepreneurs, but what's wrong with that? The difference between many Asian countries and Britain is that, among the tiger economies, inequalities of wealth and income do not co-exist with the denial of opportunity and social cohesion that so many in Britain experience. The reason for this is a conscious attempt by governments such as those in Japan, Korea and Singapore to give their workforce a stake in the country's economic success both at the workplace and in society.'[25]

Like other whirlwind visitors to the region, Mr Mandelson has extrapolated a false picture on the basis of half-digested information. He is right to say that the tiger economies have not formed a giant sweatshop. However, Mr Mandelson's tour of the region must have missed out many of the tightly packed industrial areas I have visited in Southern China, Thailand and Indonesia, where there are a great many sweatshops and very unpleasant ones at that. Nevertheless, he is right not to allow too great a generalisation to be made on this subject. As the World Bank has pointed out, the big eight Asian growth economies 'achieved unusually low and declining levels of inequality, contrary to the historical experience and contemporary evidence in other regions.'[26]

However, Mr Mandelson is wrong to say that the governments of the region made a 'conscious attempt' to give their workforce a stake in the country's economic success. This was evident before the crash but even more clearly seen afterwards, when workers were ruthlessly laid off without having the support of a social-security safety net to cushion the fall. The 'stake' they were given was no more than the promise of secure employment while times were good. There was no suggestion that the 'stake' would be worth anything if times were bad. In Japan some vigorous attempts were made to preserve the system of lifetime employment, although even this long-held tradition started fraying at the edges.

Mr Mandelson painted a picture of something resembling a shareholding democracy, but this was total rubbish. Not only do employees have practically zero say in the running of Asian companies, but even minority shareholders are notoriously treated in a shabby manner. The trickle-down effect of increasing affluence did much to alleviate poverty but, in most cases, was not accompanied by parallel advances in the development of representative government. It was precisely because the 'social cohesion' that Mr Mandelson thought he saw did not really exist that the regimes of East Asia proved so fragile when the economic dam burst and carried away the old leaderships.

Until the late 1980s there was little by way of collective bargaining in the 'Miracle' economies. Conditions of employment were determined by employers without reference to employees' organisations or government controls. The absence of legal or mutually recognised outlets for the workforce to express views and be consulted led to violent confrontations in Korea and a rash of wildcat industrial action in countries ranging from Thailand to China and Taiwan.

The cash mountain

Concern over these social and political issues was largely pushed to one side in the excitement over the growing mountains of cash flowing into East Asia. Nongovernmental organisations trying to raise these issues were given little air space. Everything that did not touch on wealth creation was considered to be peripheral.

As wealth was being created in spades there seemed to be a good case for not tolerating distractions. In 1993, the high point of the boom years, almost $15 billion in net foreign investment flowed into emerging Asian stock markets. The previous year was also a record but net flows totalled only $2 billion.

Everything was looking really rosy in 1993; Thailand's stock market shot up 88 per cent, Malaysian stocks scored a 98 per cent rise but even this was topped by Indonesian stocks, which soared 115 per cent.

Price earning ratios (p/e ratios) soared too. These ratios are the usual means for judging market valuations, a high p/e ratio suggests that the market believes that there is considerable growth to be had in share prices. The p/e ratio is the price of a company's share divided by earnings per share. In 1993 the Japanese stock market was trading on an average historic p/e ratio of 60 times. In other words investors were valuing the majority of Japanese listed companies at 60 times the amount of money they were making. Other markets were more moderately rated. Malaysia, for example, was trading on a multiple of almost 27, and Singapore was on a multiple of almost 25. The lowest rating in the region was in Hong Kong, which has a mature market and was suffering from the perception that the pending 1997 Chinese takeover increased political risk. The average p/e ratio in this market was almost 16 times.

Foreign money makes its mark

The reality was that the Asian markets were peaking in 1993 but investors clearly believed that there was considerably more growth to be found. That belief was perhaps more prevalent among overseas investors.

By 1995 foreign players accounted for the greater share of trading in most of the Asia 'Miracle' markets. According to the Indonesian stock exchange, foreigners accounted for 81 per cent of all trades that year. Half of all trades in Malaysia and the Philippines were said to have been made by foreigners. Only in South Korea, where strict controls were still placed on overseas participation, was the foreign activity minimal, accounting for no more than 6 per cent of trades.[27] In the more mature Hong Kong market, foreign players accounted for 30 per cent of turnover.[28]

Both domestic and foreign investors were making very good money and were regularly told by so-called market experts that there was more wealth to come.

Analysts with their hands tied

Most of those making these predictions were stock brokers analysts. The quality of equity research in Asia leaves a great deal to be desired. Few stockbroking houses, including those considered to be reputable, allow their analysts to pepper the pages of their reports with 'sell' recommendations. Nor, in the early 1990s, were analysts encouraged to adopt a gloomy macro outlook.

The real money was and is to be made by the investment banking side of many broking firms who rely on corporate fundraising business to boost profits. It was clear that the companies likely to be in the market for these services would not take kindly to negative recommendations. Moreover, particularly in Asia where corporate information is hard to come by, analysts had to rely on the personal contacts they established within the company they were studying. These contacts would quickly be severed at the first hint of criticism.

Because of the kind of 'ersatz' capitalism discussed above, finance houses were also very wary of publishing material that would be viewed as directly critical of government policy in countries with which they were doing business. Not only were the governments themselves a good source of business but the close ties between government and business leaders meant it was risky to criticise either party.

However, a number of big companies did issue outspoken reports on what they saw as problems in the market. Others did not. I know a fair number of analysts who work in the region and most have tales of how they were told to hold back on this or that subject – their employers did not want to be seen as 'negative'.

On rare occasions it became known that certain analysts had left companies after writing negative reports. In December 1998, for example, HSBC Securities Asia in Hong Kong parted company with Joe Zhang, its well-respected head of China research, who had just written a highly critical report on a $1 billion bond issue by the Chinese government. Having worked at China's central bank, Mr Zhang knows something about these matters. However, within days he was off the premises. Neither side would comment on the reasons for his departure. What is clear, however, is that HSBC, which owns Hong Kong's largest bank, had no wish to get on the wrong side of the territory's new sovereign state.

A friend of mine working in Thailand wrote what I thought was an extremely good paper on corporate debt in 1995. It never saw the light of day because his bosses decreed that if it were to be published the company would be accused of causing a loss of confidence in the market. Moreover, he was warned not to attempt an exercise of this kind in the future. He did as he was told, leaving the company's clients pouring money into the Thai stock market.

The quality of fund management is strained

If the quality of analysts' advice left something to be desired, what about the quality of fund management? On the surface everything looked good. Asian funds appeared to be outperforming everything else in sight. However, a spot of retrospective analysis, covering 1975 to 1995, shows that these funds, which were the leaders in the emerging market fund league tables, were actually laggards if viewed over a longer period of time. In an article in *Fortune* magazine, James Montier, the global strategist at Natwest Markets in London, is quoted as saying, 'not only are emerging markets more volatile, but over the long run you get the perverse result that you aren't rewarded for it with higher returns'.[29] This assertion was confirmed by research undertaken by the finance house Morgan Stanley Dean Witter, which looked at risk reward ratios in the period from January 1993 to May 1999. It found that in this period the average return on investments from emerging markets was around 5 per cent whereas it was around 23 per cent in the United States and just below 20 per cent in Europe, in other words, in the world's most developed markets. Yet the risk factor (measured as standard deviation) in emerging markets during this period was double that of the more mature markets.[30]

The fund managers cannot be held solely to blame for relatively poor performance because there was a tendency in the fund management industry to give diminishing degrees of independence to those managing the funds. The gut instincts that have made people like Warren Buffet such great fund managers were not allowed free play among the smart men and women handling the Asian (and for that matter other) funds. Their bosses – and, to be fair, their clients – were obsessed by performances linked to benchmark fund indexes such as the MSCI Emerging Markets index. The safest way to ensure that the funds performed close to the benchmark was to buy blue chip stocks, which made up the region's main indexes. As long as fund manager A was buying more or less the same stocks as fund manager B, they were highly likely to produce the same returns. Moreover as these markets were soaring upwards even those who demonstrated a lack of imagination in their buying strategy could be sure of securing decent returns. Head offices were not really looking for imagination. Nor were they looking for fund managers who were confidently forecasting that the bubble was about to burst.

Such predictions would have curtailed enthusiasm at the retail end of the market which brought some of the biggest inflow into funds from investors looking for specialist Asian investments. So a vicious circle of pumping up Asian markets was well in place. All the fund managers had to do was keep pressing the buttons.

In the second quarter of 1997, immediately prior to the devaluation of the Thai baht on 2 July 1997, international emerging market funds made their biggest investments ever in these markets since Standard & Poors Micropal, the international fund rating service, began tracking these funds in the first quarter of 1995. So at the beginning of 1997 a staggering $9.3 billion was poured by funds into emerging market stocks, primarily in Asian markets.[31]

When the bubble burst in 1997, Asian markets, excluding Japan, saw 36 per cent wiped off their valuations. According to Micropal, most of the eighty-three regional funds it surveys only just managed to do better than the average level of the market fall. Investors in Asian funds who lost around a third of their money could be considered to have done fairly well.

Having recovered from the shock, wise investors would have been best advised to do nothing. A study by William Reichenstein and Dovalee Dorsett concluded that 'bad periods in the market are *predictably* followed by good periods and vice-versa . . . stock prices, like peapods, have shown no tendency to head off indefinitely in one direction or the other'.[32] However, the temptation to do something is great, and as we have seen, the herd instinct in financial markets is one of the strongest instincts that makes them move.

Rational thought is hard to come by when panic breaks out in the markets. A babble of conflicting voices invariably battles to be heard. The aftermath of the 1997 crash was no different from other crisis periods. Having been overconfident, the pundits turned overpessimistic and there was the usual parade of 'experts' claiming to have foreseen the collapse. Strangely their voices were heard more loudly in the post-crash period than before.

In April 1998 the *South China Morning Post* conducted a survey of Asian regional finance-house strategists. Their consensus view was that the worst was over but continued turbulence could still be expected.[33] By the end of the year the stock markets demonstrated that the worst was far from over. Most markets were still falling, although signs of a recovery were emerging in places like Singapore, and, to a lesser extent, in Malaysia. However, the Thai market fell by almost 27 per cent in 1998, Taiwan was down almost 26 per cent and Indonesia, already flat on its back, still managed a 15 per cent fall.

Rating the raters

As for the international rating agencies, whose job it is to identify signs of boom and bust, they too failed miserably in their task.[34] Sovereign ratings were lowered only after July 1997. Most spectacular was the failure of the credit-ratings agencies to identify the problems in South Korea. As late as October 1997 South Korea enjoyed a credit rating on a par with Italy and Sweden. By the end of the year its sovereign rating slumped from these favourable levels to junk-bond level.

Of the big three international ratings agencies, Standard and Poors, Moody's and Fitch IBCA, only the last has owned up to its lack of foresight, although all three were unanimous in their misjudgement.

In January 1998 Fitch IBCA published a *mea culpa* arguing that it had been lulled into a false sense of security by the fact that Korea as a nation had a low overall debt burden: 'We used to think that a high proportion of short term debt was a worry only with highly indebted sovereigns. We were wrong.'

The agency went on to criticise the IMF for its predictive failures and said that the governments in the region had proved to be bad managers. 'We over-estimated the sophistication of Asian policymakers, who have proved good fair weather navigators but very poor sailors in a storm' said Fitch IBCA.[35]

When the credit-raters finally got around to addressing the problems of the collapse they were subject to vilification by governments who saw their ratings slip away with the immediate consequence that the cost of borrowing rose sharply. As corporate entities cannot be given better ratings than the nations in which they are based, the effect of downgrades caused increasing amounts of pain as they travelled down the line. In these circumstances the agencies have reason to be cautious in their judgement but, equally, they should have had reason to identify the looming problems and, at the very least, issue what are known as 'watches' on various countries.

Reading the tea leaves

Some readers may consider this chapter to be unfair, relying too heavily on a form of 20/20 vision denied to most mortals. Indeed looking at some of the usual economic indicators it was not obvious that Asia was on the verge of a serious reversal.

For example, there were no signs of a state fiscal crisis. On the contrary most of the nations involved in the crisis were enjoying balanced budgets; in some places, notably Hong Kong and Singapore, there were healthy budget surpluses. Secondly, inflation rates were low, as were rates of unemployment, at least in relative terms. Thirdly, most of the Miracle economies were still enjoying very high savings rates, averaging above 30 per cent. Fourthly, with the exception of the Japanese yen, most Asian currencies were trading in a relatively stable manner.

It was true that there had been a rapid deflation of assets values, primarily reflected in fast-falling property prices but this was, at the time, seen as part of the entirely manageable cycle of business activity.

Despite the appearance of wellbeing there were those who warned of what was to come and, for those prepared to do their homework, there was plenty of data that showed that the good times were about to end. The data was not sufficient to put a precise date on the end of the party; that would have been asking too much.

Even without being able to pinpoint the collapse it was possible to learn some pretty clear lessons from the history of business cycles, the most obvious being that all cycles end with a downturn. History is also littered with attempts to tame the business cycle, making it less cyclical and more stable. In the nineteenth century the adoption of the gold standard was a means to this end. In the 1930s Keynsian economics, advocating government intervention, was widely seen as a way of removing the sharp swings of the business cycle. Multinational agreements and the establishment of multinational organisations, such as the International Monetary Fund and the World Bank, represent other attempts to pacify the beast that is known as business cycles. It can be said without qualification that all these attempts have, at best, delayed the inevitable but done nothing to alter the inherent nature of cyclical behaviour in economic systems.

It follows that the more extreme behaviour of systems, as manifest in the staggering growth of the Asian economies, was going to be followed by a decline, not necessarily of the same proportion as the growth, but nevertheless of severe proportions. In their heart of hearts, even the cheerleaders for the Asian Miracle acknowledged this piece of rather obvious forecasting but they could not bring themselves also to acknowledge the fact that there were inherent problems in the making of the Miracle. Problems that would lead to such a sudden collapse.

In February 1997 the Union Bank of Switzerland issued a report entitled 'No Reason for the Asian Economic Miracle to End', in which it said that the 'economic miracle' was set for many more decades of growth.

Asian economic growth must eventually slow to world norms of technological advance. But this need not happen before Asia has fully adopted existing technologies, upgraded education levels, and taken full advantage of gains available from international trade. If East Asian nations remain open to competition and technology, an Asian 'miracle' could continue for many decades. The risks to continued above-average Asian growth lie in politics – not in economic competition from the rest of the world, temporary infrastructure bottlenecks, shortages of particular raw materials or other often-voiced concerns.

So, were there early-warning signs of political risk? Probably not for the believers in the democracy-versus-economic-growth argument. And probably not for those who believed that the system of 'ersatz capitalism' was actually an ingredient of the Miracle. For everyone else the warnings were littered all over the place. The regimes that had helped create the bubble economies were reliant on the bubble not bursting. After all if they could no longer deliver the economic goods, what reason remained for their survival? When times were tough the authoritarian regimes responded by handing out more cosy deals to cronies. It took only a few setbacks (and the devaluation of the baht did not have to be more than a minor setback) to prove their economic incompetence and lack of strategy.

And, what of the economic indicators? Did they supply clues to point to the start of the collapse?[36] The most obvious clue came from export growth figures, the engine that powered the Asian Miracle. The Big Eight Asian economies had enjoyed export growth of 20 per cent in 1995; the following year, instead of growing exports fell by 1 per cent. This indicator of events in the 'real' economy should have given some food for thought.

Meanwhile corporate profitability started to drop. From 1991 to 1996 the average return on assets in Thailand fell from 8 to 1 per cent; in other countries the fall was less sharp, although in Malaysia profitability was still rising.

A survey by the World Bank of companies in Indonesia, Korea, Malaysia, the Philippines and Thailand showed that, particularly in Thailand, up to 17 per cent of companies in the construction sector had interest costs exceeding their profits; in all other sectors reviewed there were a significant number of companies in the same situation.

Out in the bubble economy 1996 also marked the year when asset prices started falling. New property developments in a number of capital cities were having difficulty attracting buyers. The problems in the property market fed their way into the equity markets, which started coming off their peaks.

By the beginning of the following year flows of private capital were diminishing. In the first half of 1997 bond issues and syndicated loans were down by a third compared with the same period in the previous year.

Borrowings were also rising rapidly, causing debt equity ratios to double in Thailand and Malaysia, and increase by a third in Korea. By 1996 leverage or capital gearing (the difference between loans and capital) had risen to 640 per cent for the average Korean company and 320 per cent for Thai companies. In other words for every $1 owned by Korean companies, they had debts of over $6. It is a myth to pretend that this worrying increase in gearing was not known at the time. The information was there, even though the full picture was not available and some of the debts were disguised.

Less easy to quantify at the time was the quality of the loans so freely granted. The defaults were to come as was the massive provisioning for nonperforming loans. However, the high degree of bank exposure to the property sector was well known. In Indonesia, for example, some 20 per cent of bank loans in 1996 went to the property sector. Thai and Malaysian banks were not trailing far behind in the level of their exposure. As the vulnerability of banks to the property market was a matter of public knowledge, it did not take a genius to work out that sliding property prices would cause a problem.

All these factors, which were known about before the crash began, should have set alarm bells ringing. The information may not have been neatly put together but it was there for the taking. It may not have amounted to a blueprint for charting the end of the Miracle, but the red light was flashing for anyone prepared to glance up and see it.

Despite the weaknesses, as we shall see in the following chapter, there are many aspects of the Asian 'Miracle' that were real and likely to be lasting.

2

WAS IT ALL A MIRAGE?

The *fin-de-siècle* feeling

Just before the Asian financial crisis errupted in the middle of 1997 I was discussing the take-off in fine-wine sales with a drinks distributor in Thailand. He was astonished by the rapid growth of the market, as were his bosses in the United States. In the capital Bangkok the latest rage was cigars for the *nouveau riche*, who were convinced that bigger meant better. Fancy hotels and stores were establishing bijou cigar saloons. An upmarket Hong Kong retailer called Joyce Boutiques, which specialises in higher-end designer-label clothing, had just opened an enormous and very expensive store in the centre of town.

There was something suspiciously unreal about all of this. I think I can say without the benefit of hindsight that it had a *fin-de-siècle* feel. After all, it was taking place in a city where some people still counted themselves lucky to be earning a dollar a day for their work.

To have so much conspicuous affluence in the midst of so much poverty was hardly unknown but the scale of the affluence and the rapidity with which it was spreading seemed very much like a miracle, albeit for the privileged few. This spread of affluence was happening not just in Bangkok but elsewhere in the region. Visiting other capital cities I saw the rising tide of wealth making its mark in equally bizarre ways.

In the Malaysian capital Kuala Lumpur excess was a hallmark of government policy. Not content with building the world's biggest flagpole, an interesting claim to fame, the government decreed that the capital should house the world's tallest building. Within days of the decision to devalue the Thai baht in July 1997 the twin Petronas Towers were opened for business. Standing nearly 530 metres tall, they topped Chicago's Sears Tower, the previous record holder, by 10.06 metres. Some estimates put the price of this edifice as high as $700 million, more than Cambodia's national budget. The construction was an unashamed attention-seeking, morale-boosting enterprise. What it did for the people in the *kampongs* – or villages – is a matter of debate.

Yet it could be argued that Malaysia had every right to aim high and literally reach for the sky. The question being asked was whether grandiose projects like this giant office building were substituting show for substance. For example, could the money poured into the Petronas Towers project not have been better used in hundreds of electrification projects throughout the country? This kind of debate was hardly restricted to Malaysia, nor indeed to the Asian region.

The irony was that projects like the Petronas Towers and other displays of extravagance concealed something far more solid and, I believe, more lasting. Moreover, the outward signs of overindulgence overshadowed the very real improvements in living standards that were evident throughout the region. They often occurred in ways that were not as visually dramatic as the construction of vast buildings.

The real miracle

I sometimes think that the *real* miracle was that Asian business overcame the many obstacles of poor government, poor management, corruption and a lack of planning, which should by rights have held them back. I cannot help but observe that many of these problems have been turned around and described as advantages by a number of commentators who have never soiled their hands by being involved in commerce.

As my hands are thoroughly soiled and I have found myself up close and personally involved in the cutting edge of business, I see things differently. The closer I got the more unlikely it seemed that most of the companies I got to know would be likely to continue performing in the way they were. Nevertheless, they had achieved a level of business growth that was real and impressive.

At its most basic the Asian Miracle represented a level of economic growth not seen in 130 years of recorded history. Economic output in South Korea, for example, doubled in a period of just eleven years.

Compare this with the fifty-eight years it took the British to double the level of output from 1780, or the forty-seven years it took the United States to double output from 1839. The Asian achievement in part is a product of the cycle of development that has speeded up economic growth and in part an acceleration of that cycle, bringing it to new levels.

In the period following the late 1960s the Miracle economies recorded an annual average level of economic growth exceeding 6 per cent. No other group of countries has come close to this record. In the 1980s the East Asian economies were collectively growing by 7.4 per cent per year.[1] At the same time the economies of the Latin American countries, poised to become the flavour of the month among investors, were growing at a mere 1.7 per cent. The more developed economies of Europe and North America would have been delighted to see economic growth rates of 3 per cent, but were happy enough to settle for around 2 per cent in good years. Sub-Saharan Africa economies were growing by less than 0.5 per cent in this period.

In East Asia the industrial revolution, which took European nations many decades to accomplish, was achieved within a couple of decades. In 1965 East Asia accounted for 1.5 per cent of the world trade in manufactured goods; by 1986 its share had grown to 8.5 per cent. A lesser revolution was also underway in the agricultural and primary-industries sector.

The standard-of-living miracle

As a result living standards in the high-growth Asian countries rose faster and in a shorter space of time than in any other part of the world at any other time in recorded history. In 1965 average incomes in Asia were a mere 13 per cent of those earned by Americans. Just twenty-five years later, in 1990, the gap had narrowed to an extent where Asian average incomes were 26 per cent of American levels. In the tiger economies workers not only managed to leap from subsistence levels to something far above that, but they started to achieve levels of disposable income that were on a par with and beyond the levels found in many of the industrialised countries. In Korea, for example, average incomes rose fourfold between 1975 and 1995. In the same period two out of every five Indonesians were lifted out of the poverty level.

Although the so-called Miracle made some people extraordinarily rich it also made a great many poor people richer than they had ever been. Some would argue that the singular success of the Miracle was to achieve very high levels of economic growth without producing ever-expanding gaps between the rich and the poor. In East Asia the income of the poorest 20 per cent of the community was higher than in other regions, where overall income levels were the same but the poorest 20 per cent earned less. However, at the extreme ends of the poverty and affluence charts, the gap remained very wide.

The social miracle

The extraordinary increases in living standards also brought about a profound social transformation. One of the most noticeable changes, visible to anyone who has travelled around the region for the past two decades, as I have, is the very shape of the people who live in East Asia. The new, post-boom generation are taller and broader than their parents. In Singapore, where living standards increased faster than elsewhere, the average height of a 16-year-old Singaporean boy increased from 158 cm to 170 cm between 1973 and 1993, and average weights increased from 43.8 kg to 59 kg. During the same period, girls of the same age were, on average, 7 cm taller, and 8.5 kg heavier.[3] These changes are almost entirely attributable to better diet, which in turn is a direct consequence of increasing prosperity.

Dietary changes have been so profound that Asian medical experts are now worried by the phenomenon of the East importing the worst dietary habits of the West as the traditional carbohydrate-dominated foods found in Asia are replaced by fatty foods, which are contributing to the rapid growth of diseases such as diabetes and are producing heart problems.

Heart problems are also exacerbated by the rapid shift of the population from the countryside to the towns. This has resulted in poorly regulated urban growth and a massive increase in pollution. According to United Nations and World Bank figures, East Asia and the Pacific experienced by far the biggest increase in urban populations in the period stretching from 1970 to 1995. By the end of the period 31 per cent of the population were living in towns, compared with 21 per cent at the beginning of the period.[4]

Among the main social consequences of urbanisation was the freedom it gave to the women, who started pouring into towns in search of work. Not only were they more in demand than their male counterparts, especially for clothing and electronic-assembly work, but, for many, their presence in the towns provided a degree of independence unknown in the countryside. Having worked in family units without a formal system of payment they suddenly found themselves to be wage earners and as such wielded far more power than they had ever possessed before. In many cases young women became richer than the men in their families. This created new tensions and a shift in the nature of their relationships which was most definitely in the women's favour.

As conditions for women improved at the lower end of the scale they also took a turn for the better further up the social ladder. The number of female managers in Singapore has nearly tripled in the ten years ending in 1995. In Thailand, the number of women employed as managers increased five times over a period of two decades.

Asian societies remain more patriarchal than most Western societies and, in extreme cases, discrimination against females is still prevalent and alarming. This is primarily seen in China, where girl babies are killed in large numbers so that families can concentrate on male offspring (China's one-child policy is the main reason for this). It is also seen in the poor parts of Thailand, Burma and the Philippines, where some families sell their daughters into a life of prostitution. However, the situation is improving and, more than anything else, it was economic developments that helped break down some of the doors that have held back women in the workforce.

The position of women has also been altered by urbanisation and growing prosperity, which are causing a breakdown in the institution of the extended family. Prosperity means that economic circumstances no longer compel young families to move into the home of the husband's family. Moreover, in the more prosperous parts of Asia, notably Hong Kong, Singapore and Taiwan, a small army of foreign domestic workers have been imported and created an era of unprecedented opportunity for middle-class women to pursue their careers without a break while bringing up children. Indeed, the freedom this has brought to this group of women has given them opportunities much envied by their counterparts in the West, who are busy trying to juggle family and career priorities. The flip side of this coin is that many of the women they employ have had to leave their own children in places like the Philippines, Thailand and Indonesia so that they can earn the kind of money that could never be made back home. Their children are then brought up by their grand-parents, providing an extreme version of the urbanisation phenomenon in which younger family members move to the towns while the older family members and young children remain in the countryside.

Developments of this kind also have an impact on deeply held Asian notions of filial piety. Most Asian nations lack anything more than a rudimentary welfare-state network and rely on younger family members to look after the old and assume that at a very young age children will be cared for by their grandparents. The break-up of the extended family and the growing independence of family members is undermining some of these assumptions. In Singapore the government was so worried by this trend that it introduced legislation in 1995 to compel younger family members to look after their elderly parents. No other country has gone this far but it is widely recognised that the assumptions that surrounded the obligations of filial piety are being challenged, moving Asian nations in the direction of the West, although they remain far apart.

The increasing advance of urbanisation went hand in hand with a rapid growth of the middle class. Definitions of what constitutes the middle class are problematic; however, it seems most simple if based upon relatively straightforward economic measurement. In 1995 Samsung, one of the big South Korean *chaebols*, which specialises in making low-cost electronic goods, defined the middle class as being those who own or can afford to buy five basic home appliances: a washing machine, a refrigerator, a television set, a microwave oven and a video recorder (VCR). By Samsung's definition, the bulk of the South Korean population had already reached this status. The company estimated that 89 per cent of Koreans owned a washing machine, 99 per cent had refrigerators, 75 per cent had VCRs in their homes and nearly half had microwave ovens.[5]

Whether or not the Samsung definition holds water, it provides a basic guide to economic prosperity and correctly identifies ownership of certain material goods as being perceived as equating to membership of the middle class. Social class is in a far greater state of flux in Asia than in the industrialised nations. It is also better defined by wealth than in most European countries, where history lays a heavy hand on the evolution of social class. The kind of snobbery associated with social class in Britain, for example, is relatively absent from Asian societies. This even applies in those countries – such as Malaysia and Thailand – that have long-established royal families and a continuing system with feudal character-istics. Admission to the Asian middle class comes with cash, not as a pure consequence of family background. Few people would dream of looking down on the new rich, or of seeing 'old money' as somehow superior. Indeed the opposite is far more likely to be the case as most Asian societies admire those who have become rich from their own efforts rather than as a result of inheritance.

The political miracle

The growth of the middle class has also done much to challenge the rule of autocratic regimes. Although it is not fashionable to mention it these days, Karl Marx showed considerable foresight in predicting the revolutionary role of the bourgeoisie forcing the pace of change before the proletariat were ready to take power. The latter phenomenon has yet to be witnessed in Asia, which has seen peasant revolutions and middle-class uprisings but never a revolution of the proletariat. In Asia it was the middle class who literally went to the barricades to help overthrow the Marcos regime in the Philippines in 1986; it was the middle class again who were in the forefront of the protests against the military coup d'état in Thailand in 1992; and in 1987 it was the middle class in South Korea who made the difference by joining the students in protests that led to direct presidential elections.

In other words it is a myth to believe that the Asian middle class are only preoccupied with money making. As in other parts of the world, increased prosperity has led to rising expectations of good government and demands for increasing levels of *representative* government. This too is a positive result of the Asian Miracle, even if it is not recognised as such by the most enthusiastic promoters of miracle myths.

It may even be argued that the most profound and lasting consequences of rapid economic advances in East Asia have occurred at the social and political level. Moreover, they have had an impact on society that has released the genie from the bottle. Women who have found a new independence will not willingly return to their former lives. New styles of eating, new forms of entertainment and new concepts of family life cannot be so easily reversed.

Yet it is the economics of the process that exercises the greatest interest and with reason. The economic achievements are truly extraordinary and cannot be lightly ignored or under rated.

Retaining some perspective

However, before we all get too excited, it is worth repeating something that Chris Patten, the last Governor of Hong Kong, has noted. He wrote,

> what has really been happening in Asia is the recovery of ground lost over the last century or two. Asia is not springing forward from a position of strength but clawing back from what was painfully forfeited.[6]

In the early part of the nineteenth century Asia accounted for about 58 per cent of the world economy. By 1920, its share had dropped by more than half. In the 1940s it slipped back further to 19 per cent.

So, as Mr Patten says, Asia is in fact 'clawing back'. He quotes the Asian Development Bank as predicting that it will take until 2025 to return to the position where it was two centuries previously. The financial crisis of the late 1990s is a setback but not a cause for a major reversion.

Discussing the region as a whole is problematic because of the very great differences between the countries of Asia. Generalisations are dangerous and can rightly be held to ridicule as circumstances in individual countries demonstrate the folly of trying to extrapolate a general trend. However, that does not make generalisation invalid, nor is the task of identifying the components of Asian economic growth resistant to this process.

The ingredients of the miracle

Most studies that seek to pinpoint the reasons for economic success in East Asia focus on a number of common themes. Among them are the emphasis on education and creating a skilled and adaptable workforce. Secondly, most analysts point to the very high level of domestic savings in East Asia, which created a substantial degree of funding for investment purposes. Thirdly, it is widely agreed that the countries that have grown most had trade policies designed to facilitate export-led development. Fourthly, East Asian governments are seen as having pursued sound macroeconomic policies, nurturing an environment in which business found it easy to grow. Finally, although there is some disagreement on this point, many analysts point to the driving role of Japan in the growth of the rest of East Asia. On the one hand Japan has been a major source of investment and trade while on the other it has provided an Asian model for economic growth.

Beyond this there is considerable disagreement over the ingredients for Asian success. The biggest divergence of views centres on the role of government in the growth process. One school of thought holds that the hands-off, laissez-faire governmental attitude has made it possible for these countries to flourish. Another insists that, on the contrary, the state has been a guiding force. And, as we have seen, there are many who believe that the presence of authoritarian government and the absence of democracy have left Asian nations free to get on with economic development, rather than be hindered by time-consuming democratic niceties.

We will return shortly to the contested factors that are said to have helped promote growth. First, however, a quick review of the commonly agreed factors.

The human-capital ingredient

The development of what has been called 'human capital' is mainly seen in the development of education. On the one hand, in the high-growth Asian economies government policy emphasised expenditure on education; on the other Asian societies have traditionally viewed learning to be a matter of great importance and education is widely respected. The impetus for realising educational aspirations was that governments had the financial means to spread the educational net wider and declining fertility rates were putting less strain on educational resources.

With the exception of Malaysia, which devoted an average of around 4 per cent of its gross national product (GNP) to educational expenditure, most of the other high-growth economies devoted some 2 per cent, which was more or less in line with expenditure elsewhere in the world. But they got better results because of falling birth rates and because the money was better used on primary and secondary education rather than on more prestigious higher levels of education. In 1985, for example, 10 per cent of Korea's education budget was devoted to higher education, compared with 43 per cent in Venezuela. In the 1980s Indonesia was spending some

90 per cent of its educational budget on basic education, while Bolivia devoted only some 40 per cent of its expenditure to this purpose.[7]

Yet there was also a rapid development of tertiary education in universities, but this was accompanied by the channelling of resources into enhancing vocational skills. The net result of these educational policies and priorities was to produce a solid basis of literacy. This gave rise to far higher standards of literacy in East Asia than elsewhere in the developing world.[8]

In 1986, for example, a mere 18 per cent of Somalia's adult population was literate; female literacy was even lower at 6 per cent. In South Korea at this time, 96 per cent of the male adult population were literate, as were 88 per cent of the female population.[9] South Korea was not alone: all the high-growth Asian economies had very high levels of literacy, which verged close on being universal in places such as Hong Kong and Singapore and were near these levels elsewhere. Where pockets of illiteracy remained they were mainly confined to the older generation.

The savings ingredient

Turning to the second most widely identified source of Asian economic growth, it was clear that the development of high levels of domestic savings provided a source of cheap capital for Asian companies. There is considerable debate over why Asians proved to be unusually assiduous savers, with some analysts favouring cultural explanations to explain this phenomenon. However, pragmatists can see that the economic environment was conducive to savers. First, real rates of interest remained relatively good (despite wide spreads between bank lending and deposit rates), and secondly there was a relatively stable economic situation, which gave people confidence to save their money rather than spend it quickly to mitigate the consequences of inflation. Unlike Western countries, Asian states tend not to tax savings gains, thus providing an additional incentive to save. Or it may be argued that they have not fallen into the trap of creating a *dis*incentive. Also, Asian savers had reason to feel secure that their savings would not be taken away by fraud, bank failures or the like. This was an important factor for people who had experienced precisely these problems within living memory.

As a result, by 1990 the high-growth East Asian countries were seeing savings rates equivalent to over one-third of GDP. This was almost four times higher than saving rates in the Indian subcontinent and Africa, and almost double the rate in the Caribbean and Latin America and the United States.[10] In individual countries the extraordinarily high level of regional savings was impressively exceeded. In Singapore, for example, where the state imposes mandatory saving on the workforce, saving rates soared to almost 50 per cent of GDP.

The availability of cheap local sources of finance meant that for most of the high-growth Asian economies, with the significant exception of capital-awash Singapore, foreign direct investment (FDI) played a relatively small role in fixed-capital formation. In the first six years of the 1990s, FDI accounted for an average of just 0.2 per cent of Hong Kong's capital formation; the figure was 0.9 per cent for South Korea, 2.7 per cent for Taiwan, 4.1 per cent for Thailand (and this was despite much publicity about foreign capital inflows) and 5.5 per cent for Indonesia. At the other end of the scale Singapore attracted an average 29.7 per cent of its fixed capital from abroad, Malaysia 17.5 per cent and the Philippines (where domestic savings rates are lower) 17.5 per cent (some of this, however, was derived from overseas-based Filipinos).[11]

In most countries there is a more or less even split between private and public investment, but in East Asia some two-thirds of all investment came from the private sector. As it turned out, after the 1997 collapse, the debt problems produced by the massive expansion of investment lay in the private sector, whereas financial crises are normally triggered by public debt problems. We shall examine why private debt was so problematic later; however, there is no intrinsic reason why private funding should be a cause of fiscal weakness. On the contrary, some would argue that it is a more flexible and cost-efficient means of investment.

The export ingredient

So, where did all this direct investment (as opposed to indirect or portfolio investment through financial markets) go? This brings us to the third, most commonly cited reason for East Asia's economic success, namely the rapid development of export-orientated industries and government policies that encouraged the promotion of trade. Principally this involved a rapid expansion of the export of manufactured goods. Governments throughout the region were hellbent on developing export industries. Their strategies varied from the Korean policy of giving direct assistance to create large domestic manufacturing entities who could compete in world markets, to the policies of the Thai and Indonesian governments, which sought to attract foreign investors with a package of tax breaks, cheap land and so forth, so that they could develop export industries for the nation. On the other hand, in Singapore, government policy emphasised a rapid upgrading of export manufacturing stimulated by direct state participation in industry and a vigorous overseas campaign to attract foreign direct investment for export-orientated industries.

Although it is sometimes stated that East Asia managed to grow because its governments promoted open-market policies, this view does not stand up to careful scrutiny. Some of the countries who were most aggressive as exporters, such as Korea and Taiwan, were also pursuing protectionist policies up to the end of the 1980s. These policies involved crude tariff instruments; other forms of protectionism were not so crude but the net effect was to keep imports out. Understandably these barriers to free trade were kept under pressure, particularly from the United States, and were forced down. But they did provide a protective wall from behind which to build local industry.

Other places, notably Singapore, Thailand and Hong Kong, erected few barriers to trade, yet achieved the same results – although, in the case of tiny Singapore and Hong Kong, it came at the expense of high import bills and a negative trade balance on the visibles side of the books while there were big surpluses in the trade in invisibles.

Both the nations tending towards protectionism and those who did not were running relatively open economies. One useful measure of the openness of an economy to foreign competition is the ratio of black-market to official rates of foreign-currency exchange. As early as 1984, all the high-growth Asian economies showed either no difference or very little difference between the two rates, so little that in places like Hong Kong there was no reason for a black market. However, at this time Latin American emerging markets, for example in Argentina, Brazil and Mexico, all showed noticeable disparities between black-market and official rates of exchange. State-controlled economies usually suffer from significant rate differences and this was the case in places such as Vietnam and China. It was also the case in countries such as Uganda, Ghana and other parts of sub-Saharan Africa.

This push into world markets produced staggering productivity increases. According to the World Bank two-thirds of the productivity growth came as a result of physical and human-capital growth and one-third as a result of something it describes as total-factor-productivity growth (TFP) or, more prosaically, improved efficiency. Whether this was, as Paul Krugman famously put it, the result of 'perspiration, not inspiration', will be discussed later.

The macroeconomic-policy ingredient

The fourth most commonly cited reason for East Asian economic growth is that governments pursued sound macroeconomic policies which were conducive to the expansion of business. Inflation was kept low, taxes were kept low, exchange rates remained competitive and stable and, as we have seen in Chapter 1, it was argued that governments kept out of businessmen's hair, leaving them free to get on with money making. Whether or not this is correct (I personally doubt it), it can generally be stated that the governments of the region went out of their way to be business-friendly, even though this friendliness was manifest in many different ways.

The degree of friendliness to all sectors of the business community may be in question but the one thing that all businessmen tend to like is consistency and in East Asia they found a great deal of consistency because governments tended to be long-lasting. Even where the governments changed a lot, as they did in Thailand after Prem Tinsulanond stepped down from eight years in office ending in 1988, the bureaucracy that remained was strong enough to run a pretty much unchanged economic policy with little political interference causing stops and starts in policy making.

The plus side of longevity in government was the willingness to make short-term sacrifices, which in other systems would have been politically problematic, in return for longer-term gains. The flip side of this coin was that many of the long-standing governments, such as the Suharto regime in Indonesia, were dictatorships or semidictatorships which were corrupted by their long years in office and perverted the virtues of stability to make the goal the survival of their own regimes a priority at the expense of other considerations.

The Japanese ingredient

Finally and, in some parts of Asia, controversially, there is the role of Japan to be considered. Even Asians who do not have particularly warm feelings about Japan, because of World War Two, concede that Japanese invest-ment, trade and the example set by Japanese business, have had a profound impact on economic growth throughout the region.

The bulk of Japan's external trade had traditionally been with other Asian countries. Until the 1980s most of that trade involved Japanese manufactured goods going to other parts of East Asia while Japan imported natural-resource products from them. During the 1980s the pattern began to change and Japan became either the principal or second most important trading partner with most of the countries in the region.

However, Japan was not a major investor in the region until the 1990s. Before then direct investment by Japanese companies in the rest of Asia accounted for only some 12 per cent of the nation's worldwide external direct investment.[12] The bulk of Japanese money was going to the United States and Europe as a means of getting around restrictions on Japanese exports.

All this changed in the 1990s when, with a great leap, Japan became the dominant investor in the region's industries, providing the vital impetus for the creation of some of the biggest export-orientated industries. The new Japanese outflow was prompted not by trade worries but by a desire to escape high labour costs at home. The massive shift in manufacturing assembly work from Japan to Southeast Asia was described as the 'hollowing out' of Japanese industry. By the late 1990s things had reached a stage where Japan was importing two and a half times as many television sets as it was exporting, but the imports carried names such as Sony, Toshiba and Hitachi.

By 1990 Japanese direct investment in Southeast Asian countries had risen to over $7 billion, almost four times higher than four years previously. The levels of investment remained high until the later part of the 1990s, peaking in 1995 at a level of $14 billion. (It is, incidentally, interesting to note that Japanese investment flows exactly mirror rises and falls in the value of the yen.[13]) The sheer speed with which Japan adopted other parts of the region as its industrial back yard caused some alarm and revived memories of the infamous 'Greater Asia Co-Prosperity Sphere', which the Japanese tried to create when occupying many countries in Asia during World War Two.

However, no one doubted the role of Japanese companies in kick-starting industrial development in the rest of East Asia. The large Japanese corporations, and even the smaller companies who live by supplying components to the larger companies, brought new work practices to the region, dispatched hundreds of thousands of workers for training in Japan and eventually, albeit in some cases reluctantly, formed joint-venture companies which brought local partners into businesses. In so doing Japanese know-how was transferred and local companies were able to leapfrog into international markets with the knowledge and skills acquired as a result of the partnership.

The most interesting of the joint ventures is ironically one that claims to be Malaysia's indigenous national car producer. This is an alliance between the Mitsubishi Motor Corp. and Hicom, a Malaysian entity making the Proton brand of cars. In effect Proton cars are versions of Mitsubishi models and incorporate parts imported from Japan. The fortunes of Proton have been decidedly mixed but the sometimes fraught joint venture demonstrated how an East Asian nation could build a car-making industry from scratch (hitherto there had been only auto assembly in Malaysia) and do so at great speed.

It is hard to imagine how the high-growth Asian economies could have penetrated world markets quite so rapidly without the Japanese presence. Even in South Korea and Taiwan – both countries occupied for long periods by the Japanese, and still harbouring strong reservations about Japan – investment and trade with their former colonial masters provided the impetus for many local industries.

Unraveling the less tangible ingredients

There is little that is difficult to understand about the tangible reasons for the growth of East Asian economies. The problems come when one is trying to unravel the less tangible reasons, which, in some ways are more basic and less likely to be undermined by the Asian financial crisis. In fact it seems more than likely that out there in the land of the less tangible are reasons that explain both the Asian boom and why Asian economies will survive the crisis. I draw here more heavily on my own business experience and have come up with conclusions that, in many cases, have been shared with others.

Let me start with a sweeping generalisation about state of mind. Working in companies alongside Asian people, I never cease to be amazed by their sheer capacity for hard work, their focus on becoming successful and – this particularly strikes someone born in Britain – their lack of envy of those who have become rich. On the contrary, being rich is admired, and nearly everyone I have come across aspires to become rich themselves, or at least they hope and believe that their children can become rich.

I am well aware that these generalisations are dangerous and willingly concede that, in a region as large as East Asia, there are profound differences in mindset. However, the generalisations I am making largely refer to the eight high-growth economies and their people.

When I started my first business in Hong Kong my partner, who was born in China but started his working life in Hong Kong, decided to spend some months before we opened taking a menial job in a company that was a market leader in the field we were planning to enter. He wanted to make sure that he knew how the business worked at the very lowest level because this would be where most of our employees were engaged. The work was tough, distinctly unglamorous and not at all well rewarded.

I wonder what the reaction would have been from, say, a British person, wanting to start a business. First there would have been a reluctance to opt for this low-status work experience. Secondly, there might have been social awkwardness at suddenly becoming a lowly employee. And, thirdly, the effort might have been considered all too much. And then look at the matter from the other side. What would the employers have had to say? Would they have seen this behaviour as some form of industrial espionage? Would they have been annoyed when he left to start up his own business?

The answers to these questions are: first, it was not regarded as espionage because the real trade secrets of the company were well locked away; secondly, the managers of the company were not in the least dismayed by the thought of a former employee going into business on his own account. This was considered to be natural rather than errant behaviour; indeed one of the managers subsequently joined our company because he wanted to become an entrepreneur and have a share in the company rather than just being a wage earner.

There are a couple of lessons to be drawn from all this, which is admittedly an attempt to draw a wide picture from a mere microcosm. However, experiences like this are, to my certain knowledge, repeated time and time again throughout the region.

Lesson one is the preparedness to do whatever it takes to develop a business. Lesson two is that entrepreneurism is regarded as positive behaviour and is automatically accorded a level of support. It may be argued that this attitude is shared by entrepreneurs everywhere and therefore this can hardly be described as a particularly Asian characteristic. However, the fact of the matter is that there are more entrepreneurs in Asia and this attitude is therefore far more widespread and, as we shall see, also a characteristic of workforce behaviour.

Which brings me to the subject of the people who work in our company. Some work harder than others, some are brighter than others. In other words, they are like people in all other companies. However, if you were to compare their application to work with the application commonly found in companies in the industrialised countries, I am confident you would find that they simply work harder and are more diligent, both because they feel it is the thing to do and because there is peer pressure which encourages members of the workforce to maintain similarly high levels of activity.

When one of our units was performing badly it was the staff who volunteered to change working practices and cut costs, rightly seeing this as a better option than closure. They did so in anticipation that when things improved they would receive bonuses over and above their basic pay. None of this was explicitly stated but it was well understood. This attitude is rather different from one that might be found in Western companies, where employees expect the management to solve financial problems and are nervous of relinquishing gains made in wages and working conditions because they, often rightly, assume that these conditions will not be restored in good times. However, we found that our staff had a wholly realistic appreciation of how business was conducted and were prepared to make sacrifices, which would be rewarded if business improved or, at worst, their initiatives would keep them in work during a difficult economic period. In other words their approach as *employees*, was essentially an *entrepreneurial* approach. Instead of instinctively looking for ways of preserving their personal position in the face of declining business prospects, they looked at ways of improving the business and in so doing improving their position within it.

This form of pragmatism characterises how people in this region work. Expectations are rapidly adjusted in the light of surrounding realities. The determination to remain employed, whether self-employed or by a company, is strong and ensures that when the going gets tough Asian workers cling tenaciously to their work.

For many years I was adamantly opposed to the introduction of a time clock for our staff. I felt that it signified a lack of trust and involved an unnecessary piece of bureaucracy. However, my opposition finally crumbled when it was put to me that it was the staff themselves who felt uncomfortable without having a time clock to record their punctuality and, in many cases, long hours of working. There is a pride in hard work and, to Western ways of thinking, a curiously formal mindset which requires it to be acknowledged in a precise manner.

Without meaning to diminish the considerable regard I have for our employees, I do not claim that there is anything special about this group of people because I know that my experience is shared by countless other employers throughout the region.

Of course every employee is not suddenly going to become an entrepreneur, although, again from my own experience, I can think of a number of our staff who have done precisely that. One is now a supplier to the company.

Even those who do not want to strike out on their own admire wealth creation. In Britain and the United States, for example, it is common for owners of luxury cars to worry about them being scratched, not as a result of accidents but as a result of deliberate defacement by those who have no hope of ever owning such a vehicle. In Hong Kong, however, this phenomenon is unknown. Moreover, I recall that when the Hong Kong government's 1999 budget was being debated some legislators from the Frontier Party attempted to stop the government giving a proposed rebate to higher-level taxpayers. In what can only be viewed as populist gesture, they insisted that only those earning less should receive the money. However, the move was far from popular: the Democratic Party, who had planned to support their Frontier colleagues, soon withdrew their support when they saw it was greeted by a chorus of disapproval, especially from the poor, who viewed it as an idea that had more in common with the Chinese Communist Party than the traditions of Hong Kong.

Another example is drawn from Thailand, where, after the crash, an enterprising car-sales company set up a weekend market for the 'previously rich'. Desperate for cash, they flocked to Bangkok's classy Sukhumvit Road to sell their Rolex watches, Mercedes Benz cars and the like. Imagine the mocking this would have produced in most Western countries. Not in Thailand, however, where the venture was thought of as slightly amusing but perfectly sensible.

The point I am making here is that this is a region where wealth creation is enthusiastically embraced by the whole population. Not only is it accepted as a good thing in principle but there are a sufficient number of people in the region who believe that they too can become wealthy. This provides the motivation for levels of hard work that have long faded elsewhere.

There are signs that this driving force is becoming less potent, especially in highly developed Japan, where countless agonised studies have been conducted about the new youth culture, which shies away from the hard-work ethic of the elders. There has, as yet, been no need to conduct these studies elsewhere in the region.

The following chapter examines the concept of Confucianism, which is supposed to lay the ideological foundations for the Asian work ethic. This is a complex matter and I don't want to get ahead of myself, only to say at this point that it is hard to put the cart before the horse. In other words, Confucianism may well provide an intellectual explanation of what is happening – although even that is problematic – but it is not necessarily the cause of or motivation for the way people work in East Asia.

The much-overlooked immigrant factor

One overwhelming reason why the region has such strong entrepreneurial drive is the unusually high level of immigrants in all but one (South Korea) of the eight high-growth economies. By definition immigrants are a highly motivated, self-selected group of people. In the case of East Asia most were driven to migrate by economic rather than political or racial factors. For reasons that baffle me, so-called economic migrations are considered to be somehow unworthy. Maybe this is because they consist of people who set out to make money by leaving their homes. Unsurprisingly they are an unusually determined group of people. As a result of their activities they always provide considerable stimulus for the new host economies.

The result of so-called economic migration in Asia and other parts of the world is different from that in some of the countries largely populated by immigrants, such as the United States, Australia and Argentina, because the immigrants do not constitute the majority of the population but a significant and dynamic minority who have ended up exerting an economic influence that is wholly disproportionate to their numbers.

In East Asia the overwhelming bulk of the immigrants are Chinese, although they have been joined by much smaller, albeit influential, Indian communities in places such as Singapore, Malaysia and Hong Kong. It is commonplace to describe the Chinese as the 'Jews of the East' in terms of their impact on the economies in places they have settled, although the Chinese have had more impact on these economies than the Jews ever had in Europe. They could equally be said to be like the Lebanese of Africa, if their activities were compared to the role Lebanese have played in a number of African communities. People are forever seeking a racial explanation for the success of the Chinese or Jews or whoever. I am highly sceptical of this approach and believe that the success is far more understandable in the context of the situation of ethnic minorities as economic migrants.

In Mandarin the overseas Chinese are known as the *hua ch'iao*, but most of the successful Chinese migrants are from the South. In Cantonese they are known as *wah kiu*, but they also call themselves '*tong yan*'. This is interesting because their self-description literally translates as 'people of the Tang dynasty', arguably the most successful of the Chinese dynasties, which lasted 289 years until 907. It was a time when the Chinese empire stretched from Mongolia in the North to Singkiang, taking in much of what is now Korea, to Annam in the South, and exerted a great political influence over India.[14]

Like the Jews and like all other prominent immigrant communities, the Chinese in Asia have had their fair share of problems. Ironically it was in Thailand, where the Chinese are most assimilated, that the term 'Jews of the East' was coined by King Vajiravudh in a vitriolic racist essay written in 1915. However, discrimination and prejudice has not thwarted Chinese commercial success, a success that has added immeasurably to the dynamism of the communities in which it has been achieved.

It is not easy to be precise in measuring the overseas Chinese impact on East Asian economies, not least because it has been the subject of exaggeration among both those with racist and those with Chinese chauvinist motives.

In 1994 the Chinese-language *Forbes Zibenjia* magazine analysed the 1000 biggest companies listed on ten Asian stock exchanges – Bangkok, Hong Kong, Jakarta, Kuala Lumpur, Manila, Seoul, Shanghai, Shenzhen, Singapore and Taipei. It was conducting the kind of exercise that greatly appeals to some Chinese readers by finding out how much of the wealth on these exchanges was under ethnic Chinese control. The conclusion was that they accounted for 42 per cent of total market capitalisation amounting to some \$541 billion.[15]

The majority of companies listed on the Thai, Indonesian, Malaysian and Philippine stock exchanges are controlled by ethnic Chinese (this is also true in Hong Kong, Taiwan and Singapore, but these are majority Chinese communities). However, Chinese influence is not confined to big business: it is even more noticeable among the smaller and medium-sized enterprises that make up the bulk of Asian companies. One estimate, which strikes me as exaggerated, states that 90 per cent of these companies are controlled by ethnic Chinese.[16] Even if this is not the case and, say, is exaggerated by a third, it still represents an enormous disparity between the actual size of Chinese populations and the economic influence they wield.

In Indonesia, for example, ethnic Chinese make up at most 4 per cent of the population yet are said to control around two-thirds of the economy. This control made the Chinese the target of racially motivated violence during the Indonesian riots of 1998 and 1999. The poor and disposed who poured out on the streets to loot Chinese-owned businesses and seek Chinese blood were hardly contemplating the contribution the Chinese had made to the economy: rather they were focusing on their supposedly privileged position within it. Incidentally, the anti-Chinese violence in Indonesia serves to underline a basic point about the attitude of the poor towards the rich. There were no outbreaks of class-based violence in Indonesia: all attacks were racially or religiously motivated. Despite the fact that many of those who benefited from the largesse of the disgraced Suharto family were Muslim Indonesians, their premises were not looted, nor were they personally attacked.

What the overseas Chinese brought to Asian economies was an immigrant's determination to succeed and a capacity for hard work which realised these aspirations. Moreover, the connections between Chinese clans created a ready made network for international trade and co-operation.

Most of these Asian overseas Chinese communities are now entering their third or fourth generation. The hunger of the early immigrants has been replaced by the affluence and easy life of their descendants. This must have blunted their drive, yet the Chinese continue to be a dynamic element in Asian economies even though, as we shall see, the traditional style of Chinese business organisation, ideally suited to getting businesses going, is far less suitable as a model for sustaining really big businesses and making them global players.

In Malaysia the Prime Minister, Dr Mahathir Mohamad, set out with single-minded determination to break the Chinese control over the economy by introducing a series of policies discriminating against the Chinese and giving preference to *Bumiputras*, or indigenous Malays. The policy had mixed results. Although it clearly succeeded in achieving a large degree of redistribution of wealth, it did not so clearly provide an impetus to new wealth creation.

In Thailand design and default arising from high levels of integration of the indigenous and Chinese communities produced a much better infusion of Chinese business acumen within the mainstream of activity. In the past Thai governments pursued policies of active anti-Chinese discrimination, which were widely seen as failures.

So, in considering the intangibles that have made for high growth in Asian economies, we have principally been talking about attitude and the infusion of a dynamic immigrant element, which has reinforced positive attitudes and assisted in kick-starting business development and created flourishing businesses.

Doing best by doing least?

From here we return to the question of the contested elements that are believed to have been ingredients of the Asian Economic Miracle. The basic division is between those who maintain that government did best by doing least and giving businessmen the freedom to go out and develop the economy, and those who argue that, contrary to popular myth, Asian governments were extraordinarily interventionist and by intervening steered their economies on to paths of success.

There is little argument about the degree of government intervention in places such as South Korea and Singapore but it is usually assumed that in places like Hong Kong the government kept its distance. This too is a myth. I recall with a wry smile the anger of Don Curran, vice-president of United Airlines, when in 1999 he announced that his company was finally giving up the unequal struggle of trying to provide an air service between Hong Kong and Delhi in an industry where the government goes out of its way to help Cathay Pacific Airways, the territory's de facto flag carrier. 'The claim that Hong Kong follows a laissez-faire policy is one of the biggest myths in Asia,' he exploded. 'It may be true if you or I want to open a shop selling bootlaces, when you can get the paperwork done in the morning and be in business by the afternoon. But if you want to challenge one of the vested interests it is different.'

Mr Curran is quite wrong about the problems of opening a small shop, as I discovered when trying to open a tiny sandwich shop and found myself going to court with hundreds of others once a month for four months to pay a fine for not operating with a valid licence, which was hard to get because it was forever pending in the in-tray of some indolent bureaucrat.

The truth is that the former colony is a place riddled by government-created monopolies and restrictive practices, which in part have promoted growth and in part held it back. By its ownership of all land and a system of land disposals that favour only the biggest companies, the government has succeeded in creating a concentration of economic power in the hands of just five corporations who are primarily property companies but also hold utilities monopolies and have dominant positions in many other sectors. The arch monetarist and free-market advocate Milton Friedman really had the wool pulled over his eyes when he uttered his famous comment, 'To see how a free market really works, Hong Kong is the place to go.'

Hong Kong even has monopolies regulating rice imports and driving schools, and, until 2001, will have an officially sanctioned banking cartel controlling retail banks' deposit rates. Hong Kong was among the last of the more developed countries to lift the telecommunications monopoly. This, remember, was happening in the supposedly freest economy in the world.

On the other hand it can be argued that government interventionism of a high order did much to stimulate economic growth. The utility monopolies provided a solid level of infrastructure on which businesses were built. By providing government-owned homes for half the population and charging low rents, the state kept down labour costs, which would have rapidly escalated out of control if the workforce had been left to the mercy of the market. And it may even be argued that the government assisted economic development by encouraging the growth of large companies under the aegis of land disposal, government contract and other policies which were biased towards the larger corporate players.

Elsewhere, where less grandiose claims of economic freedom were being made, the hand of the state was not far from the economic rudder. This was certainly the case in Indonesia, where the Suharto regime crisscrossed the economy with monopolies handed out to the President's cronies. And it was also true in Malaysia, where government intervention in business became the norm rather than the exception for industries seen by Dr Mahathir as key to national development.

Yet despite high levels of government intervention in these economies they performed spectacularly well. The classic example of the flip side of this coin is provided, ironically, by the People's Republic of China, which is governed by the world's largest Communist Party and is supposed to adhere to socialist economics. Yet China has shown how much the government can do by doing very little. In effect the 'open-door' economic policies initiated by Deng Xiaoping in the late 1970s simply meant state withdrawal from large sectors of the economy and a self-denying ordinance on the part of the government not to get involved in the high-growth, export-orientated industries that sprang up throughout Southern China. Mr Deng claimed, with what to me looks like delicious irony, that his economic-reform policies explained 'what socialism is in terms never used by the founders of Marxism-Leninism'.[17] For reasons of political expediency Mr Deng held the red flag high and in its shadow allowed industry and agriculture to develop free of state control. In every sector where the state withdrew, productivity and growth rose like a rocket.

It is not surprising that the withdrawal of the state from economic activity had such a positive effect (although the results were far more mixed in the former Eastern-bloc countries) but it can be said to provide support for the theory that the less government has to do with the economy, the more it is likely to grow.

My view about the development of the high-growth Asian economies is that it is too simplistic to assert that Asian economies did well because the state kept out of business. This argument is not supported by the facts that show that governments in the region were rarely hands-off. Moreover, as the famous World Bank 'Asian Miracle' study has demonstrated, the effects of intervention were far from being negative. Therefore it seems more reasonable to be fair and acknowledge that the so-called Miracle came about in part with government assistance and in part despite government intervention because the driving force of entrepreneurial spirit was too strong to be thwarted by the bureaucrats.

The real economy and the financial sector

Some commentators have argued that the Asian Miracle happened because Asian financial markets created an enormous pool of capital to fuel economic development. This argument seems to be fundamentally shaky. The reality is that an enormous gap emerged dividing what can be described as real economic development and the financial sector – or, to be more precise, the equities part of the financial sector. What was happening was that the equity markets were draining funds from productive investment and bringing down some companies which, on the merits of their productive capacity and market for their goods, should have been solvent but were dragged under by crippling debt, some of which was caused by reckless market speculation and some by the sudden surge of higher interest-rate charges. Interest rates rocketed throughout the region in 1998 and, as the rating agencies steadily, albeit belatedly, raised their Asian sovereign-risk ratings and corporate-credit ratings, borrowings became increasingly more expensive.

Meanwhile, as we have seen in Chapter 1, stock-market investors were driving share prices up to levels that bore little resemblance to corporate performance. This lack of connection, however, pales in comparison with an even more telling indicator which compares stock-market capitalisation, i.e. the combined price of all shares listed on a stock exchange, with gross domestic product. In what can only be described as a sane world stock-market capitalisation should be no more than a fraction of a nation's economic output. There certainly seems no case for the corporate value of listed companies (as reflected in their share price) to exceed GDP.

However, looking at figures for the heady year of 1995, it is possible to see that half of the stock markets in the eight Asian high-growth economies had stock-market capitalisations far exceeding the size of their domestic economies.[18] Most spectacularly the Malaysian stock market was capitalised at a level more than two and a half times greater than the nation's GDP. The Hong Kong stock market's level was more than double GDP, while Singapore managed to have stock-market capitalisation at a level that equated to 177 per cent of GDP. It should be quickly stated that at this time both British and United States stock-market capitalisation figures were also high: in the case of Britain the stock market equated to 127 per cent of GDP and in the US the stock market's capitalisation was almost the same as the nation's GDP. The difference here is that both of these exchanges have a large number of overseas companies listed, which inflates capitalisation, whereas the number of overseas listings is minimal on Asian exchanges. Secondly, public companies in Britain and the United States account for a higher proportion of output than in the Asian nations and so it is understandable that stock-market capitalisation should more closely match GDP.

It may be argued that the enormous amount of money going into Asian stock-markets was providing masses of private capital for the development of industries and services. This is simply not the case. In East Asia, for example, the bulk of financing for private-sector infrastructure developments has not only not come from stock markets but not even from local sources.[19] Even where new capital is being raised as a result of new share issues, very small amounts of the money collected from shareholders goes into financing new projects, although a greater proportion is utilised for debt reduction. Generally speaking, however, the main beneficiaries of initial public offerings (IPOs) are the original owners of the companies who take the opportunity to realise their capital. This issue is more thoroughly examined in Chapter 5.

The Asian debt market, although growing, is relatively underdeveloped and has been kicked in the shins by the emergence of the financial crisis, so this too is a rather limited source of funds.

As we have seen above the real investment comes from the small army of savers in East Asia who have created a pool of cheaply raised capital.

It would therefore be wrong to paint a picture of Asian growth as being based on the activities of the people who invest in equity markets. On the contrary, the financial markets have proved to be something worse than a distraction.

This brings us back to the central question posed in this chapter: was it all a mirage? Clearly it was not, despite efforts, conscious or otherwise, to cloud the real achievements of Asian economic growth in a mist of market make-believe and extravagant spending.

It seems to me that the most lasting aspects of the Miracle and its most solid underpinnings remain battered but intact. The level of economic activity generated in the last three decades, particularly the last two, has lifted East Asian economies on to a higher plateau which has not been demolished. The attitudes of the people who did the lifting are still the same and still conducive to making these economies perform well.

This brings us on to the question to be discussed in the next chapter, namely whether these attitudes are derived from some special Asian value system and whether it is a system with its roots in Confucian thought.

3

ASIAN VALUES AND CONFUSION
ABOUT CONFUCIUS

Why *Asian* values?

It is hard to be precise about when 'Asian values' came into vogue, or more
to the point, for our present purposes, when they were brought into play
as an explanation for Asian economic success. However, what is clear is
that talk of Asian values became closely tied up with talk of the Asian
Miracle. It may even be argued that the Asian-values vogue, which peaked
in the mid-1990s, sought to provide an intellectual rationale for the Asian
Miracle or even a moral basis for what was then perceived as the relentless
rise of the Pacific Century.

If this is so the corollary must be that the Asian financial crisis proved
the shaky foundations of so-called Asian values, or, worse, that they lay at
the root of the economic debacle. The problem with the great Asian
Values Debate is similar to that surrounding the great Asian Miracle
Debate, namely that the exaggerated claims and inflated notions
surrounding both debates obscure the real achievements of Asian
economic growth and blur the important cultural differences in Asia that
have contributed to economic success.

In 1995, when the Asian Miracle looked unstoppable, Anwar Ibrahim,
the former deputy premier of Malaysia, perceptively identified the reasons
why the Asian values debate got going. 'Prosperity is a confidence
booster,' he said. 'And this renewed self-esteem has spawned a growing
desire among Asians to share the burden of reshaping the world, rather
than being shaped by others as was the case in the past.'[1]

In the desire to reshape the world some Asian leaders deemed it
necessary to identify specifically Asian characteristics which they believed

brought a unique regional contribution to the global assortment of value systems. Quite apart from the dubious proposition that Asia, embracing such a mass of diverse cultures, could have a single values system, there is also a problem over whether some of the values described as being Asian are any different from universal values. We shall return to that topic later.

However, let us deal now with what may be described as the central tenet of the Asian values system, namely the idea that the individual is less important than the family, which is portrayed as the most important entity in society. In the West, it is alleged, it is the other way around.

'Eastern societies believe that the individual exists in the context of family,' said the former Singaporean Prime Minister Lee Kuan Yew in a famous interview. 'He is not pristine and separate. The family is part of the extended family, and then friends and the wider society. The ruler or the government does not try to provide for a person what the family best provides.'[2] From this idea flow many others, which suggest that Asians are prepared to sacrifice individual desires to the common good, and that sacrifices for the family will be made at the expense of individual fulfilment.

This line of thought is then stretched into the economic arena, where, so it is said, economic entities work better because they are an extension of the family. In some cases this is literally the case because a very high proportion of Asians, particularly in the agricultural sector, work in family units. However, the proposition is more dubious when it is suggested that corporate entities have become another kind of family creating new bonds of loyalty, filial obedience and the like.

New ideas sold as old

It may be thought that if there were something as distinct as a philosophy of collective Asian values they should have been around for a very long time. However, this is not so. Very little was heard about Asian values until, in the late 1980s, Lee Kuan Yew in Singapore and Prime Minister Mahathir Mohamad in Malaysia started to talk a great deal about this concept. Significantly their thoughts tended to focus on how Asian values contrasted with a Western value system. 'It is a rebellion against domination; it is Asia standing up to its former masters,'[3] wrote John Naisbitt, one of the most enthusiastic peddlers of Asian myths. A rather different view was expressed by Anwar Ibrahim, who fell from grace after crossing swords with his boss Mahathir Mohamad. He said, 'while there is no denying the widespread acceptance of the thesis positing a clash of civilisations, rather than a mutually beneficial dialogue, between an emergent Asia and a statist West, there appears to be no foundation for this rather hysterical scenario. In fact, such a populist endorsement is a consequence of the pandering to the paranoia and insecurities of those who succumb to stereotyping.'[4]

Rejecting Western ideology?

However the proponents of the Asian-values idea go further. They see this idea not only as part of the battle against Western hegemony but also as an expression of something superior to the supposedly collective Western ideology, which was previously imposed on Asian minds. Kishore Mahububani, one of Singapore's most senior diplomats and a lucid participant in the Asian-values debate, puts it this way:

> It is difficult for a European or North American to understand the momentousness of the psychological revolution in East Asia because they cannot step into East Asian minds. Their minds have been wrapped in colonialism. They have never struggled with the subconscious assumption that perhaps they are second rate human beings, never good enough to be number one. The growing realisation of East Asians that they can do anything as well, if not better than, other cultures, has led to an explosion of self confidence.[5]

Mr Mahububani, if he wishes to be consistent, must, presumably, believe that process works both ways and so East Asians find it difficult to understand Western concepts such as the rule of law. Strangely, he does not say this.

Moreover, according to Lee Kuan Yew, who might be described as the grandfather of Asian values, 'Westerners have abandoned an ethical basis for society, believing that all problems are solvable by good government, which we in the East never believed possible.'[6] Here, Mr Lee is putting his distinctive spin on the Confucian 'one-man' thesis, which postulates that, if the leader (there need only be one) is the right man for the task, he will exert his moral authority to solve all problems. Confucians never believed that the solution lay in institutions but were reliant on the moral leadership of a single person.

It is not stretching things too far to believe that Mr Lee very much saw himself in this role. He is modest enough, however, not to say this.

A fig leaf for authoritarianism?

Yet he makes a number of extravagant claims which lead to equally extravagant claims on the other side of the argument, where it is asserted that Asian values are no more than a fig leaf covering all the worst facets of Asian society. 'Behind the rhetoric of Asian values lay, and still lies, a smokescreen designed to obscure balance sheets that won't stand scrutiny, something called crony capitalism as a way of doing business,' said Richard Holbrooke, the rather blunt US ambassador to the United Nations who in a previous incarnation popped up in Hong Kong in March 1998 in his new capacity as vice-chairman of Credit Suisse First Boston.[7]

Other critics say that the concept of Asian values is nothing more than a cloak to drape over the notion of authoritarian government and to justify the lack of political freedom, which is the hallmark of these governments. Confucianism, with its emphasis on hierarchical authority, seems to provide some intellectual justification for those who like authoritarianism.

A special Asian craving for stability?

This draws the debate over Asian values into a clash of views over whether political liberty encourages or suppresses the development of economic growth. It is also part of a debate over whether Asians have a special craving for stability. Fulfilling this craving is said to have provided the underpinning for economic growth.

Again it is Lee Kuan Yew, who has outlined this argument in the most unequivocal of terms. 'In the East,' he said, 'the main object is to have a well ordered society so that everyone can have maximum enjoyment of his freedoms. This freedom can only exist in an ordered state and not in a national state of contention and anarchy.'[8] Actually Mr Lee has stolen this idea, almost to the word, from the liberal theorist John Rawls, a leading American philosopher who elaborated it in his famous book, *Theory of Justice*. To the best of my knowledge John Rawls has never been known as an 'Eastern' philosopher.

There is nothing wrong with Mr Lee appropriating Western ideas, although it seems a bit rich to term them as 'Eastern' concepts. Nevertheless this notion brings us to the nub of the Asian-values debate at the political level. Advocates of Asian values, like Lee Kuan Yew, assert that stability is the priority and to secure stability there may be a need for some sacrifice in terms of personal liberty. This idea draws heavily on the Confucian notion that society is best managed by a ruler who is not really a ruler but a moral guide whose moral guidance needs to be followed without questioning to avoid chaos. In these circumstances there is space for personal liberty but freedom of thought is not considered to be necessary.

Moreover it is suggested that democracy and democratic values are Western imports which can not easily be grafted on to Eastern systems of government. As ever, on the other side of the equation is Anwar Ibrahim. Referring to those making this suggestion, he responded: 'Under the cloak of Asian values, they disdainfully dismiss the universal humanitarian ideals taught by all the major traditions of Asia as being nothing but new-fangled Western inventions, introduced by Occidentals in order to maintain their dominance.'[9] Mr Anwar is not alone in the anti-Asian-values camp when he maintains that Asia has a perfectly good democratic tradition of its own, without needing Western references to discover democracy. 'It's as if Asians are happy to live under authoritarian rule and have always done so,' Abdul Razak Baginda, the Executive Director of the Malaysian Research Centre in Kuala Lumpur, told me. 'We are the same as everyone else. We want to live in freedom. If they say that we do not, they are not doing justice to Asians.'

The sophisticated version of the Asian-values proponents' claims about democracy is that democracy is all very well but it cannot be introduced, in the so-called Western sense, until economic development is further down the road. Again it is Mr Anwar who has a succinct answer to this: 'The pursuit of economic prosperity is no justification for the persistent and flagrant deprivation of political and civil liberties. In fact, increasing wealth should be the occasion for the extension of freedoms to all spheres, these being the legitimate expectations of a civil society. Some would argue that, in resisting democratisation, the people are not sophisticated enough to practise democracy. To this, Dr Sun Yat Sen (the founder of the Chinese republic) replied earlier this century, 'Alas! This is like telling a child that he cannot go to school because he is illiterate.'[10]

Interesting as it is, this debate about values may seem to be little more than a rather esoteric sideshow. Yet it is more than that because, as we shall shortly see, the countries most engaged in this debate have devoted considerable effort to creating a national ideology out of their views. Secondly, if the context of Asian economic development is to be adequately understood, it is also necessary to understand the intellectual climate in which these economies were nurtured.

Singapore searches for new values

In the case of Singapore it can be argued that the seeds of the Asian-values concept were sown in the early 1980s before the debate even got under way. Lee Kuan Yew, then still Prime Minister, dispatched his old comrade-in-arms Goh Keng Swee, then Deputy Prime Minister, to produce a report on moral education. Mr Lee was worried that the younger generation was becoming too Westernised and too detached from their Eastern roots. 'Why does Singapore need an ideology or shared values?' asked an editorial in the state-produced *Singapore Bulletin*, 'The answer, simply put, is to ensure our future survival . . . As a cosmopolitan city state, Singapore is wide open to external influences and values, both good and bad.'[11]

Mr Goh duly produced his report and recommended that Confucianism should be placed more firmly on the school curriculum (as it was for example in Taiwan, before finally being removed as a compulsory subject in 1999). In Singapore Confucianism already had a place in the classroom but Mr Goh maintained that its place was not prominent enough. At first this proposal had little effect. Both parents and students showed scant interest in the Confucian preoccupations of Messers Goh and Lee. However, Lee Kuan Yew was not prepared to let the issue simply fade away. It was decreed that religious knowledge was to be phased out as a compulsory subject and a secular moral-education course was to be brought in. Children were to be taught about Asian values. They would learn about the need for uncritical acceptance of authority and have inculcated in them a respect for elders, parents, the family, teachers, scholars and, of course, the state. These were held to be Confucian values.

Many Confucians, many different Confucian ideas

However, as with Christianity, Judaism and Islam and other great religions that are guided by a holy grail, the holy grail has never succeeded in producing a single interpretation. Confucianism has its large band of scholars and, like the Talmudic scholars of Judaism, who delight in splitting hairs over the interpretation of Jewish law, they crawl through the works of the great master Confucius and come up with greatly differing conclusions. Indeed there is a whole body of work called Confucian thought, which sheds more mystery than light upon the thoughts of the Chinese philosopher.

The big difference between the Talmud and the *Analects*, which is sometimes described as the Confucian 'bible', is that even its most enthusiastic adherents do not dare attribute divine origins to this work. In fact practically all scholars agree that it was not written by the great man himself but was compiled at least a hundred years after his death by a number of disciples trying to reconcile the intense debate that raged even then over what the Sage really meant.

Moreover, the core classics of the Confucian 'church' are in fact four works, including the work of Mencius. Interestingly the authoritarian ideology, so popular among modern day semidetached Confucians, comes from Xunzi, the great critic of Mencius.

So, it is hard to speak of a Confucian bible as such but there is a body of work (scholars are engaged in lively debate on what should be included here) which, like the New Testament for Christians and the Koran for Muslims, contains enough to make them open to differing interpretation by those holding widely divergent views. That a Chinese Communist and a right-wing Korean dictator could both point to the thoughts of Confucius as the source of their inspiration is no more surprising than the Bible being cited as the ideological underpinnings of the socialist radicalism of the worker priests in Latin America and the source of justification for right-wing fundamentalist Christians who go around bombing abortion clinics in the United States.

It is therefore somewhat pointless to allege that there is only one true interpretation of Confucianism, or, to put it more controversially, that Confucianism provides the authentic basis for the new-fangled Asian-values concept. In essence Confucianism sought to provide an ethical or moral approach for creating social order. However, as many Confucianism scholars have noted, Master Kung, or Kung Futse, as Confucius is known in Chinese, had distinctly political motives, although it is doubtful whether these extended to a desire for holding office. He lived in troubled times (479–551 BC) when the reigning Chou Dynasty was losing its grip on power and chaos lurked throughout the empire. The Master was understandably concerned about this and concluded that stability could be achieved only by the restoration of a highly moral feudal order where a ruler set an example for his people.[12]

The emphasis Confucius is supposed to have placed on order and hierarchy was understandably well received by the autocracies of the late twentieth century. This is so even though the modern semidetached Confucians fail to acknowledge that the Master was more concerned with education and example to promote good behaviour rather than punishment to ensure compliance.

These latter-day Confucians also greatly warmed to the idea of the need for the individual to be subjected to the greater needs of society, which they interpreted as being subjugation to the needs of the state. However, there was no concept of the state in Confucian thought – this is a modern-day invention. The Confucian concept is not one of having a ruler in charge of a state but of a more global entity including 'all under heaven'. Yet this universal approach has been swept aside and Confucianism has been wheeled out for the political purpose of justifying autocracy. Moreover, selective reading of Confucian works allowed the modern enthusiasts to overlook references to the need for a force to mitigate the autocratic powers of the ruler. Traditional Confucian scholars, rather immodestly, saw this role as being performed by themselves.

At the economic level Confucianism also proved to be a useful intellectual tool for societies bent on rapid growth, requiring hard work and an absence of demands for workers' rights. Thus the idea of the Confucian work ethic was heavily promoted. As we shall see later, however, Confucianism, if anything, provided an intellectual barrier to economic development.

Confucianism versus authoritarianism

It is not the intention here to provide anything like a comprehensive guide to the contradictions in Confucian thought that suggest why, for example, authoritarian governments were taking liberties with the Master in claiming that his teachings provided all the necessary justification for their form of rule. However, it is hard to resist reproducing a couple of passages from the thoughts of Confucius, which provide equally good, if not better, arguments against the kind of authoritarian governments favoured by people who describe themselves as Confucians.

If the government is not 'right', then the sovereign's position is threatened, and when the sovereign's position is threatened, the powerful officials become arrogant and the minor officials begin to steal. We should then see criminals punished by severe sentences and the general morality of the people degenerates and there would be a general absence of standards.

Confucius then describes how a breakdown of social order ensues and how the ruling class no longer attends to its 'proper' functions, leading to a lack of loyalty to the sovereign and flight from the crumbling state over which the sovereign rules. He concludes: 'This is called a "sickly state".'[13]

If the word 'sovereign' were replaced by 'president' this description would, for example, perfectly fit the last decade of rule by the Suharto regime in Indonesia or it would even more precisely fit Burma under military rule in present times – this being the Burma, renamed Myanmar, which was welcomed into the Association of South East Asian Nations (ASEAN) in 1997 despite its atrocious record of human-rights violations and almost total government mismanagement.

And what of notions of unquestioning obedience which are supposed to form part of the Confucian work ethic? 'The superior man', says Confucius, 'is liberal towards others' opinion but does not completely agree with them; the inferior man completely agrees with others', but is not liberal towards them.'[14]

It may also be argued that Confucius was not exactly an advocate of the kind of voracious wealth creation that became the hallmark of the Asian Miracle. 'The gentleman seeks neither a full belly nor a comfortable home,' said the Master. 'If wealth were a permissible pursuit, I would be willing to act as a guard holding a whip outside the market place. If it is not, I shall follow my own preferences.' the *Analects*, VII.12.)

It is not difficult to find other sayings of Confucius that can be used to serve the purposes of the Asian-values advocates and authoritarians because he was essentially a philosopher who favoured precisely this form of rule, albeit conducted by upright, moral and just rulers.

Dusting off the shelves

The interest for those trying to make sense of whether there really is a particular set of Asian values that give rise to economic growth is in the way that Confucian thought and other Asian-based philosophies have been interpreted. 'In this renewed search for civil society,' said Mr Anwar, 'we have dusted off the shelves the ideals and values expounded by our ancient philosophers and championed by the early figures of the Asian Renaissance: poets, thinkers and statesmen such as Tagore, Iqbal, Rizal, Sun Yat Sen and Gandhi. They demonstrated that Asia and Asian traditions are very much part and parcel of a world built on the dignity of man, an ideal which in the recent past had been purportedly the exclusive domain of the West.'[15]

Although Confucius is probably the most influential figure in the dusting-off process, non-Chinese societies and Asian societies that have not been strongly infused with the Chinese cultural tradition, such as Indonesia, Malaysia and Thailand, have more difficulty identifying with Confucius than countries such as Japan, Korea and Vietnam, which were heavily influenced by China. Nevertheless, the degree to which Asian governments shared common thinking on value systems is striking.

Developing new national ideologies

Some of these governments have elevated their thinking into a form of national ideology. The Indonesians were prominent in this field with the development of *Pancasila*, which was originally seen by President Sukarno, its leading proponent, as an ideology owing as much to the American Declaration of Independence as to the Communist Manifesto.[16] It is hard to find evidence for this when the five principles of *Pancasila* are examined but it is interesting that President Sukarno (who preceded Suharto) sought to present Indonesia's ideology as being derived from Western thought. The principles are: belief in the one and only God, just and civilised humanitarianism, unity, democracy guided by wisdom through deliberation and representation, and social justice.

The government that replaced the Sukarno administration in 1965 decided to stick with *Pancasila* but, as has been the fate of other holy grails, the new Suharto regime liked the form but wanted to change the substance. So, in 1978 an official reinterpretation of *Pancasila* was published, which stressed that it meant avoiding, among other things, 'free-flight liberalism'. The same year the President established a *Pancasila* commission charged with providing advice on how the national ideology could be transmitted to the new generation and considering how it should be implemented. This body soon started churning out papers stressing the specifically Indonesian nature of *Pancasila*, a philosophy 'dug up from Indonesia's own soil'.[17] In practice *Pancasila* was interpreted as a means of propagating unity in this immensely diverse nation and, although it is hard to find this reflected in the words of the five principles, it was a dogma that stressed loyalty to the state, meaning loyalty to the Suharto regime.

Malaysia was also preoccupied with a means of securing national unity in the wake of the 1969 anti-Chinese race riots. This gave rise to the proclamation of the Five Principles of Malaysian Nationhood, or *Rukunegara*. The principles are: belief in God, loyalty to King and Country (Malaysia still has a rotating monarchy), the supremacy of the constitution, the rule of law, and finally that most Confucian of virtues, mutual respect and good social behaviour.

Rukunegara is not as much talked about as *Pancasila*, although they are similar. However, when government ministers refer to the national ideology they tend to dwell on the themes of national unity, national development and, increasingly, belief in Islam. Like the former Suharto regime in Indonesia, the Malaysia government, which, since independence, has been headed by the United Malay National Organisation (UMNO), largely equates notions of stability and national development as being synonymous with its own rule.

In Singapore this equation is not only made explicit but the point is made repeatedly during election times by the ruling People's Action Party. The Singaporean government came relatively late in the day to the business of creating an official national ideology and did so at a time when the whole Asian-values debate was well under way. On 15 January 1991, the government laid out to Parliament the final version of its 'Shared Values' ideology. It too has used the magic number of five for this exercise but has gone further than its neighbours in devising an almost explicitly Confucian set of ideas. The five values are: Nation before community and society above self, the family as the basic unit of society, community support and respect for the individual, consensus not conflict, and bearing in mind that Singapore also has a problem with ethnic diversity, the fifth value stresses racial and religious harmony.

Conscious of ethnic sensitivities, the Singapore government declines to describe these values as Confucian per se. In an official government publication it explains the position in these terms:

> The five core values are common denominators of the value systems of all the ethnic groups here. Just as the Chinese will interpret the core values in terms of Confucian teachings, so the Malays will view them in terms of Malay traditions and Islamic teachings, and the Indians in terms of Indian traditions.[18]

As ever, the official Singapore propaganda machine is being slightly generous with the truth but not totally misleading for it is indeed possible to find elements of these values in other cultural teachings and philosophies, not least Western ideologies, which are conveniently not mentioned for the government's purposes.

Abdul Razak Baginda, who mockingly describes 'Asian Values', as his 'favourite subject', told me that he was not surprised to see that the Asian-values concept took off in Singapore and Malaysia, 'arguably the most Westernised countries in Asia', which were desperately searching for their roots. 'In Malaysia we have difficulties in tracing where we come from; in Singapore there is a mixture of Malays, Chinese and Indians.' They needed to identify something that could be said to be binding the nation together.

However as Mr Abdul Razak pointed out, 'It is conceptually very difficult to define values based on geography.' Moreover, the whole process of defining the unique nature of Asian values has required a degree of contortionism that is straining even the most athletic of minds.

Ignoring universal values

Indeed ignoring the universality of certain values became a part of the general amnesia that prevailed in Asia when Asian values were still in vogue. The ignorance of this approach is similar to that displayed by those who seek to deny the influence of Greek and Roman ideas in the development of Western Christian philosophy. To ignore the precedents is to assume that all ideologies develop in a vacuum. To be generous it may be that this denial of precedence is more a matter of sloppy thinking than a deliberate attempt to mislead. That certainly seemed to be the case with Hong Kong's head of government.

Shortly before taking over as the Chief Executive of the newly formed Special Administrative Region of Hong Kong in 1997, Tung Chee-hwa regaled a business audience with his interpretation of 'Chinese values'. He said, 'These values have been with us for thousands of years and are as relevant today as they have ever been: trust, love and respect for our family and our elders, integrity, honesty and loyalty towards all; commitment to education and a strong desire to improve and advance oneself; a belief in order and stability; and an emphasis on obligations to the community rather than rights of the individual; a preference for consultation rather than open confrontation.'[19]

I was among a small group of journalists who met Mr Tung after he had made this speech. We asked what he thought was distinctive about this set of values, which sounded suspiciously like good old-fashioned ideals propagated in Britain and elsewhere in the Victorian era and were still lingering in contemporary times. Mr Tung was somewhat taken aback by this question and 'accused' us of drawing him into a philosophical debate. The simple fact of the matter was that he, like many others who were so busy mindlessly trotting out the Asian- or Chinese-values line, had really given little thought to what it actually meant.

This lack of intellectual rigour may also explain the lack of historical perspective among those who propagate the Asian-values idea. Many of them seem to be unaware of how ideas have developed in even relatively recent history. This ignorance may help to explain why they cannot see the similarities that so-called Asian values share with the prevailing ideas of Victorian Britain, when the Industrial Revolution had triumphed and the empire was being built. Nor do they seem to know anything about the German sociologist Max Weber's turn-of-the-century work on the Protestant work ethic and the development of capitalism, which formed the basis for many subsequent sociological studies (however, some of those who were well aware of Weber actually interpreted the Asian-values idea as a *negation* of his theories – this is all very puzzling).

Weber's work throws interesting light on the development of capitalism in Asia. In other words it may well be that Asian values are in fact universal values. Not only are they universal but they are better understood as a set of values that prevail at this particular stage of economic development rather than at this particular geographical location.

If this is so, it makes sense, for example, for nations working hard on economic development to place an emphasis on diligence, thrift and self-improvement, to name but three values cited as being somehow particularly Asian.

Looking at the flip side of the values debate also brings us back to questions of history and different values fitting different stages of development. Lee Kuan Yew and Mahathir Mohamad talk a lot about how the West (that single entity that supposedly brackets countries as diverse as Portugal and the United States into a shared existence) has seen moral values fall, leading to crime, lack of respect for elders and wide-spread social problems such as divorce and drug abuse. When Kim Dae Jung was an opposition leader, before becoming the President of South Korea, he addressed this question in a wonderfully pointed essay:

> Moral breakdown is attributed not to inherent shortcomings of Western cultures but to those of industrial society. The fact that Lee's Singapore, a small city state, needs a near totalitarian police state to assert control over its citizens contradicts his assertion that everything would be all right if governments refrain from interfering in the private affairs of the family'.

Indeed as Mr Kim pointed out, this too is a myth: 'Asian governments intrude much more than Western governments into the daily affairs of individuals and their families.'[20]

There is also evidence that the kind of moral breakdown experienced in the West is being replicated in the East. Drug addiction is a major problem in East Asian states ranging from Burma to Thailand to Indonesia. Prostitution, already at very high levels in Asia, is on the increase. Hong Kong, for example, is faced with an unprecedented flood of divorce cases. Japan is worried by an outbreak of youth crime and child pornography and in squeaky-clean Singapore the authorities are scratching their heads wondering how to prevent the population downloading pornography from the World Wide Web.

The real Asian differences

Somehow, deeply embedded Asian values have not prevented any of the above from happening. Yet there are certain Asian attitudes that are very different from those in the West and may survive an even greater degree of industrialisation and urbanisation. On the one hand Eastern people seem to be more interested in spiritualism, and even – as is the case for most Chinese – where religion plays only a peripheral part in spiritual beliefs, spiritualism forms a central point of reference in people's lives. There is much discussion over how this may impact on economic development, a discussion that goes beyond the scope of this book.

However there are two outstanding Asian characteristics that do seem to have a more direct impact. They are respect and discipline. There can be little doubt that Asians tend to have greater respect for elders, authority and learned people than their Western counterparts. They are also more likely to accept discipline and follow orders without question than many people in the West.

I remember a friend telling me how surprised she was on arriving from Britain to take up a teaching job in a Hong Kong school. 'As soon as I got in the classroom,' she said, 'all the children bowed and chanted "Good morning, ma'am." I was lucky if any of the kids even noticed my arrival when I was back in London.' I asked her whether Victorian schools in Britain, famous for their levels of discipline, would have followed the same practice. She promised to get back to me. Finally she did, explaining that it had taken some time because she got very interested in the subject. The answer was that children did not bow but they did leap to their feet when a teacher entered the room. The reason she became so interested in the subject was that the more she read, the more she found that what she was experiencing was the norm in Britain – around a century ago.

Therefore, even the elements of discipline and obedience, which seem to be markedly Asian characteristics, may be modified as the region's economies develop. It is foolish to assume that national characteristics are set in aspic and that morals, cultural norms and the like are established once and for all time. This brings us to the central absurdity of the Asian-values claims, namely the idea that they are a fixed point of reference, created somewhere in the ether and never changing. 'Nothing in human history is permanent,' noted Kim Dae Jung.

For the time being, however, the Asian characteristics of respect and discipline have created obedient and industrious workforces, ideal for low-technological production, which is repetitive, boring and demands unquestioning workers to ensure that the production lines roll without interruption. No wonder Japanese companies like employing Asian work-ers and American companies felt so pleased to be removed from the more assertive attitudes of their domestic workforce.

However, Asian economies, particularly the high-growth ones, are poised to move to a higher plane of the productive process. At this level the qualities of obedience and discipline may be less valued than those demanding creative thinking and initiative. We shall examine this question more carefully in the following chapter.

Asian values and economic growth

For the time being let us briefly consider whether Asian values and the Confucian tradition could be seen as fundamentally inimical to economic growth. It is argued, as we have seen above, that Confucius was opposed to vigorous economic development and was certainly not an advocate of avid wealth creation.

Indeed he seems to have had some of the disdain for money makers that was characteristic of the European aristocracy as they observed the unfolding industrial revolution and were appalled by the men of commerce and industry who made it happen. The Asian landlord class and the traditional ruling elites, generally speaking, have been hostile to change and reactionary in the true sense of the word by resisting change as a matter of principle. There are, of course, exceptions such as the rule of the reformist King Chulalongkorn of Thailand and the revolutionary period of the Meiji Restoration in Japan, both of which occurred in the mid-nineteenth century. However, had it been left to Asia's traditional elites, trying to preserve their increasingly archaic value systems, economic development would have been stalled even more than it was.

Frank Tipton quotes a wonderful line from the Qing-dynasty doyen of Chinese diplomats, Li Hongzhang, who was curious about Western ideas and wanted to see some of them applied to China: 'The gentry class forbids the local people to use Western methods and machines, so that eventually the people will not be able to do anything . . . Scholars and men of letters always criticise me for harbouring strange knowledge and for being queer and unusual. It really is difficult to understand the minds of some Chinese.'[22] Poor old Mr Li went down in Chinese history with even greater ignominy for having been the emissary who signed the infamous treaty handing over the Hong Kong New Territories to the British in 1898. No one ever gave him credit for inadvertently creating the most prosperous piece of territory in China and one that, thanks to his treaty, was returned to China in 1997.

Mr Li was not alone in being thought of as 'queer and unusual' among Asian reformers. It took the outbreak of world war, civil wars and other traumatic forms of change to shake the old ways and bring Asia into the twentieth century very much as a poor continent that actually became poorer as the century progressed. It cannot be said that ideology alone was responsible for holding back Asian economic development – far from it. The point, however, is that it is hardly plausible to state that Asia had an ideology that was conducive to economic growth.

In short it seems to me that the Asian-values advocates are either deliberately or unconsciously guilty of having produced a spurious explanation for economic growth, asserting, on the one hand, that positive universal values are somehow 'Asian' and on the other that universal values relating to political freedom and liberty are not appropriate for the people of Asia while they are working to develop their economies.

Despite this there are in Asian cultures, as in all other cultures, distinctive features. Some of these, discussed above, have proved conducive to business development, particularly at the early stages of mass industrial production. Other cultural vestiges can be described as reactionary and a hindrance to the further development of Asian economies. The alleged dichotomy between freedom and economic growth is false and certainly not proven in Asia, where authoritarian societies, such as that which prevails in Singapore, have done just as well as libertarian societies, such as that which prevailed in Hong Kong. Moreover, in some Asian societies, such as the Philippines, the end of authoritarian government also marked the beginning of greater economic growth; in others, such as Taiwan, it made little difference; and in Burma, for example, authoritarian government has led to one of the most dismal economic performances of any Southeast Asian nation. In other words the link is not proven either way.

If what is described as Asian values is viewed as little more than the mindset of a group of countries undergoing rapid and radical economic development, there is reason to talk of some sort of common values system. This, however, does not make it a *uniquely Asian* values system.

If there is confusion about Confucius, there is even more confusion over the Asian-values debate. Moving from the theoretical level to the cutting edge of business, the following chapter will examine how the thinking of those who run businesses in Asia has led to fundamental weakness in Asian companies.

4

ASIAN CORPORATE MYTHS

Myths at both ends

In the 1970s a British television company made a film about Hong Kong which suggested that the whole place was covered in sweatshops where poor oppressed workers were ruthlessly exploited. The then colonial government was furious and launched a publicity drive to prove that the film was badly flawed. For once the official propaganda machine got it right. The film makers had dipped into the wrong era, grasped at straws and produced a marvellous piece of history dressed up as current affairs.

Film makers and journalists still trek to Asia is search of exploitation and have little difficulty finding it. The problem is that they simply do not understand what is happening. They see crowded, crumbling factories packed tight with industrious workers slaving away and conclude that they are observing something that is morally wrong. If they would pause and think, they would realise that, in most cases, they are observing people greatly improving their standard of living. Yes, the conditions are often appalling and, yes, surprise, surprise in these nations of rampant capitalism, the workers are paid but the merest fraction of what their bosses earn.

However, it is a myth to see the fast-growing countries of Asia as forming a giant sweatshop. Yet this is a common image.

Equally common is an assumption that figures right at the other end of the exaggeration scale. Here the picture of exploitation gives way to an equally absurd image of Asia housing a beehive of efficient, highly productive companies whose hallmark is flexibility and the easy adoption of new technology. The truth is that even the biggest Asian companies are not particularly efficient, they are not highly productive and they are often strangers to new technology.

An 'easy sell' in the go-go years

Yet in the go-go years Asian companies made a great deal of money and were fêted around the world as examples of a new generation of money-making machines. In its study of Asian markets the finance house Morgan Stanley Dean Witter talks of how Asia was 'an easy sell in the late 1980s and the early 1990s'. It continues, 'The lure of outsized earnings growth in Asia was irresistible – especially when combined with low taxes, no (visible) fiscal problems, a flexible (not to say docile) labour force, stable currencies and pro-business governments.'[1]

Closer examination showed that what looked like a sleek money-making machine was nothing more than a rather rusty vehicle riding the asset wave. Companies plugged into rising asset prices, notably in equity and property markets, and hung on for dear life as these prices soared into the outer stratosphere. As we shall see in the following chapter, some companies simply abandoned their focus on their core activities and plunged into share trading. Others simply played the property market. In Hong Kong, where the entire stock exchange is anchored in the property market, property developers' profit margins were staggering. In 1993 they soared to around 80 per cent. In some Asian markets property prices were literally doubling in the space of just two years. No genius was required to make money in these circumstances: all that was required was sufficient funding to get into the game.

The companies who got into the game were hardly providing an example of a new type of enterprise management which could serve as a model for those hoping to reproduce Asia's money-making ideas else-where in the world.

The myths at ground level

If the myth makers were to spend just a little time actually visiting companies in Asia what would they see? A number of things strike first-time visitors. In Korea, for example, they may be struck by the fact that most employees of big companies are wearing uniforms and that those who are not, wear close to identical suits denoting their status as members of senior management.

Elsewhere in Asia a visitor may be somewhat surprised by going to the headquarters of a large corporation and being confronted by a set of shabby, run-down premises covered in stacks of files and paper spilling out in every direction.

If none of this makes much of an impression, even the most incurious visitor may wonder why there are so many people sitting around with seemingly little to do, even though a great many of them are bent over their desks industriously scribbling or apparently engaged on a specific task, which often turns out to be little more than copying slips of paper or filling in one of the endless forms that big Asian companies generate within their horrendously complex bureaucracies. Such is the level of distrust of employees and the reluctance to delegate even the smallest degree of responsibility that even in the biggest companies' staff have to fill in requisition forms to obtain postage stamps, to make phone calls and to perform elementary tasks such as applying for permission to call a customer.

Often superficial impressions can be misleading but in this case, although it is hideously generalised, what we have is a matter of what you see is what you get. In other words what you see is a tremendous muddle, a great deal of nonproductive effort, an impressive sense of discipline and diligence and not much evidence of the environment for strategic planning or creative thinking that is usually required to propel companies into new areas of growth.

Structural problems

Herein lay the roots of a crisis much more fundamentally serious than the financial crisis that swept through Asia in the late 1990s. It is a crisis of management, a crisis that lies at the very heart of the way business is conducted in Asia. The effect of the financial crisis was to lay bare what had been covered up during the good times when money making was easy. In extreme cases the crippling effect of mounting debts in badly managed businesses forced them to go under. Elsewhere the crisis merely highlighted management weaknesses, which were either fixed or fixable.

The problems are structural. They stem from an extraordinary absence of strategic planning, which in turn means that research and development is generally neglected, marketing is an obscure subject and product development often consists of no more than going to trade shows, collecting other manufacturers' samples and studying how they can be reproduced at a lower price.

Typically Asian companies suffer from a rigid pyramid-management structure with all decisions, even comparatively minor ones, taken right at the top. Unlike many Western corporations, Asian companies tend to be run directly by their owners, not a set of professional managers or a vast mass of shareholders. The owners retain tight control and tolerate very little delegation of power. There are some advantages here: for example, this kind of structure is very useful for deal making because the person at the top of the pyramid can move fast and act decisively. This is not the case in most large Japanese and Western companies, where managements report to boards and subcommittees and so forth, a process that con-siderably slows down decision-making for big issues. Western companies, however, tend to speed up the decision-making process for smaller issues by delegating power to line managers who have no need to constantly refer upwards.

It may be thought that the bigger companies get, the more professional they become. In many of Asia's biggest companies the reverse is true. They start out as small trading companies working efficiently in a limited number of areas, or maybe they are single-product manufacturers subcontracting for a large-product producer. The larger company provides a template or blueprint and the smaller company goes off and efficiently churns out the specified number of items required.

As they start to make money, these smaller companies look for other things to do. Some, often under state guidance, as in the case of South Korea, seek synergy and try to build up a series of companies which interact and complement each other. This, however, is not typical. It is far more likely the successful smaller company will plunge into the property market, then cast around for cheap assets which can be added to a portfolio of corporate holdings that has little synergy. If they are really ambitious they will try to buy a small bank or other kind of finance house to provide a source of cheap funds for their expansion programmes, and if they are really successful they will start picking up quite large businesses that have run into trouble and are therefore available at fire-sale prices. The end result is that a fairly typical Asian conglomerate will have an enormous hotchpotch of unrelated operations under its wing. Because the holdings are so disparate it is hard to add value to their operations or create the kind of critical mass propelling them towards greater efficiency or higher levels of productivity.

Large companies – small-company mentality

Asia is awash with large companies burdened by a small-company mentality. They are companies with little long-term vision and a get-rich-quick mentality which makes them reluctant to accept the need for long-term investment. Among the many people I have talked to about this subject, the person who sticks in my mind is Liu Fu-kuen, a Taiwanese-born medical researcher who moved to the United States so that he could pursue his interest in DNA research involving a process of trying to clone and synthesise genes. He ended up working for a leading biotechnology company called Amgen and developed an award-winning revolutionary drug for people suffering from kidney failure. His drug, known as Epotein, reproduces a hormone called erythropoietin, which naturally creates oxygen supply for patients who suffer from anaemia because of the lack of oxygen reaching their red blood cells. This problem typically affects those receiving kidney treatment. However, once they start taking Epotein they need fewer blood transfusions.

After gaining his doctorate in the United States, Dr Liu went back to Taiwan hoping that he could develop a career in a local biotechnology company but he could not find one that would provide the sort of resources he needed for his research. His problem, as he put it, was that most Taiwanese investors 'are looking for short-term gains not long term goals'. He found US business to be 'more risk taking – they allow researchers to spend a lot of money'. The development cost of Epotein, for example, was $350 million.

In an ideal world he would have liked to develop the drug in Taiwan but he could not find anyone to back him. The resource he was offering was the human brain. 'There is great potential in many Asian companies but you can't get them to recognise how to utilise the potential of the brain.'

Little research – little development

Dr Liu's experience is far from unique – indeed Taiwan is not half as bad as some other Asian countries when it comes to levels of investment in new development. Asian companies, outside Japan, have an appalling record for investment in research and development. This is despite the fact that a direct link between R&D expenditures and business growth is fairly well established.

A study conducted in Taiwan found that between 1970 and 1986 R&D expenditure contributed an average of almost 22 per cent to the added value of goods produced. In the United States expenditure on research and development was found to be *the* decisive factor in creating productivity growth.[2]

American companies, especially those that are still growing, do not regard heavy R & D expenditure as a luxury. On the contrary, it is at the very heart of their corporate strategy. According to two American researchers who studied the growth of research and development activity in US industry, 'The greatest share of the recent increases in R&D commitments are the result of industry's growing realization that the structural and operational changes made in the late-1980s and early-1990s are not the only road to profitability. R&D managers are realizing that continued investment in research will be required for long-term industrial survival.'[3]

During the boom years of the Asian Miracle when funds were flowing into the region, and there was certainly no shortage of capital, expenditure on research and development in the high-growth Asian economies either *declined* or remained extremely low by international standards. Why bother with boring old R&D, promising long-term returns and involving a lot of up-front capital, when fortunes could be made overnight on the stock market or literally within months by speculating in the property market? When the window of opportunity for future investment in company development occurred, the people who ran Asian companies made sure the windows were tightly shut.

In Malaysia, for example, official figures show that less was spent on R &

D in 1996 than in 1994. Combined public- and private-sector expenditure fell by 9.7 per cent. This meant, in terms of percentage of gross domestic product (the usual comparative measurement), Malaysia spent just 0.22 per cent of its GDP on R&D in 1996, 0.34 per cent in 1994, and 0.37 per cent in 1992.[4]

In Hong Kong, which prides itself on running a technologically advanced economy, R&D expenditure is tiny. In 1996–7 local companies invested a mere $406 million on research and development, equivalent to 0.27 per cent of gross domestic product. A survey conducted in 1994 found that a third of Hong Kong companies spent nothing at all on R&D, and even this figure may not reflect the whole picture because very small companies were not included in the survey. Surveys do not appear to have been conducted since then – presumably the last exercise was too depressing.[5]

Hong Kong's level of R&D expenditure is low but not extraordinarily so by Asian standards. Even in Singapore, where the government gives considerable incentives for R&D activity, the record is not impressive: 1997 was a good year for the island state, yet only 1.33 per cent of GDP was devoted to R&D expenditure, while the national target is 2 per cent by 2005.[6]

The Taiwanese government also lays out the red carpet for overseas and domestic investors prepared to put money into research and development. Yet in 1997 its total expenditure reached 1.8 per cent. This is the same proportion spent in Britain that year, the lowest ever recorded for research and development in the United Kingdom.[7]

In the United States R&D expenditure reached over 2.6 per cent of GDP in 1998 and is still rising. This puts it on a par with countries such as France and Germany, but below the global leader Sweden, which devotes around 3 per cent of GDP to research.

In the past Japan has bettered Sweden's research spending record but in 1997 its R&D expenditure had fallen to just below 3 per cent, while South Korea, the other Asian leader in R&D expenditure, was spending 2.7 per cent. It is no coincidence that Japan and Korea are the only two Asian countries to have established global brand-label companies.

Not only that but Japanese companies, in particular, have taken their R&D programmes overseas both to tap into sources of expertise not available in Japan and to better understand the markets of target export destinations. According to Jetro, the Japanese external trade organisation, the number of overseas R&D centres in Europe for Japanese companies rose from 73 in 1990 to 285 in 1994. Honda Motors, which is particularly strong in the United States market, has taken the bold step, in Japanese terms, of establishing an autonomous R&D centre in America for product development.

The results of this high level of expenditure on R&D are most evident as companies pump out new state-of-the-art products but are also reflected in figures for patent registration, which give some idea of what products are to come. In 1996, according to the Organisation for Economic Co-operation and Development (OECD), US companies registered one-third more electronic patents than Japanese companies and twenty times more than companies from Taiwan.[8]

While examining comparative records of R&D expenditure may not be a perfect way of assessing how companies and countries remain competitive it is certainly a good indicator. According to a report commissioned by the OECD,

> recent surveys of companies confirm that strong R&D expenditure is only one part of the innovation effort of countries; marketing and product design are other important factors. In addition, it appears that an increasing share of national R&D effort is being undertaken by small firms which are often not included in these surveys, and that R&D is still imperfectly measured in certain parts of the economy, not least in the services sector. In spite of this shortcoming R&D expenditure remains the best and most broadly available indicator of innovative activity.[9]

The problem in Asia is that not only are levels of R&D expenditure low but resources devoted to marketing and product design are also minimal. Some very large Asian companies do not even have marketing departments and where they do their function is severely curtailed. I remember asking one director of a large listed company in Hong Kong what was the role of the marketing department. He thought about this for a moment and said, 'Oh yes, they're the girls who organise our parties for clients and staff'.

Few global brands

Japanese companies and the larger Korean companies are much more like Western organisations in terms of the resources they devote to business development. They may well have done so as a consequence of government bullying to ensure that resources were poured into research and development but the results speak for themselves. Even in the depths of Japan's late-1990s recession, the country was still home to industrial world leaders and to some of the most respected brands in the global market. The Japanese economic lift-off did not come when companies were busy trying to make cheaper cars and cheaper electronic goods but when they started making products that were better than anything else in the market. Korea is still at the level of competing on price but with brands such as Goldstar and Samsung it has developed good-quality, distinctive global brands.

How many global brands have emerged from the rest of Asia? The answer is practically none. However, attempts at brand creation have a long history in Asia. One of the earliest Asian attempts at global brand making looked as if it had a chance of success. In the mid-1920s Aw Boon Haw, a Burmese-Chinese, moved to Singapore and started making Tiger Balm, a cure-all soothing ointment which became a permanent fixture in households throughout Asia and then spread to other parts of the world. Like other strong brand names, Tiger Balm used its good image to introduce a whole range of pharmaceutical products, including the Chen K'uai, or So Speedy laxative. As the company grew it diversified, most famously into the newspaper business, where Tiger Balm's trademark tiger brand was also incorporated on to the newspaper mastheads.

In 1954 Aw Boon Haw died and the empire fragmented because of fierce squabbling between the family members inheriting the Tiger Balm fortune. Remarkably the main Tiger Balm brand survived this squabbling and penetrated new markets, while consolidating its hold on the well-established Asian markets. The company fell into the hands of Aw Cheng Chye, Aw Boon Haw's nephew. Like many second-generation family business managers, he was no business genius. In 1971 he sold a 46 per cent stake in the company to Slater Walker Securities, run by the notorious (but very smart) Jim Slater, a British wheeler-dealer. Slater Walker acquired another 5 per cent of the company and pushed the Aws out of the controlling seat. Cheng Chye had been lured by the prospect of instant riches to be derived from getting a stake in Slater Walker. However, the new owner quickly ran it into the ground and collapsed under a heap of debts and criminal convictions for its managers. (We shall see in the following chapter what happened to Sally Aw, one of Aw Boon Haw's daughters, who also saw her business collapse in an ignominious fashion). The Tiger Balm brand has survived not because of but despite the way the company that created it was run. However, its full potential has never been realised.

In less dramatic and more successful circumstances it could be argued that Singapore Airlines and Cathay Pacific in Hong Kong have created strong brands in the airlines business, but brands of this kind are hard to expand.

In the Philippines the San Miguel beer brand has established something approaching global penetration, although it is mainly regional and, as we shall see, the company has been undermined by a management that is seemingly careless of the brand it has created. Hong Kong has also developed a couple of regional brands, such as the clothing retailer Giordano. Singapore has become a world market leader in the relatively anonymous business of producing sound cards for computers with the emergence of Creative Technology Ltd. and Aztech. Taiwan, however, is home to a couple of truly global bands, such as the Acer computer company and the Tatung electronics manufacturer. Acer, incidentally was the only non-Japanese product brand to qualify for cross-Asia 'super-brand' status in the large *Reader's Digest* 'Asia's Super Brands Survey' of 1999.[10] These examples of Asian brands are very much exceptions to the rule.

It may be argued that the high-growth Asian economies have not really had sufficient time to establish global brands, that the upgrading of production lines will follow as time goes by and that, in turn, superior products will become world-leading brands. This may be so but the evidence to hand is that the necessary investment in R&D is not being made, nor is there much evidence of strategic marketing taking hold.

The Japanese way

If a comparison were to be made with Japan at a time when it was at a roughly similar level of development to some of its Asian neighbours today it would rapidly become clear that it did not make the leap forward by a process of osmosis but by dint of conscious effort and investment. Money was poured into research and development, often with the help of the powerful Ministry of International Trade and Industry (MITI).

Development of new products and the upgrading of industrial production was a major preoccupation of Japanese companies. One of the myths of Japanese industrial development is that high-growth industries were given a leg-up as a result of government-funded R&D under MITI's aegis. In fact both the British and American governments contributed more than double the proportion of state (as opposed to private) R&D expenditure, compared with the amount handed over by Japan's MITI in the 1980s. Whereas the British and American governments paid for roughly half the research-and-development work going on in their countries, the Japanese state's contribution amounted to about 22 per cent of the total, meaning that the rest was funded by private companies.[11]

The main reason for this was that Japan spent little on military R&D, which tends to be state-funded. It has been convincingly argued that one of the reasons for Japan's (and to a lesser extent Germany's) industrial success has been that so much of its R&D effort has been channelled directly into the civilian industrial sector while the other major industrial nations devoted the bulk or greater proportion of their R&D expenditure to military purposes.

However, this is slightly beside the point for our current purposes. The point is that in the 1970s and early 1980s Japanese companies invested heavily in research and development, more heavily in general than companies elsewhere in the world. In 1974 Japanese companies registered more patents than any other country. By 1982 Japanese companies had registered 105,905 patents, almost twice as many as the United States, which fell to second place in the world patent stakes. In the same year 440,219 applications for patents were made by Japanese entities, four times as many as the applications from the US.[12]

As a result of this enormous effort Japan's economic miracle came when Japanese companies started producing quality products. Japanese brand names now stand for quality, not for economy. They carry a premium because they are worth it. Japanese automotive companies, for example, not only had the temerity to take on the world's biggest mass producers of cars but succeeded in making a better car. Honda, for example, beat every other car maker in the United States by producing its Accord model, the best-selling car in America during the early 1990s. Toyota and Nissan have since taken on Europe's luxury-car makers, such as Daimler Benz and BMW, and produced world-beating bestsellers under the Lexus and Infiniti marques.

Not only did Japanese companies make Herculean efforts to produce better-quality goods but they typically seized on downturns in the market to step up their R&D effort. For example, when the semiconductor slump reached Japan in 1985, the big chip makers, such as Fujitsu and NEC, poured money into researching and developing the next stage of chip production.

Even after years of economic decline and falling corporate profitability in the late 1990s, Japanese companies have retained their R&D effort, albeit at a slightly reduced rate. There is no parallel evidence of other Asian companies using the 1990s production glut as an incentive to step up R&D to make them more competitive. On the contrary, many companies in these countries are cutting back on their research investment programmes.

The great productivity myth

Even the apologists for Asia's abysmal management practices and the cheerleaders for the Asian Miracle idea will admit that Asian companies have a poor R&D record but maintain that their great strength lay in an impressive ability to increase productivity.

This brings us to another of the Asian corporate fairy stories, the great productivity myth. Measuring and assessing productivity is a much-debated topic put into some interesting perspective by William Baumol, an economist at Princeton University. He studied productivity trends in seventy-two countries over a period spanning practically a century, starting in 1870. What he found may not sound surprising but it is illuminating in the light of the confused debate over Asian productivity. In summary, Dr Baumol concluded that countries with the lowest rates of productivity in 1870 subsequently registered the highest rates of productivity improvement, while those with the highest rates in 1870 registered the lowest rates from then on. He found that the defining measure of productivity was GDP per work hour. Using this measure the United States has topped the productivity league table of industrialised nations, even though Japan had the best and most consistent record of productivity increases.[13]

Therefore it seems reasonable to conclude that the excitement over productivity in the high-growth Asian economies comes from ignoring the low base from which these increases occurred.

However, it is a fact that the high-growth Asian economies have succeeded in achieving considerable productivity improvements. How they did it is the subject of another vigorous debate. Before examining the productivity record, we will briefly outline the parameters of the debate. At the one extreme is the view that increases in productivity were basically derived from a massive input of capital, which made production more efficient, less labour-intensive, leading to higher output per worker. In addition improvements to 'human capital', meaning essentially a better-educated workforce, led to more efficient working. At the other end of the debate there is the view that the influx of capital was only one among a number of factors leading to greater productivity but that the crucial factor was the better utilisation of capital resources in Asia, leading to greater efficiencies. In other words Asian companies and primary-product makers organised themselves more efficiently and better exploited the tools to hand in order to achieve impressive productivity increases.

Two Australian economists, Malcolm Dowling and Peter Summers, have studied the considerable literature in which these arguments have been debated and concluded that the two positions are not as far apart as they may appear to be.[14] Looking at what is called total productivity factor (TPF) – i.e. increases in productivity that cannot be accounted for by increases in inputs (primarily capital) – they found that even those who disagreed on the reasons for productivity increase tended to produce similar estimates of TPF increases. Secondly, TPF increases were affected by differing levels of development between nations, the external trade environment (levels of protectionism etc.) and more problematic factors such as the different ways of measuring capital and labour in these countries. Thirdly, they concluded that, in periods of rapid economic growth and periods where the international exchange of technology was more rapid, TPF rose more quickly. They concluded that capital inputs were 'equally if not more important in explaining the high and sustained level of exemplary economic performance in Asia'. Finally, they found that the introduction of new technology gave a particular push to economic growth at the early stages of economic development.

In other words there is some evidence that Asian companies made good use of the resources placed in their hands as a result of increased investment, and there were some external factors propelling economic growth, but the overwhelming reason for productivity increases was down to the increased level of human and physical capital which came to fruition in the high-growth economies from the mid-1980s onwards.

If this is so it follows that once the tap of inputs has been turned off or the flow has been reduced, rises in productivity will fall. Only where TPF accounts for the bulk of productivity increases can they be sustained without a constant infusion of investment. At the end of the day TPF increases boil down to better management of resources or, to put it even more simply, better management.

The World Bank estimates that only a third of productivity increases in Asian high-growth economies can be attributed to TPF.[15] Others have argued that the proportion is higher, particularly in the agricultural sector, which is often overlooked in discussions about productivity. There are no clear answers here but even those who are part of the Miracle cheerleading brigade concede that the overwhelming bulk of the productivity improvement was derived from an unprecedented level of resources being poured into economic growth.

Big companies but not world-class

The result was to produce rapid corporate growth and big increases in output but not, in general, to develop world-class companies. This is not because companies have failed to grow or because of the preponderance of small and medium-sized enterprises in Asia, but because the companies that *have* grown tend to be second-rate.

A global study by the American finance house Morgan Stanley Dean Witter surveyed the world's listed companies in search of those with what it described as a 'competitive edge', defined by the study as 'companies with a sustainable, global competitive advantage'. This generally well-regarded piece of research turned up a mere ten companies from the eight high-growth Asian economies. The only Hong Kong company in the list was Cathay Pacific, which is part of the British-controlled Swire Pacific group. Taiwan produced five contenders: China Steel, Nan Ya Plastics and three hi-tech groups – Quanta Computer, Siliconware Precision and TSMC. Singapore scored with Asia Pulp and Paper and Singapore Airlines, and Korea also had two entries: Pohang Iron & Steel and Samsung, one of the *chaebols*.[16]

It may be that Asian companies (outside Japan) are still too immature to be global contenders. However, in terms of market capitalisation, size of assets and other indicators of size, they are very much on a par with global players in other regions. Nevertheless, companies in the former 'Miracle' economies are way behind in terms of product development, manage-ment skills and practically all the other qualities needed to make them true global market contenders.

Hotchpotch conglomerates

Practically all the largest companies in the eight former high-growth Asian economies (outside South Korea, which has more focused conglomerates in the shape of the *chaebols*) are what I call hotchpotch conglomerates. Most really successful corporations elsewhere in the world have a core business activity and a policy of diversification that either supports the business of the main activity or, in the case of a declining industry, such as steelmaking or the tobacco industry in the United States, the diversification policy establishes new businesses with decision-making power centres within the newer parts of the corporation.

In 1997 *Asia Inc* magazine, in conjunction with the management consultants Arthur D. Little, began a search for Asia's fifty most competitive companies. The most striking thing about the survey is that not one of Asia's hotchpotch conglomerates made it into the list above a ranking of fortieth place. This is despite the fact that these conglomerates are the biggest and often cited as the most successful companies in Asia.

Every high-ranking company, such as the Sony Corp. of Japan, at number one, and Acer Inc. of Taiwan, at number two, and the Honda Motor Co. of Japan at number three, have well-defined businesses based on branded products with a good reputation for quality. They have developed by adding value to their initial investment and making the business competitive through innovation, product development and improvements to the production process.[17]

This is not the case with the hotchpotch Asian conglomerates, which grow by acquisition, typically adding little value to their investments and adding to the bottom line by deal making rather than building the companies within their embrace.

The Cheung Kong group in Hong Kong

Of the better Asian conglomerates, the Cheung Kong group of companies in Hong Kong, arguably the most powerful grouping in the territory, has succeeded in building some of its businesses but remains a sprawling ill-defined mass. Its activities are based on property development but include telecommunications, ownership of major ports in Hong Kong and Europe, retailing activities spanning grocery to drug stores, control of one of Hong Kong's electricity-generating companies, running hotels, control of Husky Oil of Canada and a banking operation.

In some respects Cheung Kong is better managed than the average Asian hotchpotch conglomerate and has the benefit of being run by Li Ka-Shing, one of Asia's most consummate deal makers. However, even Mr Li, known locally in mock affection as 'Superman', cannot possibly be intimate with the complexities of all these businesses. The only visible delegation of substantive power has been to Mr Li's oldest son, Victor, who nevertheless remains very much in his father's shadow. The youngest son, Richard, has also been given some responsibilities but was packed off with a wad of cash to start his own businesses.

The people around Mr Li are very discreet and rarely criticise him, but, in a departure from the code of silence, Rick Siemens, a Canadian who helped launch Mr Li's Hutchison Whampoa subsidiary into the tele-communications business, spoke of the problems he encountered: 'K.S. [Ka-shing], for all his strengths – you know a poor guy who became the fourth richest guy in the world – did it on the back of property. He knows nothing about technology and therefore he just didn't trust us. He thought we were leading him into a black hole or direction where he felt he had no understanding and it was going to take away from him becoming the wealthiest guy in the world.'[18]

Mr Siemens parted company with Hutchison and went on to found the highly successful Hong Kong-based telecommunications group called Distacom, which developed the Sunday mobile-telephone brand.

The structure of Cheung Kong and the diversity of its business is far from a-typical among Asian companies. Indeed, a quick glance at *any* of the biggest conglomerates in the previously high-growth Asian economies shows the same pattern writ large.

The Salim group in Indonesia

In Indonesia the biggest group of companies belongs to Liem Sioe Liong (also known by his Indonesian name, Sudono Salim). Mr Liem's Salim group started from humble beginnings trading in soap. It soon moved into textiles and banking, then flour milling and cement, then, as with all Asian conglomerates, it became a big property player. In all the group consists of some seventy-five major operating companies, located in twenty-four countries. It has major automotive and shipping interests, a large agribusiness and the usual mass of smaller activities which are all under the thumb of the ageing Mr Liem, although in theory his son Anthony is supposed to be in charge of much of the empire. The most interesting aspect of Anthony Salim's accession is that he is the third son rather than the first, meaning his father broke the normal dynastic rules of succession in passing over Anthony's two older brothers. In so doing he at least indicated an interest in competence, even though the search for a competent successor was narrowed down to a choice of his own sons.

The Charoen Pokphand group in Thailand

Dynastic rules were, however, rigorously observed at Thailand's largest multinational. The Charoen Pokphand group is run by Dhanin Chear-avanont. To be fair to him it can be argued that he broke the normal rule of second-generation company owners doing worse than the founders by greatly expanding the business his father started. The company is a major force in Thailand, was the biggest foreign investor in China, and an influential player in Hong Kong. Its roots lie in agribusiness but it is also a major motorcycle manufacturer (although at the time of writing it was getting out of this business), has many retailing operations, large petrochemical investments and a growing presence in the telecommunications business and, of course, lots of property on its books. Control from the top is rigid and overseas operations remain under the firm management of family members.

The political hotchpotch conglomerates

Cheung Kong, the Salim Group and Charoen Pokphand are among the better of the hotchpotch conglomerates. Far worse, and equally widespread, are what might be called the political hotchpotch conglomerates. These are large companies spliced together on the back of political influence and governmental patronage whose idea of added value is to call up the Presidential palace or Prime Minister's office to ask for another concession to run something or other or to put pressure on another company to make it sell a proportion of its equity to the politically favoured conglomerate. If these companies were on the sidelines of Asian business they could be regarded as little more than a poor joke but they are at the very heart of the corporate structure in East Asia and have ways of making better-run companies arrange shotgun weddings with them.

Citic Pacific in Hong Kong

Of the political hotchpotch conglomerates, one of the least badly run is Hong Kong-based Citic Pacific. This is the locally listed offshoot of the Chinese state-controlled China International Trust and Investment Corp. (CITIC), established by Deng Xiaoping's pet capitalist entrepreneur Rong Yiren. Mr Rong, who later became one of China's vice-presidents, was charged with creating a corporation run on capitalist lines to introduce market-discipline-type practices into Chinese companies. It ended up investing a great deal of its money overseas and in Hong Kong, where Larry Yung, Mr Rong's son, was sent to oversee local operations.

Brandishing his red-chip connections in Peking, Mr Yung had little difficulty establishing ties with some of Hong Kong's leading tycoons, including Li Ka-shing, who helped him establish Citic Pacific. The company is little more than a warehouse for investments in leading companies, such as the local airline and one of the electricity-generating companies. There are also stakes in a clutch of infrastructure companies, a bank and a local trading company which deals in everything from cars to grocery products.

Naturally, Citic Pacific also became a big-league property-market player. Not only does it have absolutely no core activity but, as far as I can see, it has never added any value to its investments. It attracts partners because of its political clout, or, more accurately, its *perceived* political clout, with Hong Kong's new masters in Peking. The companies in which it has stakes seek an alliance with Citic Pacific as a means of acquiring political insurance. They are certainly not hoping to benefit from an infusion of management skills.

The complexities of China's feudal political system cast some doubt on the value of the political insurance offered by CITIC but, as Hong Kong was undergoing a transfer from British to Chinese rule in the 1990s when it was founded, it was understandable that big business in the former colony should be interested in acquiring some degree of political patronage even if local businessmen were not sufficiently savvy about Chinese politics to appreciate how problematic this was going to be.[19]

The Renong group in Malaysia

The same cannot be said for the political connections of the Malaysian Renong Bhd. group, founded by Halim Saad, a protégé of Daim Zainuddin, Malaysia's former finance minister and in-house financial guru for Prime Minister Mahathir after he relinquished the finance portfolio. Renong was largely controlled by the ruling UMNO party, through a series of nominee corporate holdings which the party owns. Unlike Citic Pacific, it actually has a core activity consisting of infrastructure-development companies. As all of Malaysia's major infrastructure projects are awarded by the government, it was hardly surprising to find Renong getting the lion's share. Even though it was spoon-fed the most plum of Malaysia's plum projects it was so badly managed that it was practically pushed into bankruptcy by the financial crisis and ultimately bailed out by the government.

In its heyday Renong had twelve listed companies under its wing, ranging from infrastructure developments to telecommunications to oil and gas, power engineering and, as ever, property development. Investors flocked to buy shares under the Renong umbrella for the simple reason that they believed that the UMNO-controlled government would look after its own investments. They certainly were not investing in Mr Halim's entrepreneurial genius.

The Humpuss group in Indonesia

The same could be said, but even more forcefully, for Indonesian investors who snapped up shares in the Humpuss group run by Hutomo Mandala Purtra, better known as 'Tommy' Suharto. Those wanting to do business in

Indonesia also rushed to form alliances with his five other brothers and sisters, who formed part of Indonesia's biggest business organisation, 'Suharto Inc.', a concept rather than an entity. Put simply 'Suharto Inc.' was the means by which members of former President Suharto's family plundered the wealth of Indonesia in a number of ways. They were granted state-controlled monopolies, awarded contracts for government projects, given access to preferential funding and, in some cases, simply handed ready-made businesses to run.

The example of the Humpuss group is taken for no other reason than that this is the company best known to Western businessmen who were queuing up to do business with young 'Tommy', 'a really smart guy', as he was described to me by an Italian executive in the infrastructure business, before he discovered that he was not actually going to get any contracts in Indonesia. One estimate states that 'Tommy' had interests in at least 127 companies.[20] His hotchpotch conglomerate makes Citic Pacific's holdings look like a business plan drawn up at the Harvard Business School. Humpuss covered everything from water bottling to tourism, airlines, petrochemicals and so on. However, the most outrageous of the projects awarded to young 'Tommy' was the national car project. Like Malaysia, with its Proton cars, Indonesia was supposed to have its own indigenous national car. The Malaysians, as we have seen, modelled theirs on the Mitsubishi Lancer and gradually increased the level of local content as the cars were being assembled at a plant near the capital Kuala Lumpur. 'Tommy's' short-cut approach was to import the entire car from Kia Motors in South Korea; the local content was represented by a badge bearing the name 'Timor'. He did not even bother to set up a factory but gladly accepted all the tax breaks and tariff benefits accorded to the production of a locally made car.

After the downfall of President Suharto in 1998, the future of 'Tommy's' empire is in some doubt. At the time of writing he was already facing legal action and the more absurd of his projects had simply withered away.

The point is, however, that Humpuss was considered to be a perfectly normal company, courted by bevies of Western and Asian businessmen who quickly overcame any aversion they may have had to the stench of nepotism. It was among the worst of a very bad bunch of political hotchpotch conglomerates.

Running everything from the top

The best Asian companies are of course better, but hardly inspiring. Look at an organisational chart of a typical Asian company, assuming such a document exists, and you will see an enormous number of legs to the chart. Whereas a company organised on Western lines would be likely to be divided neatly into functional areas with a decision-making centre located at the top of each area, Asian companies tend to focus all decision making in one centre so that, for example, in the case of Cheung Kong, the people at the top are taking decisions about industries as diverse as property development, telecommunications, port management, pharmaceuticals and grocery retailing, electricity generation and a host of more minor activities. It is quite impossible for one person – or in this case one person, his two sons and a very small group of advisers – to really know enough about each of these industries to make sufficiently well-informed decisions. Yet there is no other power centre and the input from the operational units is not always delivered directly to those who make the decisions, nor is it necessarily given the same weight as input from family members who are close to the chairman.

Running much smaller businesses at the other end of the spectrum, I observe with fascination the degree to which the manner bigger companies are run gets in the way of what they are doing. For example, it is very difficult for me as the owner of a small business to directly contact anyone with real decision-making powers in the big property companies that rent premises to our business. This means that the smallest problem with the premises is hard to resolve. Bigger problems, such as rent levels and terms and conditions, are hard to negotiate because those actually conducting the negotiations have to follow policies handed down from above, allowing no flexibility for discussion. The net result is that in good times, when space is at a premium, the landlords have no trouble filling their buildings and getting the terms they want. In bad times, such as those that followed the 1997 economic downturn, they quickly lose tenants like ourselves because it is hard to reach an agreement with a middle-level manager who has no authority to make the sorts of deals that fill buildings when the tenant has plenty of choice and plenty of bargaining power.

It is the same situation when dealing with a large supplier. Positions of inflexibility are adopted and business is lost because it is hard to get directly in touch with sufficiently senior managers with whom sensible arrangements could be made.

Trying to win in deal making

The problem is compounded because of a mentality that is widespread and regards making deals not as a business of giving both sides something that they both want but gives one side a 'victory'. A subordinate who can report a 'victory' to his or her boss is seen as having done a better job than someone who says that both sides have emerged happy with the deal.

This in turn impacts on longer-term business relationships because they tend not to be based on mutual trust and respect but mutual convenience or lack of choice by one of the parties involved. The consequence of this is that as soon as the situation changes, as it did in the late 1990s, businesses like my own had no compunction in changing suppliers or indeed forcing existing business partners into new arrangements, because we were well aware that, if the boot had been on the other foot, we would have been subjected to changed arrangements that were not to our advantage.

In other words these attitudes lead to inherently unstable business relationships, which cannot withstand adverse conditions.

Building relationships

However, one of the biggest myths about Asian companies is that they derive strength from building relationships with business partners and cultivating mutual trust. This delusion arises out of confusion. In most cases these relationships are formed between relatives or, particularly in the case of Chinese-owned companies, business is often conducted between members of clan groups. This process is often referred to as the 'guanxi' style of Chinese entrepreneurial networking. In China itself guanxi is usually taken to mean good political connections; elsewhere, among the Chinese diaspora, guanxi tends to refer to the business networks forged on the basis of family and clan. The relationships are reinforced by cross holdings between family- and clan-controlled companies that create a bond of mutual benefit not available to outsiders.

In these circumstances certain standards of behaviour apply and lead to more long-lasting business relationships. Because a basic level of trust exists only in a limited circle, and is notably absent from the conduct of business outside this circle, a barrier to expanding the scope of the business is being erected. Indeed this mentality ensures that the scope of close business relationships is very confined. The idea of forming a close partnership with people outside the circle, which is quite common in other business communities, is absent.

Cultural misunderstandings

The irony here is that in many management textbooks Asian businesses are characterised as being less aggressive than Western business organisations and having a stronger sense of consensus building between business partners. This is another myth. It is born out of cultural misunderstandings to do with language and the way Asians, as opposed to Westerners, approach matters of disagreement. Whereas the common Western approach is to confront problems directly and use pretty direct language to try to sort them out, most Asian cultures favour a more indirect, less confrontational approach. This does not mean that they are not confrontational but they do not wish to appear so. Everyone who has done business in Asia can summon up countless tales of how difficult it is to resolve problems or get to the heart of a deal when one of the parties declines to be explicit about their concerns.

Indeed there are all sorts of helpful handbooks designed for Westerners which give advice on this matter. A good example comes from *The Economist*'s Business Traveller's Guides series. Here is some of the guide's advice on doing business in Thailand (although it could apply to most countries in the region):

> Do not show anger or irritation or offer blunt criticism. Anger not only breaks all the rules about avoidance of conflict, it also causes considerable, possibly irreparable, loss of face to whoever displays it. Criticism similarly smacks of confrontation. Such discourtesy may be met with studied politeness, but this only disguises the cost.[21]

This is perfectly good advice and illustrates the problem rather than the means of solving it.

Face

The nub of the matter is face. If it were possible to identify the biggest 'invisible' cost of doing business in Asia, face-related issues would figure close to the top of the list, if not *at* the top. It is hard to exaggerate the degree to which face issues bedevil the efficient and logical conduct of business in Asian companies.

Yet the preservation of face can hardly be described as an unworthy aspiration. Min Chen describes the importance of face in this way: 'The central goal of Confucianism is to achieve social harmony, which depends not only on the maintenance of correct relationships among individuals but also on the protection of an individual's "face" or one's dignity, self respect and prestige.'[22]

The importance of face is not confined to the directly Confucian-influenced societies, nor, although it is often overlooked, can it be said that Western societies have no concept of face. The preservation of dignity is not the exclusive preserve of Asians.

The problem of face in the business world is that it stifles initiative, causes positions to be taken that cannot be changed and generally imposes a layer of complexity on business relationships that limits their potential.

To take a few random examples of how this works in practice is to see why face creates a fundamental barrier to the full development of Asian companies. If a junior employee in a company has a good idea, or has a better idea than one of his or her superiors, it will often be suppressed because of the loss of face it may cause to the superior.

True, there are ways round the problem, such as having the junior pretend that the idea comes from the superior. However, the overbearing problem of face is that it stifles creative thinking precisely because it gives rise to the prospect of loss of face. Why bother to think creatively about problem solving when it will only cause problems for the person coming up with a solution?

Another example is so common that it would be amusing were it not so damaging. A senior company official makes a mistake, say, in misquoting for a contract. It might be thought that the way to solve this problem would simply be to correct the quote. However, this is not done because of the loss of face it entails. The company therefore has to find ways of working around the mistake, which are time-consuming, damaging to the business and, in almost all cases, far less satisfactory than rectifying the error. Of course, if the error is made by a subordinate, that person can be hauled up and put through the mill.

The repercussions can be quite terrifying. For this reason everyone in the company, besides the boss – who is allowed to make mistakes – spends a great deal of time avoiding mistakes and makes the avoidance of errors their main priority. They follow the rules to the letter even in cases where they know the rules make no sense. Thus there is no incentive to find a better way of doing things because the rewards are likely to be far less than the consequences of doing something in the wrong way.

I have been involved in many dealings where the boss has had what can only be described as a crazy idea. There is no question of thwarting this idea because it would cause enormous loss of face. Even if the idea produces disastrous consequences no one is allowed to mention them because of loss of face. Therefore the company has the choice of either blundering further down the hazardous path laid out by the boss or finding a way to take another path while pretending that the original course of action is being followed. At best, therefore, much time and effort has to be devoted to a totally unnecessary course of action.

It is also quite likely that face problems could be found in a company organised on Western lines. However, the Western method of corporate organisation is less likely to allow matters of face to overshadow all other considerations, whereas in Asian companies it is the norm.

As a Westerner who has worked in Asian companies and run businesses that relate almost entirely to companies run on Asian lines, my most frequent response to face problems is to feel a sense of enormous frustration. I get equally frustrated when I, as a boss, do something stupid and do not get told about my errors by employees. Friends tell me to be more relaxed about these things: maybe I should be 'more culturally sensitive'; after all, this is the Asian way of doing things and it works, or sort of works, for everyone else in the region. To my mind this is like saying there is no point in fixing a slow puncture in a tyre because you can always keep adding air and the wheel will still turn. I see the puncture as a problem that needs putting right, not just because it causes constant inconvenience but because ultimately it will become a large puncture which will stop the wheel turning.

Autocrats and crisis management

The reason why face problems loom so large is because they directly relate to the hierarchical nature of Asian companies and the personal style of management that places personal priorities above those of the corporate entity.

In times of crisis or business downturn, the autocratic way of running companies causes even more serious problems. A company run by an autocratic boss and a band of sycophantic yes-men is hardly best placed to unravel the decisions that have led to the downturn in business. An interesting article in *Asia Inc* magazine looked at the yes-men phenomenon in the aftermath of the Asian financial crisis. Among those quoted was Alex Liu, a vice-president at the A.T. Kearney management consultancy in Hong Kong. Talking about why the Korean *chaebols* were among the companies hardest hit by the crisis, he said, 'All Korean companies are shining examples of organisations run by autocratic leaders who led them on to incredible shareholder-value destruction.' In the same article Dick Warburton, chairman of David Jones, the Australian department-store chain, said, 'The yes-man culture isolates a manager from meaningful debate and honest criticism. He ceases to know what's really going on. It can be a cancer in the whole organisation'. Just in case it was assumed that this is a particularly Asian management phenomenon, Mr Warburton estimated that no more than 20 per cent of Australian managers are 'true leaders', not surrounded by yes-men.[23]

Keeping it in the family

Many of Asia's biggest companies are run by businessmen of extraordinary talent and so it may be argued that all they need is a bunch of yes-men around them to execute the orders they have so cleverly devised. However, it would be stretching this observation to a fantastic degree to believe that all these people have sons and other relatives of equal talent. Yet the norm in Asian companies, outside Japan, is for the sons, and very occasionally the daughters of the bosses, to be brought in as board members and, in time, assume control of the organisations. Some of them may have acquired business-school training or other professional qualifications; some may even have learned the business from the bottom up – in as much as the boss's son can ever be said to be experiencing his father's business as a normal lowly worker.

However, it is hard to think of more than a handful of these second- and third-generation business owners who match up to the business acumen of their fathers. Born to wealth and influence, they tend to lack the poverty-driven ambition of the older generation, and it would be unnatural if they retained it. The bottom line is that most of the new owners of the businesses are people of less talent and drive than the older owners. Moreover where the sons of elderly businessmen have been handed the company to run, they often find that their fathers are still pulling the strings.

In one extreme case I know of in Hong Kong, the 'old man' dispatched video tapes for his managers to watch so that they could hear his thoughts on what they were doing even though he was living overseas. Moreover, the fathers have a tendency to be second-guessing their sons and will have installed loyal family retainers who report back to the fathers as they monitor the activities of their sons. This hardly seems like a prescription for efficient management yet it is widespread and so commonplace that it is not regarded as strange.

The other major consequence of these arrangements is that people with real talent in many Asian companies cannot hope to rise to the very top because they are not family members. A World Bank research paper found that two-thirds of large East Asian companies controlled by family shareholders were run by managements consisting of family members.[24]

In some companies nonfamily members cannot even aspire to senior management if they do not come from the same clan or district as the family that controls the business. This waste of talent is regarded as far less of a loss than the fear of 'outsiders' gaining control over the company.

Even the biggest businesses in Asia, outside Japan, are essentially family businesses. In Hong Kong 70 per cent of listed companies are family-controlled, 67 per cent of Indonesia companies are in this position, 52 per cent in Thailand, 43 per cent in Malaysia, 46 per cent in the Philippines and 45 per cent in both Singapore and Taiwan.[25]

Most exceptions to this rule among big companies are either political hotchpotch conglomerates, forged together as an alliance of interests associated with the government, or foreign-owned companies based in Asia.

Even public companies tend to be little more than family companies with a small group of minority shareholders whose interests are decidedly subservient to those of the majority shareholder, as we shall see in the following chapter. Even in Hong Kong, where the stock market is supposed to follow standards as high as those in any of the world's other leading financial markets, a 'public company' needs to float only 25 per cent of its equity to qualify for a listing. An astonishingly high proportion of listed companies do precisely that, retaining three-quarters of the shares in the hands of the majority shareholder.

To put it bluntly, family-owned companies, which have many virtues, are not intrinsically likely to be professionally managed companies, or, as Gordon Redding, the former head of the business school at Hong Kong University, incisively put it, 'a family company is constitutionally incapable of building sophisticated cars'.

Going outside the family

The other side of the coin is the proposition that big companies run by professional managers, armed with business-school diplomas, are constitutionally incapable of doing a deal without spending so much time on due diligence that they often lose sight of the original purpose of the deal and end up walking away from it because they have made it too complex.

The challenge is somehow to find a middle way between these two extremes. It has sometimes been attempted through joint ventures between family-owned Asian conglomerates and Western multinationals. The results of such alliances are not inspiring. The Wharf group in Hong Kong, founded by the late shipping tycoon Sir Y.K. Pao, and now run by his sons-in-law (he had no sons and, naturally, there was no question of the daughters running the companies), has attempted a couple of joint ventures of this kind. They have ended in tears and litigation.

More famous, and equally ill fated, have been the alliances between Korean and American automotive companies. Ford of the United States was once bitten by an aborted deal with Hyundai and then bitten again when it consummated a less than satisfactory partnership with Kia. General Motors fared no better with its failed marriage to Daewoo. Both sides have lurid stories to tell about who was to blame but the basic problem was an insurmountable difference in management styles, which simply could not be resolved.

When Asian companies have ventured out of their region and tried imposing their style of management on Western companies they acquired there was a similar lack of success. Yeo Hiap Seng, a highly successful Singaporean food and beverages conglomerate, sought to broaden its horizons by acquiring a series of 'Oriental-style' food labels from the giant RJR Nabisco corporation in the United States back in 1989. They plunged into the business, only to emerge two years later with losses that were so heavy that they undermined the profitability of the parent company back home.

Only companies that have actually started their own operations overseas have been able to make them work. Acer of Taiwan provides a classic example of this. At the end of the 1980s it acquired an American computer company which had developed the moderately successful Altos brand. After trying to run it on Taiwanese-Acer lines problems with the previous management became intolerable. However, when Acer started its own factories in the United States it managed far better.

The fallout from the financial crisis is starting to bring some overseas companies into the management of Asian companies as the price for their rescue. This too is problematic and will be discussed later in the book.

Bringing in the consultants, bringing in 'Western-style' management

Aside from joint ventures with foreign companies, the more plausible method of securing management improvements comes from within companies and does not rely on external partners. For better or worse, depending on your view of the capability of management consultancies, they started seeing greater demand for their services in the 1990s. Whether they were able to give good advice is a matter of debate but the fact that they were being called in at all suggests a recognition of the problem.

One of the few leading Asian businessmen to publicly air the heretical view that Asian companies need a more 'Western' management style is Charnchai Charuvastr, the head of the Thai-based Samart Corp. Speaking to a conference in the Malaysian capital Kuala Lumpur at the end of 1997, he said that to survive the crisis his fellow entrepreneurs had to 'implement the same refocusing, restructuring and re-engineering of their businesses as our Western counterparts'. Even more controversially he added, 'Instead of good management, many of our businesses relied too much on the connections and the Chinese enterprise style of networking . . . Instead of being competitive we relied on concessions and protected markets.'[26]

Mr Charnchai is unusual in speaking so bluntly but is far from being alone in recognising the need for a change in management methods. Professional managers are being brought in to a greater degree and some companies are generally becoming more professional in the way they run their businesses. Good examples of this process are found in two clothing retail chains based in Hong Kong, Giordano and Espirit, both of which were founded by young entrepreneurs but, from the beginning, organised their business on lines that would be instantly recognisable to anyone familiar with the way international corporations are run. Both companies devoted a great deal of resources to marketing, created distinctive brand names and have built regional multinational businesses. They are no less tightly controlled than other Asian businesses in terms of ownership, nor are they lacking in well-defined management control from the top, but they have devolved power and responsibility and they have created an atmosphere that fosters rather than discourages initiative from staff. Even lowly staff have opportunities for providing input into corporate policy.

On a much larger scale Samsung in Korea, one of the big *chaebols*, took the bold step of creating five regional headquarters in 1995. It thus institutionalised devolution of management power and created a management structure that funnelled fewer decisions into the bottleneck at the top of the pyramid. It also went some way to make promotion and reward within the company a less arbitrary and personal process than it is in most Korean companies by creating laid-down performance criteria.

It is politically incorrect to say that companies that have gone further down the 'Western-management' route are the most likely to succeed. However, the outstanding examples of corporate success in Asia, namely in Japan, suggests that this is precisely the route most likely to produce results. Yet it is inaccurate to describe the Japanese style of management as a 'Western' style because Japanese companies have added local characteristics and introduced innovations and new styles of management, which make the local corporate structure appropriate to Japanese conditions.

At their core successful Japanese companies are very different from companies elsewhere in Asia, with the possible exception of South Korea. The larger corporations conform to many of the norms found in multinational companies regardless of national origin. Indeed what is striking about the 'Japanese-management-style' literature is how little attention is paid to the very basic Japanese management practices that are the same as those followed in Western companies. In the period after World War Two the big Japanese companies decided to emulate the example of corporate organisation in the West, mainly in the United States. They diligently sent out teams to discover the secrets of how big Western corporations worked and then studied ways of adapting them to Japanese conditions. The result is that most leading Japanese companies are basically managed on lines that mirror the biggest corporations anywhere in the world.

However, Japanese companies have, of course, added some distinctive management styles and practices that have been taken up and copied by companies outside Japan. These include such practices as quality circles, low-inventory methods and standardised facilities for white- and blue-collar workers. Other distinctively Japanese management practices, such as the policy of lifetime employment, the intensely complex *ringisho* style of decision-making, involving endless circulation and endorsement of proposals, have not been adopted outside Japan. Meanwhile, they are being dropped inside Japan itself as companies face up to the conse-quences of a decade of economic decline.

As a result it is questionable whether it is even appropriate to talk of a 'Western' management style – it may make more sense to regard it as a global management style with origins in the West, because the Western nations were first to experience an industrial revolution. Looked at from the other side of the coin it is equally valid to argue that many of the management practices labelled as 'Asian' were equally characteristic in the West during the earlier period of the Industrial Revolution, when hierarchical control was the norm, nepotism was the norm, devolution of management power was minimal and so on.

This means that 'Western' and 'Asian' management styles are better understood not as geographical phenomena but as management styles evolving from certain stages of economic development. Seen in this light, concerns over the political correctness of criticising 'Asian' management styles seem rather tedious.

Indeed it can also be argued that some of the more worthwhile aspects of the so-called 'Asian' style of management are no more than practices and ways of doings things that are typical of relatively newly industrialis-ing societies. These are practices that have been abandoned in the larger corporations, which dominate business life in the West, but were present in an earlier era.

Is small beautiful?

Now that the pendulum has swung so far in the other direction and the biggest of the corporations in the industrialised societies are run by committees, carefully devised management schedules and a bevy of rules and regulations, there is a feeling that they have lost something. The small-is-beautiful movement in management theory, which has many adherents in the West, is essentially a movement looking to find lessons from the past for dealing with the complexities of modern life. It reflects a feeling that big companies have become too complex and too unwieldy to remain efficient. 'The fundamental task', wrote E.F. Schumacher, the founder of the movement, 'is to achieve smallness within big organisations.'[27]

In some ways he seemed to be almost singing a paean to the way Asian companies are run in his insistence that corporations need to give space for entrepreneurship to flourish: 'Without the magnanimity of disorder, the happy abandon, the entrepreneurship venturing into the unknown and incalculable, without the risk and gamble, the creative imagination rushing in where bureaucratic angels fear to tread – without this, life is a mockery and a disgrace.'[28]

Not only that but also there is a feeling that big corporations no longer have the instincts that served the early-day capitalists so well. The new managers, it is argued, have lost touch with their businesses and see reality only in terms of their balance sheets and other data flowing through computer terminals. Asian businesses, run by old-style entrepreneurs, typically pay little attention to large piles of data and use their instinct to find good deals and keep the business prospering by seizing opportunities that they see on the ground rather than floating through the cybernet ether.

Learning from Asian business

Western managers trying to recreate some of this feeling for business and trying to find a way of making their businesses more manageable may well look to 'Asian' ways of doing things, even if it turns out that the 'Asian' ways are no more than the ways of their predecessors in the West.

In 1996 the US-based management consultants McKinsey produced a report aimed at trying to find out why the typical transnational style of corporate management was encountering difficulties in emerging markets. The report concluded that the big multinationals lacked the agility of their local competitors. It found, perhaps unsurprisingly, that local competitors have better government connections, better access to local distribution channels, were more in tune with their markets and were more flexible in conducting business.

The report said that the top-heavy multinational style of management from head office, from where experts were parachuted into emerging markets and tried to impose international standards on their business dealings in Asia, was likely to fail. The solution? Reintroduce the old system of country managers to be their eyes and ears and know more about local conditions. 'New product ideas and marketing best practices – the competitive lifeblood of any multinational – are usually generated in the field by people who observe and listen attentively to customers, not by company-culture-bound executives at global HQ.'[29] The good people from McKinsey believe that country managers need to be entrepreneurial types, 'flexible, streetwise self starters', in other words something close to what is described as the traditional model of an Asian manager.

This all sounds pretty obvious, but then much of what management consultants say is obvious, albeit not implemented until they come in and say it. In this instance McKinsey is basically saying that one model of management does not fit all and that managers based close to the roots of the business are likely to know more about local markets than those in faraway countries. This falls short of being a revolutionary insight but it implicitly makes the perfectly valid observation that some of the world's biggest companies have convinced themselves that they can run the world from their home bases, whereas, to be successful in places like Asia, they need to be, well, more like Asian companies.

Whether this means that companies need to have Asian-type ownership structures is a more dubious proposition. However, there are at least a couple of plausible arguments for this form of ownership, which leads to the kind of continuity of management often lost in big corporations where the managers keep changing. There is also something to be said for the loyalty that family-run companies often generate from their staff. The speed of decision-making that is inherent in a pyramid structure of control not only enhances the ability to make major deals quickly but also reduces the cost of deal making.

Although inheritance of company control is very much a feature of

Asian businesses, it is also a typical feature of early and developing capitalism that was common in Europe right up until the early to middle part of the twentieth century, when the concept of professional management took hold. Here again this brings into question the very assumption that there is something vastly different about Asian management styles.

Can Asian companies change?

The great unknown in Asia is whether local companies will follow the path away from owner-managers and towards the introduction of professional managers and generally become more professional in their management. There is little current evidence to suggest that this is happening yet in Asia outside Japan. It must therefore be assumed that, at least for the meantime, many Asian companies will suffer from a dilution of managerial talent at the very time when it is needed to lift their business on to the next stage of development.

Companies in other Asian countries borrowed a great deal from Japan in their efforts to establish large industrial enterprises but, as we have seen, they notoriously failed to borrow a long-term perspective requiring strategic planning and investment in research and development. There was little reason to worry about this while they could rely on simply putting together products at low cost, and hope that high-volume production would keep the coffers full. However, the high-growth Asian economies have passed the stage where their costs can be kept lower than those of rival production centres.

In Hong Kong, for example, the manufacturers stalled the inevitable need to become engaged in greater value-added production by quite literally shifting their machinery across the border into Southern China and putting it back to work on cheaper land with a lower-cost workforce. However, costs have started rising in China, pushing Hong Kong companies ever further north. However far they go, there will always be another production centre that is cheaper and more efficient.

For a time it looked as though Vietnam was going to be the great, new, low-cost production centre in Asia, a process thwarted by the sheer incompetence of the Vietnamese government, which made life increasingly difficult for foreign investors.

In the meantime most of the former high-growth Asian economies (excluding Hong Kong) have seen costs fall rapidly because of currency devaluations. Thus they have again become that much more competitive.

In the longer term, however, the high-growth economies have no choice but to move towards more sophisticated manufacturing processes. Some companies are doing this and in some countries, notably Singapore and Taiwan, they are being propelled into higher added-value production by a mixture of government guidance, incentive and straight-forward assistance. Elsewhere it seems that even the impact of the Asian financial crisis has been insufficient to shake some of Asia's biggest hotchpotch conglomerates out of their lethargy. Their strategic planning consists of little more than waiting for the property-market cycle to pick up again in the hope that the good times will return and they will be able to make a killing out of doing very little.

It is a simple fact of life that in the long run good companies survive and bad companies perish. This seems to be so obvious that it should not need saying. Yet not only the owners of many Asian companies but the people who invest in them seem to believe that the root to riches lies in companies that are well connected with governments, have an ability to make a quick buck and in general are deal makers rather than makers of anything more substantial. These are the people who would have rushed to invest in one of the 118 new railway companies that attracted funds during Britain's railway mania of 1846–7. They would have been the same people who saw their investments dwindle to a level where they were hardly worth the paper they were printed on once the bubble burst.

When the Asian bubble burst in 1997 it revealed much of the inherent weakness in Asian companies but it failed to flush out some of the corporate problems that will ultimately cause even greater losses to investors and, as the financial crisis showed, cause real problems for the economy as a whole.

Investors seem to learn little from history but they might pause to contemplate the advice consistently proffered by Warren Buffet, the American fund manager who is one of the outstanding investors of the later part of the twentieth century. He insists that he does not invest in shares but in companies. The distinction is important because he simply ignores short-term share-price fluctuations and focuses on long-term profitability growth. At the end of the day share prices are nothing more than a reflection of underlying corporate profitability and asset value. Therefore it follows that a highly successful fund manager, such as Mr Buffet, should have the ability to pick companies that, over time, offer value.

The depressing thing about most listed companies in Asia is that they offer more excitement in terms of the fluctuation of their share price than in terms of consistently adding to their value.

In the following chapter we will see not only why this is so but also why Asian equity markets have helped distort rather than encourage the development of companies. Moreover we shall see how these companies tend to treat their investors. Generally speaking it is not a pretty sight.

5

OTHER PEOPLE'S MONEY

Visiting the casinos

Some of the biggest casinos in the world rejoice in the title of 'stock markets'. Many of them are in Asia, where equity markets raise little capital for productive purposes but are centres of high-level and sophisticated gambling.

In the heady pre-crash days I visited stockbroking offices in Taipei, the capital of Taiwan, Shenzhen and Shanghai in China, Bangkok in Thailand and in some other Thai cities to the north of the capital. What I found in all these places was an atmosphere that resembled that of a casino.

There were none of the discreet practices that allowed money to change hands at the click of a computer mouse, nor were orders being calmly taken over the telephone. Instead there were large halls filled with eager and anxious punters. Rows of plastic chairs were laid out in front of what looked like electronic scoreboards. In fact these 'scoreboards' were showing movements in share prices. Big movements sometimes elicited a gasp of surprise from the packed rooms where people sat clutching pieces of paper and mobile telephones. Some women brought along their children because they were settling in for a day in front of the screens. They brought food and toys to keep the children distracted while they got on with the business of buying and selling shares, sometimes turning over their holdings in a matter of minutes. When the market got really hot there was a rush for sales counters, usually located behind bars, as found in a high-security bank where tellers need to be kept at a safe distance from the public.

At my local bank branch, located in a small town in Hong Kong's New

Territories, one desk was allocated to a securities order taker. Getting to the front of the queue to place an order was no easy matter, nor was it easy to gain access to the monitor, linked to the stock exchange. The affable man sitting behind the desk got to know me because I was one of his few foreign customers, and it made me stick out uncomfortably from the crowd. Even more embarrassing was the interest other customers took in the orders I was placing. He explained to me that this was because they imagined that I had some special insider knowledge just because I was a foreigner.

The unedifying truth was that I was simply joining the fun of the casino. I did so by junking all the knowledge about reading balance sheets that had been drummed into me while working at the *Investors Chronicle*, Britain's best financial journalists' kindergarten. This kind of analysis was irrelevant in a bull market like the one rampaging through Asia. Yet it could be argued I was a relatively sophisticated investor – at least I knew the names of the companies I was buying into. Moreover, I had a method, which, without false modesty, I can describe as pretty brainless and rudimentary. It consisted of looking for companies with low price–earnings ratios and buying their shares. This was not because I was mesmerised by price–earnings ratios but because I knew that a great many people in the market were stock picking using this method. Therefore all I had to do was the same. It may not have been brilliant but it worked nine times out of ten. An even better method of money making in this volatile market was simply to wait for a moment when prices fell for some extraneous reason, thus causing the herd to stampede towards the exit. All that was required then was to smartly place some buy orders and wait for the upturn as they recovered.

The simple truth was that you did not have to be brilliant to make money out of shares in those heady days. Everyone was betting on rumour, and tips circulated wildly. People looked for ridiculous indicators, such as the share-buying and selling preferences of a lone *gweilo* (usually translated as 'foreign devil', although it in fact means 'ghost person') turning up at a small Hong Kong bank branch.

The big joke is that when Asian stock markets started going south there was an enormous amount of nonsense talked about foreign investors being responsible for speculative share buying while, by inference, it was suggested that domestic investors were somehow longer-term holders of equities. The truth is and was that both foreign and domestic investors were speculating wildly. However, it is arguable that some of the larger overseas fund managers were more 'responsible' as investors if for no other reason than that it is more difficult to shift the large positions in various stocks as opposed to trading in smaller lots, which are easily absorbed by the market. We shall see later that figures support the claim that the bulk of the sell-off during the crisis came from domestic investors.

Back in the late 1980s and early to mid-1990s the whole atmosphere was frenzied. It was a frenzy affecting international and domestic players. Yet, as is the case everywhere in the world, it was the smaller players who were the most reckless. People bought shares on the basis of being tipped off about a particular stock code, they often did not even know the names of the companies they were buying.

Those who had no time to spend at the offices of stockbroking companies or offices of unlicensed stockbrokers, which also proliferated, had telephone accounts. Many managers complained that staff were spending far too much time on the telephone share dealing when they should have been attending to their duties.

Even more worrying was the fact that people were mortgaging their homes to raise cash for share dealing. Many were playing the margin game by buying options and futures contracts, requiring only a fraction of the cost of the contract to be put up at the time of purchase, in the hope that by the time the contract or option came to fruition – or, as was more usually the case, by the time a sale was made – the price would have moved heavily in favour of the buyer, meaning that more money would not have to be found and heavy profits would be carted away.

This was what the share-buying frenzy of the mid-1990s looked like from ground level. As ever, it was the smaller investors who got caught and crushed in the rush for the exit when the markets slammed into reverse. However, the rush was so big that it was not only smaller investors who got their fingers burned. The pressure on the markets was intense from every direction

Stock markets are jittery places everywhere in the world and are intrinsically subject to volatility; nowhere is this more so than in the stock markets of the eight high-growth Asian economies. In New York and London investors take note when the market moves between one and two per cent in a single day; in most Asian markets this kind of movement denotes a dull day of trading. The swings in share prices became more extreme during both the financial crisis itself and the 'recovery', which began in 1999. The so-called recovery was in many ways more volatile because trading volumes had reduced and smaller movements in share prices were therefore magnified.

It may be argued that, because stock markets so closely resembled casinos, it mattered little what happened to them. We will shortly see the extent to which the funny money pouring into equity markets was becoming increasingly detached from the economic reality that is supposed to underlie these markets. Yet it would be misguided to think of stock markets as nothing more than casinos. It is too glib, and thinking on these lines will make it difficult to understand why the crisis in the markets led to far wider repercussions.

Caveat emptor

The Latin term *caveat emptor*, or 'let the buyer beware', should be writ large over every stock exchange in East Asia. Of course it is not. That is why the Asian financial crisis, unlike previous financial crises, which were triggered by government debt problems, started in the private sector and focused on listed companies, which, in theory, should have been more transparent in their activities. There is really no excuse for the way companies got into the mess that eventually escalated into a panic which spread across the region. The main reason why nothing was done to put things right was simply that too many of these companies were doing things they should not have been doing; too many of them had cosy relations with the authorities who were supposed to be regulating them; and too many influential people were making a great deal of money out of the situation that prevailed post-1997.

Minority shareholders, including those from big international institutions, went along with their shabby treatment by majority shareholders both because they never held the shares long enough to develop any real concern about the companies they were investing in and because in the good times the returns from their holdings left them little to complain about. Moreover, the reality is that there is little minority shareholders can do unless they can gain support from the big institutions, who are usually disinclined to make waves. The larger of the minority shareholders quite like the privileged access they often get to the companies in which they have holdings and are not enthusiastic about upsetting these cosy arrangements.

Capital markets? You must be joking!

The simple fact of the matter is that Asian stock markets, outside Japan, do not primarily exist for the purpose for which stock markets were created. In other words their main function is not to raise money for fixed-capital formation. Most of the companies coming to the markets have no problem raising capital or obtaining credit lines on favourable terms from elsewhere. This does not apply to the political hotchpotch conglomerates, discussed in the previous chapter, because these companies need a great amount of money for, at the end of the day, they have no real business. They need money, which can be raised most advantageously in the capital markets to buy into other people's businesses.

Why on earth do companies, with ready access to cash, go to the trouble of obtaining a stock-market listing? The answer is simple: the company owners want to cash in some of the capital they have tied up in their companies and when the stock markets were booming they were able to do so on very favourable terms.

However, as we shall see, they want to have their cake and eat it. In practice this means they want to attract investors to help them realise their investment in private companies, and occasionally to provide a cheap source of new funds through capital-raising issues, but they also want to keep control over their companies and cede practically no measure of control to minority shareholders.

Asian company owners are not alone in wanting to line their pockets by floating companies. Indeed it is perfectly reasonable for people who have put a lot of time, effort and cash into building companies to want to reap some benefit from their long-term investment. However, when the main purpose of a floatation is simply to pocket the proceeds it diminishes the prospects for new investors to share in solidly based, long-term, corporate growth.

In stock markets devoted to fundraising for long-term capital investment, admittedly a diminishing aspiration even in well-developed markets, there is some logic and purpose to the functioning of the stock exchanges. In markets that exist primarily to raise money for no purpose other than to fill the coffers of already rich families, the logic of the market becomes diffused and its operations increasingly come to resemble those of a casino where the purpose is the same, i.e. to get rich quickly without having to produce anything resembling goods or services.

Are these statements too sweeping? Is this judgement too harsh? The only way to judge this is to look at how effective Asian stock markets have been in fulfilling their function as capital markets – this is, after all, how they are described.

No one can question the impressive growth of Asian stock exchanges, especially in the mid-1980s when the take-off began. (By then Hong Kong and Singapore, like Japan, were already well established and had taken off at an earlier stage.) In the period 1981 to 1987 the average annual growth of world stock-market capitalisation was 16 per cent; at the same time Asian markets were growing by 30 per cent per year. In 1981 they accounted for 17.4 per cent of world market capitalisation; six years later they accounted for 34 per cent.[1] At times the rise in the size of Asian stock-market capitalisation was dazzling. For example, in 1989, the capitalisation of the Indonesian market rose by 823 per cent. Between 1985 and 1990 the Korean, Taiwanese and Thai stock markets enjoyed an annual market-capitalisation growth rate exceeding 70 per cent.[2]

Capitalisation grew mainly because of rising share prices and because of a flood of new listings. Together they produced a boom in equity-portfolio flows to the high-growth Asian economies. In Malaysia in 1990 net equity flows totalled $293 million; by 1993 the annual total was $3700 million. Even more dramatic was the increase in equity flows to South Korea, which totalled $518 million in 1990, rising to $6029 million in 1993. Even the Philippines, which is usually the Cinderella at the 'East Asian Investment Ball', managed a spectacular increase in net equity flows from zero in 1990 to $1082 million in 1993.[3]

So, there is little doubt that equity investment was pouring into Asia, but how much of it was going into fixed-capital investment? According to the World Bank, very little. The Bank's 1995 survey of the Asian bond market looked at the sources of corporate financing and concluded that, on average, East Asian companies financed 40 per cent of investments from internally generated funds, 40 per cent from bank loans, some 10 per cent from issuing new equity and slightly less than 10 per cent from bond issues, mainly in the domestic market.[4]

Funding from bond issues provided much the same amount of capital as that coming from stock markets, despite the fact that the bond market was a fraction of the size of the equity market. The total capitalisation of seven high-growth Asian stock markets (minus Taiwan) but plus China was $1073 million in 1994, whereas the size of the bond market was just $338 million.[5] It is not difficult to work out which of the two markets was more efficient in capital raising.

In a mature market it would not be remarkable if only 10 per cent of investment was derived from the stock markets. However, in an emerging market – which precisely because it is emerging is heavily biased towards new issues – this low level of fundraising for investment is rather striking.

Even though the World Bank report was written while Asian stock markets were booming, it suggested that the proportion of investment capital likely to be raised by the stock markets would remain at around 10 per cent. This may turn out to be an overestimate if the findings of a poll conducted in early 1999, among 200 leading companies in Asia, is correct. It found that these companies were expecting to derive no more than 8 per cent of their funding from equity markets.[6]

Economic growth versus stock-market growth

One of the more glib assumptions coming from the propagators of Asian Miracle myths is that the growth of stock markets in the region helped stimulate economic growth. However, there is a growing body of evidence to suggest precisely the contrary. In other words stock market investors and the people who floated companies fed off the rising economic prosperity in Asia rather than devoting their funds to ways of creating more wealth. There is a strong correlation between increasing stock-market capitalisation in the region and levels of economic growth.[7] Were it the case that the markets were fuelling economic growth, the rise in capitalisation should have *preceded* GDP increases. Instead, market growth reflected rising income levels. So economic growth and stock-market growth followed parallel lines. Instead of fuelling new investment, stock markets provided a home for the surplus cash generated by the booming economies.

Only a small proportion of the cash raised went back into fixed investment, although as stock-market investors made money from shares they helped raise domestic consumption with the proceeds from their gains. This is turn provided a very real stimulant to economic growth.

The low proportion of financing from equity sources and the high proportion from debt instruments, typically around 50 per cent, was described by Jim Wolfensohn, the President of the World Bank, as a major sign of 'sickness in corporate governance'.[8] Borrowings are high because so little of the funds raised through equity issues are devoted to investment purposes and, in any case, the issuers of the equity are generally reluctant to release too many shares into the public's hands because they are loath to lose control over their companies.

The real source of finance for corporate growth was not equity but cheap loans. Thus in the period before the bubble burst East Asian companies were running at ludicrously high debt-to-equity ratios. In 1996 the average debt-to-equity ratio in South Korean companies was 3.5 to 1, in Thailand it was 2.3 to 1 and in Indonesia it was 1.9 to 1.[9] In the developed economies corporate debt and equity ratios are roughly equal.

Where did all the money go?

If so little of the money raised in equity markets is used for corporate long-term investment, what is being done with the rest? Besides disappearing straight into the pockets of the company's founders, much of it, as we shall we see, goes everywhere but into developing the businesses of the listed companies.

Even at the time of listing when companies are soliciting new investors they give little away about the purposes for which they are seeking funds. Read any of the telephone-book-sized prospectuses written for new share issues in Asia and you will see the section headed 'purpose of the offering' littered with phrases such as 'to provide for working capital', or 'to reduce the company's borrowings' or 'to make provision for future expansion plans'. Rarely do the companies specify that so much is required to build, say, a factory, or that such and such amount is required to develop a new generation of widgets in the field the company happens to be in. Despite a mountain of detail about practically everything else that you really need to know little about, the crucial questions concerning the use of the proceeds for the funds raised are barely mentioned.

Hong Kong: investing in what?

A random perusal of initial-public-offering (IPO) documents in Hong Kong, supposedly the best-regulated market in Asia, illustrates the problem. In 1996 Li Ka-shing's Cheung Kong group (one of the hotchpotch conglomerates mentioned in the previous chapter) spun off a new entity called Cheung Kong Infrastructure Holdings. It sought to raise HK$4,158 million (US$533 million), of which HK$1,125 million was 'to meet the capital contribution requirements of the group relative to Road and Power business'. The balance, i.e., the remaining three-quarters, was 'for potential investments in the future and for general corporate purposes.'[10] That is the sum total of information on the use of proceeds provided to potential investors in a company about to be floated by Hong Kong's most powerful business conglomerate.

The market was still buoyant in 1996 when this company was floated. Investors were in no mood to read the small print so they rushed to buy shares in a company that had the magic name Li Ka-shing attached to it and promised, or vaguely promised, untold riches in the Chinese infrastructure market. The heavy oversubscription for this offer had absolutely nothing to do with investors' views over the potential development of the company and everything to do with the lure of a quick buck, which was sure to be made and was indeed made by putting two stock-market buzz words together (in this case Li Ka-shing and China). In the short term those lucky enough to be allocated the new shares could get rid of them very quickly. In the longer term investors were in effect paying for a piece of asset juggling (because the new company's assets were spun off from asset holdings already in the group) and given no clear idea at all as to why this juggling would produce a better company.

Just over a year later the Hong Kong conglomerate, the Lai Sun group, hit upon another ingenious asset-juggling scheme but this time on even thinner grounds. In October 1997, after the crash was triggered by the Thai baht devaluation but before the contagion really hit Hong Kong, Lai Sun launched a company called Lai Fung Holdings. In effect this new company simply took out Lai Sun's property-development projects in Guangzhou and Shanghai and placed them in a new entity. Did Lai Sun have plans to develop these holdings and add value to the company? There was no way of telling by looking at the IPO document. The company said it needed HK$793 million (US$102 million) for 'acquisition of additional land, development and construction costs in relation to future projects'.

Were any projects actually under consideration? It seems unlikely because the company quickly added a rider saying that if the money raised was not immediately used it would be put on short-term deposit.[11] In other words the funds raised at minimal cost would pay good dividends to the majority shareholders in Lai Sun and then spend some time sitting in a bank earning interest. Lai Fung turned out to be a real turkey, which immediately had to issue convertible warrants to increase its capital base. Within a year of being floated it posted a 93 per cent profits fall and within two years was so short of cash that it was the subject of another furious round of asset reshuffling aimed at keeping it afloat. The hapless investors in Lai Fung should have troubled to read the small print.

Incidentally, the Lai Sun group is controlled by Lim Por-yen, who was convicted of bribery in Taiwan's biggest ever corruption trial. He is one of Hong Kong's more influential business leaders who sat on advisory committees established by the Chinese government. While his trial was underway Tung Chee-hwa, Hong Kong's Chief Executive, made public statements of concern about his welfare. It seems that even in relatively clean Hong Kong the heady mixture of politics and business produces raised eyebrows, if nothing else.

The corruption practised by leading businessmen may not directly hamper the interests of shareholders in their companies but its toleration by the political leadership creates an atmosphere that is not conducive to the best business climate.

There is no suggestion of illegal activities in the floatation of Cheung Kong Infrastructure or Lai Fung but this does detract from the dubious nature of these IPOs, which almost certainly did not result in real new investment. However, it cannot be overstressed the degree to which these two examples are in no way exceptional. It is not at all difficult to turn up even more vague instances of capital raising from the stock market for purposes other than business development.

Singapore: investing in what?

Meanwhile in Singapore the hottest IPO to have been launched in 1998 was that of an entity called the Mid-Continent Equipment Group, a company making oilfield equipment and supplying spares. Even though the Singapore stock market was suffering from a bout of post-crisis depression, the issue was oversubscribed by nineteen times. Indeed Mid-Continent shares looked like a bargain to the investors, who at one stage pushed the share price up to almost six times beyond the offer price. What seemed to be keen demand for a company with a perfectly ordinary business turned out to be nothing more than a share ramp organised by five people who effectively cornered the offer, with the help of as many as twenty stockbrokers who knowingly, or unknowingly, helped the five share manipulators make it appear that demand for the shares was hot when in fact all that was happening was that they had deliberately created a very tight market to push up the price. The saga ended when the company was delisted within months of its listing and the police were called in. Here then was a classic case of an IPO whose main purpose turned out to be simply to manipulate the market and this was happening in the aftermath of the crisis when, so we were told, everyone was much more wary of market ramps.

The rights-issue scam

Often more abused than IPOs are rights issues, which in theory exist to provide fresh funds for corporate development and expand the shareholder base. The word 'rights' in Asian markets can only possibly be uttered in irony: this is because in practice rights issues are very often used to get shareholders to pay up for pieces of corporate juggling to the advantage of the majority shareholder. In the process minority shareholders usually find that their equity has been diluted and they are faced with the unreasonable choice of either stumping up more funds to retain the size of the holding they previously had (or they are forced to get rid of their holdings at less than a fair value) or facing the alternative of seeing their equity stake diminish.

There was a big vogue for rights issues in Asian markets during the mid-1980s and early 1990s. It was a classic product of a booming market awash with cash. There was no cheaper way for companies to raise funds and no better way for the majority shareholders to sell private assets to their public companies at inflated prices. The public companies were then obliged to make rights issues to pay for these assets.

One of the most notorious rights issuers during this time was a young mainland Chinese businessman called Zhou Beifang, who burst into Hong Kong at the end of the 1980s and quickly built up a nest of listed companies under the umbrella of the Shougang group. Shougang, with origins as a Chinese-based steel maker, rode the crest of the so-called 'Red Chip' wave. Mr Zhou was a frequent visitor to the market for fresh capital, so frequent that we are spoiled for choice in examining the low-grade nature of the rights issues made by his companies. Among the biggest was a rights issue announced in 1993 by Shougang Concord International Enterprises Co. Investors were asked for HK$1889.7 million (US$242 million). Roughly two-thirds of this amount was required to buy two companies: First Level and Santi. The former company was being acquired from Shougang Hong Kong and the second from another connected company owned by Shougang Hong Kong and Cheung Kong. The balance of the proceeds from the rights issue was to be spent on reducing borrowings, increasing the registered capital and 'further expansion of the group when suitable opportunities arise'.[12]

Like all Shougang deals this one bore the hallmarks of complexity, advantage to the majority shareholder and little benefit to minorities. I was writing a commentary column for the Hong Kong-based Sunday version of the *South China Morning Post* at the time and raised a number of questions about Shougang's complex dealings. Like most journalists, who are generally starved of feedback on their work, I was delighted to have received some comments from readers on this matter until I realised that one of them wanted to know how to get in touch with the company because they were so obviously 'smart' and another was indignant that I had dragged Mr Li's companies into the commentary. So much, then, for writing what I thought were useful warning pointers to investors.

'Real' investment

Ironically there is an upside to a situation in which the equity markets contribute only a small level of the funds for fixed-capital investment. This is that when the markets went into free fall it had relatively little impact on longer-term investment in East Asian companies, particularly in terms of foreign direct investment (FDI), which, unlike foreign portfolio investment, hardly faltered in the wake of the Asian financial crisis. Although this was the first regional decline in FDI flows since the mid-1980s, foreign investment coming into East, South and Southeast Asia in 1998 still totalled $78 billion, compared with $84 billion in 1997, but above the $76 billion recorded in 1996.[13] The question of FDI flows will be examined in more detail later.

It has proved more difficult to find figures for domestically derived capital formation throughout the region but historically speaking it is the case that FDI flows tend to be less volatile then domestic investment flows. In the aftermath of the financial crisis the real cost of borrowing rose sharply and there was a squeeze on the availability of credit. It is highly likely that domestic capital formation was considerably reduced, although, again based on past trends, it probably did not fall to the same degree as the decline in equity markets.

When companies talk vaguely of using the proceeds of capital-raising issues to 'finance increases in working capital' or to 'reduce borrowing levels' or, and this is one of my favourites, 'to give the Group capital to take advantage of opportunities as they arise', they are not entirely misleading investors. All these purposes are perfectly legitimate for a company wishing to relieve investors of their cash. Problems set in, as we shall see from examples below, when majority shareholders in listed companies take the view that the best opportunities that arise are found in private companies under their control. They then proceed either to sell assets from their private companies to the public companies at inflated prices or to buy assets from the public companies at modest prices and transfer them to the private companies.

Using shareholders' cash for a gamble

So far, so bad. But what happens when the people who run the public companies simply take shareholders' money and use it to gamble on the stock and property markets? This was a common occurrence in the sunshine days of the Asian Miracle. While money was being made from these gambles no one complained.

Of course the situation changed when the markets turned down, money ceased to be made and considerable losses became the order of the day. They were usually discreetly mentioned in subsequently published company accounts but rarely highlighted by the large band of notably uncritical people whose business it is to notice these things. They go by the misleading title of stockbrokers' analysts. There are notable exceptions but, as we shall see below, there is little reason to exempt most analysts from criticism for failing to sniff out corporate incompetence.

It beats me why there was never a bigger hue and cry about the frittering away of shareholders' funds on what can only be described as high-level gambling. One of the most amusing examples came from the Hong Kong-based South China Morning Post (Holdings), whose main business, being a newspaper publisher, is to raise a hue and cry when newsworthy matters require a public airing. The company is controlled by the Malaysian businessman Robert Kuok. In the financial year 1997/8 over half the profits were wiped out when provisions had to be made for share-trading losses, which in turn contributed to a profit fall approaching 50 per cent.[14]

Also in Hong Kong shareholders in Chinese Estates Holdings had a nasty shock when they saw that the profit attributable to shareholders in 1998 had been virtually cut in half to HK$515 million (US$66 million). This was largely due to losses of HK$691 million (US$88.5 million) incurred as a result of share and derivatives trading.[15] The company is run by the wheeling and dealing Lau brothers, who appear to have been spending a great deal of the time in the financial markets although the business of the company is supposed to be property development.

Many people talk reverentially about 'the market' and 'market views' being the ultimate arbiter of business sense, but any close examination of Asian stock markets should dispel any notions of reverence. They are like markets everywhere else in the world in that they are driven by greed and fear but, considering the volumes of money that pour through them and the international sources of these funds, they are unusual in the degree to which the people who run Asian markets provide institutional complicity to the exercise of greed and fear.

Abusing minority shareholders

As we have seen in the previous chapter, Asian companies typically are run on highly centralised lines with little delegation of authority. The idea of giving authority to minority shareholders is anathema to the people who run these companies. Moreover, most listed companies are in effect family businesses that have survived on the basis of strong family and kin ties, which are not governed with legalistic rules and regulations. When Robert Gilmore retired as deputy chairman of Hong Kong's Securities and Futures Commission in 1995 he said, as politely as it can be said, that 'some companies certainly do not treat shareholders as owners'.

However, at least in theory, public companies need to run on quite formal lines, based in company law, which allows for accountability, transparency and the disclosure of information. Many of the families who run Asian public companies do not understand this, do not wish to understand this or are willfully looking for ways to circumvent having to run their companies in this manner.

I received my first practical lesson in the relationship between Asian listed companies and their shareholders at the beginning of 1987 when I moved to Hong Kong. Having studied a list of company annual general meetings (AGMs), I thought I ought to go to a few to get a feel of how companies interacted with their shareholders. Better start with one of the bigger entities, I thought. The meeting was held in the old Hong Kong Hilton Hotel. I arrived five minutes late and to my relief saw, or thought I saw, that the meeting had not started. 'When will the meeting begin?' I asked someone who looked like a company official. 'It's finished,' she replied. How could that be? I enquired. She looked at me as though I was very stupid. This AGM was no different from any other: it lasted two minutes. Really, just two minutes? Yes, why bother to stretch it out?

I then asked to see the person who dealt with the media. Eventually someone was found. He did not seem pleased to see me but politely explained that the AGM was not open to the press. I muttered something about its being a *public* company and that it seemed strange that its annual meeting was being held behind closed doors, even though it had every right to do so. He shrugged his shoulders.

Desperate to derive some benefit from turning up, I asked whether I could talk to the chief finance officer or one of the other executive directors. 'What for?' he asked. 'To talk about the results,' I replied. 'Why?' I had never been asked that particular question before. Coming from Britain I was used to the idea that talking about their results was something that companies automatically did. While I was struggling with a response he suggested I should help myself to the buffet, which was under siege by people I assumed were shareholders. 'Please help yourself,' he urged. 'No need to see anybody, just enjoy yourself.'

I was rather put out by all this and started making enquiries about the way AGMs were conducted in Hong Kong. Were they all really this perfunctory? Old Hong Kong hands in the finance industry were amused by my naivety. One solemnly assured me that some meetings lasted as long as five minutes; another advised me to attend an AGM where decent sushi was served. Everyone took it for granted that annual general meetings were little more than a joke. They certainly were not an occasion for company directors to impart information to their shareholders, nor were directors really happy even to answer questions. After all, they had laid on a buffet at some expense – what more could shareholders want?

The crash course in shareholder relations quickly produced the realisation that held true not only for Hong Kong companies but for most other companies in the region. It was that minority shareholders may well have equity in public companies but, as Mr Gilmore observed, they most certainly were not treated in any way as owners.

Quite a lot flows from this. However, what mainly flows is the simple fact that the interests of minority shareholders are rarely considered by the majority shareholders, who treat public companies as private companies.

In this spirit shareholders' funds are routinely used to make cheap loans to the majority shareholders and their private companies. When the going gets tough it is not unknown for majority shareholders to get their public companies to buy up assets in the private companies that are loss making or in some other way troubled. Equally common is the practice of getting the public company to pay lavish salaries to the majority shareholders who are also the company's directors.

However, minority shareholders are not supposed to be treated like this. Walter Woon, a legal academic and Member of Parliament in Singapore, laid out the role that minority shareholders are supposed to play in companies:

> A company is, theoretically, a democracy. Theoretically, the people who own the company call the shots. The shareholders are the ones who appoint directors, approve directors' fees and declare dividends.
>
> They have the right (in the case of public companies) to remove directors by ordinary resolution. They appoint the auditors and fix their remuneration. In practice, things are seldom so neat.
>
> Corporate democracy is capitalist democracy. The larger the shareholding, the greater the voting power. This is the golden rule; he who has the gold makes the rules.[16]

Picking examples of minority-shareholder abuse in Asia leaves the diligent researcher quite spoiled for choice. The examples given below are not the most extreme, nor are they atypical: they have been chosen to illustrate many of the usual ways in which controlling shareholders have taken minorities for a ride.

Unsurprisingly some of Asia's worst-managed companies turned out to be the most abusive of their shareholders. Renong, the Malaysian political hotchpotch conglomerate discussed in the previous chapter, was sinking under a mountain by the end of 1997. Its solution was to get shareholders in United Engineers (Malaysia), a subsidiary, to bail out the parent. The benefit to United Engineers' minority shareholders was nil but this did not stop so-called independent advisers recommending the scheme. United Engineers then became involved in another audacious scheme, as we shall see shortly.

On a much smaller but infinitely more audacious scale is the example of the sale of the Hong Kong-based Sing Tao newspaper group in 1999. Sally Aw, the daughter of the group's founder, presided over a steady diminution of the company's profitability culminating, in 1998, in losses totalling HK$116 million (US$14.9 million). Meanwhile, she was being sued for the recovery of personal debts totalling some HK$274 million (US$35 million) and had just escaped being charged for a corruption offence in relation to an intriguing fraud aimed at deceiving advertisers in the *Hongkong Standard* newspaper, which was part of the group.

A consortium led by the Dublin-listed China Enterprise Development Fund (CEDF) tried to buy Sing Tao. Negotiations were going well until Miss Aw realised that there would be no place for her once the company was sold. Considering that she had brought the company to its knees, it might appear reasonable that she should have no preferential role in the company's restructuring.

However, Miss Aw shopped around and found another interested purchaser in the shape of Lazard Asia, which agreed to pay her HK$262 million (US$33.5 million) for her 50 per cent stake in the company. In so doing she was offered a 23 per cent premium on the price Lazard was offering minority shareholders. However, the great deal for Miss Aw did not end there. She was also given a contract to act as a consultant to Sing Tao for a period of six years at an annual salary of HK$9 million (US$1.15 million) and she was furnished with a HK$58m (US$7.4 million) loan to assist in the repayment of her debts. It is not difficult to see why the deal offered by Lazard's was acceptable to Miss Aw, but it is extremely difficult to see why the deal offered by CEDF would not have suited minority shareholders better. Faced with the choice of taking the offer made by Lazard or seeing the Sing Tao share price fall through the floor, leaving them with nothing, the minority shareholders grudgingly accepted the offer.[17] Although there was some attempt to get the courts to block the deal and some talk of getting the Securities and Futures Commission to intervene, it soon fizzled out.

The post-crisis period provided a host of other examples of majority shareholders working hard to salvage their personal situations, usually caused by high levels of indebtedness. They sought to do so at the expense of their minority shareholders. A mirror image of the Sing Tao case was being played out in Singapore. The company in question came from an equally famous background. Jack Chia-MPH, was founded by Jack Chiarapurk, better known as Jack Chia, a well-known entrepreneur operating in the days when Singapore still produced entrepreneurs. His family had succeeded in pretty much turning the fortune he made into a mountain of debt. In 1998 their problems became so acute that they were forced to call in the accountants Price Waterhouse to examine the possibilities of restructuring. This is usually a polite way of saying that they were looking for a method of keeping the company from going under.

However, it was not the company itself that was in trouble but the majority shareholders. The family's debts were steadily mounting and the banks were leaning on them to pay back the money. They were forced to farm out their shares in Jack Chia-MPH as collateral against the loans. Offers were made to the family to buy out their interest in the company but they were loath to lose control. Instead they were keen on proposals to hive off the most profitable parts of the company, including a highly profitable Australian residential-property subsidiary called AV Jennings. In so doing they could have given a boost to the company's cash position, albeit depriving it of longer-term earnings.

Then the Chias wanted to sell their privately held Hong Kong-based pharmaceutical firm, Pharmacon, to the public company thus reducing their own liquidity problems. None of this was designed to promote the interests of minority shareholders. Moreover, it is questionable whether the accountants, in the guise of independent advisers, were really looking after the company's interests or those of the Chia family.

One favourite way in which majority shareholders help themselves to the funds of listed companies is to pay themselves substantial sums of money in directors' fees. During the heady years of the 1990s when everyone was making money, this produced little more than wry smiles, but after things turned bad there was not a great deal to smile about. This was certainly the case for minority shareholders in Hong Kong-listed Kwong Sang Hong International. First they saw their company being sold for a song to Chinese Enterprises, controlled by the controversial Lau brothers, and to Anita Shum, a private investor. It used to belong to the collapsed Peregrine group, whose affairs are discussed in the following chapter. In May 1999 they were informed that the company was deeply in the red and that no dividend would be paid. However, the directors felt able to announce a 1200 per cent increase in directors' fees, although the sum involved was relatively modest. Minority shareholders were so incensed that they actually managed to make the company's AGM last for an hour, as opposed to the customary few minutes. However, the anger of the few who bothered to turn up to the meeting was not sufficient to change the outcome.

Another post-crisis example of getting minorities to pay for the consequences of the crisis also comes from Hong Kong. In April 1999 Dickson Concepts, the luxury-goods retailer, announced a scheme under which Dickson Poon, the majority shareholder, would buy all the company's non-Asian assets, including the famous British Harvey Nichols stores, and leave the listed company with all the loss-making Asian assets.[18]

In return the shareholders were to be paid exactly the amount the non-Asian assets were valued at by the company's 'independent' advisers. Putting to one side the matter of how these valuations were reached, what was striking about the whole deal was that Mr Poon was not required to pay the kind of premium for these assets that any third-party buyer would most definitely have had to pay. Not only that but he structured the offer to minorities in such a way that most of the money he needed to raise to buy the companies from the listed company would be provided by a special dividend of which, as the largest shareholder, he would get the lion's share.

Why, it may be asked, did not the minority shareholders rise up in revolt? As in practically every other case they did not do so because they were leaderless, because they feared that the majority shareholder had reached an understanding with the few institutional shareholders who had a stake in Dickson and because most of them were prepared to take the money and run rather than gamble on a prolonged fight to keep the profit-making parts of the company out of Mr Poon's hands while there was a risk that the price of the shares would sink as the battle ensued.

These examples of trampling on minority shareholders' interests are deliberately taken from Hong Kong and Singapore, the two places in the region with the highest level of transparency and the most stringent regulatory environment. Picking examples from elsewhere in the region is too easy because minority-shareholder abuse is the norm. Moreover, at least in Hong Kong and Singapore there is some prospect of appealing to an independent regulatory authority.

One of the biggest pieces of 'daylight robbery' emerged from the debris of the financial crash in Singapore. It began when in September 1998 Malaysia imposed capital controls which had the effect of freezing trading in Malaysian shares on Singapore's Central Limit Order Book (CLOB) over-the-counter market (previously the two stock exchanges were linked but, when they split, trading by Singaporeans in the Malaysian market was done via CLOB). Fearing that Singaporean investors would dump their Malaysian shares and further depress already falling share prices in Kuala Lumpur, the government simply decreed that these shares could not be sold.

In effect Singaporean investors were trapped in a hinterland between holding worthless shares and yet retaining ownership rights over shares that in Malaysia itself were rising in value. In April 1999 a so-called solution was offered by a Malaysian businessman called Akhbar Khan, which effectively gave the Singaporeans an opportunity to sell their shares at a discount of at least 50 per cent to the prices then prevailing in Kuala Lumpur. 'No one should touch this deal,' an unnamed head of equity sales at a European-owned bank in Singapore told the Reuters news agency. 'It's daylight robbery.'[19]

Indeed it was robbery on a grand scale but it was robbery without menace, or could be presented as such by Mr Akhbar, who argued that he was a bulk buyer taking a huge gamble through huge exposure to the market. Mr Akhbar may have seemed like an unlikely person to be engaging in such large-scale share purchasing. Hitherto he had been better known as the owner of the Hugo Boss luxury-goods franchise in Malaysia, not exactly a high-profile investment-banking corporation. However, he was also a close associate of Daim Zainuddin, the finance minister of Malaysia. In fact Mr Akhbar has good political connections in a number of places but not good enough to persuade Singaporean share-holders to go for his dubious deal.

Once the Akhbar offer failed another popped up. Again it came from companies with strong political connections: Telekom Malaysia and United Engineers, who offered to swap the frozen CLOB shares for their own, albeit at a premium price of 30 per cent. Singaporean estimates calculated that this would mean accepting a 42 per cent discount on their Malaysian holdings if they accepted the offer. Unsurprisingly this offer was also viewed unfavourably in Singapore.[20]

It was a political act that froze the CLOB shares and it seems it was politics that will ultimately rob shareholders. Dr Mahathir Mohamad, the Malaysian Prime Minister, was typically unapologetic. He accused CLOB shareholders of causing the big fall in Malaysian share prices. 'They did nothing to bring up the value of the shares,' he said. 'In fact, it was they who brought down the price of their own shares so they deserve that price in shares.'[21]

Here was an extreme example of state-sponsored abuse of minority shareholders. Others are more subtle but the very idea that a government, which sponsors the creation of equity markets, should tolerate – nay, encourage – such flagrant disregard for shareholders' rights gives some idea why public companies do so. Unlike governments, they do not have a mandate to safeguard the public interest.

Below-par professional advisers

This brings us to the whole gamut of so-called respectable financial and legal professionals who aid and abet the majority shareholders although they really should know better. Some of the best-known names in the global accounting business sign off company accounts that, to put it generously, do not give an accurate picture of the businesses they are supposed to be describing. Legal firms append their names to share-offering prospectuses knowing full well that much needs to be disclosed that has not been disclosed. Investment banks send out their most senior people to juggle and conjure with figures and words that mislead rather than inform potential investors. Property consultants, who are meticulous in making property valuations in London and New York, are transformed when called upon to value a property in, say, Dalian in China or Kota Kinabalu in Malaysia, for the purposes of asset-value assessment. Here they are faced with a far less certain set of rules for assessing prices, so what do they do? In general they simply accept the valuation proffered by the company asking for the valuation.

Topping off this liturgy of professional negligence is the generally astonishingly low quality of brokers' analysts' reports in Asia. In Chapter 1 we looked at reasons why analysts are constrained in the type of commentaries they are able to make on individual stocks and markets, but the question of competence was not considered.

This is thrown into some doubt by a survey released in May 1999 by Barra, the company that publishes *The Estimate Directory*, a reference book compiling estimates made by stockbrokers' analysts, which found that 20 to 40 per cent of analysts covering Asian markets did nothing more than base their forecasts of company performance on whatever was the consensus view. In other words their so-called research consisted of nothing more than reprinting the findings of others.[22]

To be fair it may be unreasonable to blame the analysts themselves because the companies they work for are notoriously herdlike in their behaviour and love sticking closely to consensus views rather than boldly going off on their own. An analyst may well produce forecasts that differ from those of the herd but his or her boss may equally well suggest that the estimate be moved closer to the consensus. Brokers should be providing a vital link with the investing public and should generate first-class independent information. The reality looks more like a babble of confused and misleading information.

Were the problems of incompetence among professionals such as investment banks, accountants and lawyers confined to small hole-in-the-wall companies they could be shrugged off more easily. However, international companies have been signing off sets of accounts, share-offer documents and the like that are nothing short of a disgrace.

It is rarely easy to pinpoint where the problems lie. They tend to get exposed, if at all, after disaster strikes as it did when the Hong Kong-listed – but Chinese state-controlled – Guangdong Trust and Investment Corporation (GITIC) went under at the end of 1998. At the beginning of 1999 GITIC published accounts that showed the difference between the book value of its assets, as confirmed by its accountants, and the estimated level of recovery that could be expected from selling these assets. It is bad enough, for example, that loans totalling 11,307 million yuan ($1,362 million) would produce only 2134 million yuan for creditors – but what of the cash and bank balances, with a book value of 149.5 million yuan, which would yield a mere 35 million yuan?[23] How on earth can cash and bank balances be worth less than a quarter of their listed book value. Yet some perfectly respectable accountants signed off on these figures.

In May 1999 one of the world's biggest accountancy companies, Deloitte Touche Tohmatsu, announced that it was taking the unprecedented step of withdrawing its 1997 audit report for Guangnan (Holdings), another failed Hong Kong-listed, Chinese state-controlled company. Deloitte made its decision *after* the Guangdong provincial government called in another big accountancy firm, KPMG, to investigate the company's affairs. KPMG found a number of glaring discrepancies. Deloitte, whose statutory duty it was to investigate discrepancies before signing off on an audit, said that Guangnan was unwilling to stand by representations it had made at the time of the audit. In other words it was, according to the accountants, not at all their fault.[24]

Having made this discovery two years after the event was of little comfort to Guangnan shareholders. It is notoriously difficult to audit the affairs of Chinese government-controlled companies, but this is also a common problem when it comes to finding out what is happening inside other companies in the region. According to Michael Backman they may not even be trying too hard. He wrote, 'one of the greatest problems for auditors in Asia is the tendency for listed firms to shop around for the auditor most likely to do their bidding.'[25] Moreover, as Mr Backman rightly points out, Asian auditors are tied into a mass of business and political connections that challenge their independence.

It is dangerous to make sweeping statements, but one that can be made in confidence is that practically every company that has collapsed both before and after the Asian crisis showed signs of problems that warranted further investigation by the professionals who are supposed to do this sort of thing. Even in cases where there was some attempt at investigation there was little follow-through.

In 1999 the Hong Kong stock exchange conducted a survey of the annual reports issued by all the 672 companies listed in 1997. It found that 7 per cent of these companies, 42 in total, had had their accounts qualified by auditors who offered either a 'qualified opinion' or reflected a 'fundamental uncertainty' about the accounts they were auditing.[26] There is no record of any follow up action being taken on any of these reports.

Nine months before this survey was published Laura Cha, the deputy chairwoman of Hong Kong's SFC, expressed the commission's frustration in dealing with financial advisers, particularly merchant banks, whom she described as poorly qualified and lacking in experience, forcing the commission to step in and protect shareholder rights by stopping 'a number of deals which were unfair to minority shareholders'.[27]

So-called 'independent' directors

Public companies are obliged to appoint independent directors who are charged with the responsibility of preventing this type of unfairness and are supposed to act as a safeguard for minority shareholders. As we shall see, in Korea, activists have been pressing for minority shareholders to appoint their own representatives to these posts. They want to do so because throughout the region it is rare to the point of being startling to find a so-called independent director who is not closely connected to the majority shareholder. In other regions where majority shareholders do not hold such a large proportion of the equity, independent directors are likely to be both more independent and more influential in exercising their duties. However, in Asian companies they are paid to keep quiet and are often well rewarded for maintaining their silence.

In circumstances where a company is about to embark on a connected transaction, a so-called 'independent committee' is usually formed to pass judgement on the merits of that transaction and forward their conclusion to minority shareholders who have the power to veto these connected transactions. I searched high and low without success to find one, just one, example of an independent committee recommending against a connected transaction. However unfair they have been to the minority shareholders, these independents, in practice almost always nonexecutive directors of the company in question, judge the transaction to be fair and to the benefit of all.

Insider trading

The absence of safeguards in the shape of truly independent company directors is but one way of ensuring that abuses are allowed to flourish. Some abuses are so profound and so widespread that they have ceased to be a matter of comment. Top of the list is the nightmare of insider trading.

Having acted as a consultant to a number of public companies I never ceased to be amazed by the consistent and casual way in which I was routinely offered insider information. I frankly found it embarrassing and often pretended not to understand what I was being told. I have asked others in a similar position whether they have had the same experience. In all cases the answer came back in the affirmative.

Insider trading is treated very seriously, particularly in the United States, but in Asian countries it is considered a bit of a perk or an understandable consequence of the way companies are run. Although theoretically frowned upon, in most Asian countries insider trading either carries no penalty, aside from a reprimand, or, where a penalty is imposed in the rare instances in which action is taken, it tends to be light.

However, the effects of insider trading are considerable. Because it is so widespread it means that shareholders with no connection to the companies they invest in are consistently offered second-class deals. They can buy into the market only after insiders have taken positions and are able to get out only after insiders have taken their profit or minimised their losses and run.

Before the 1997 crash I asked a senior stockbroker in Thailand what was his estimate of the level of domestic trades that were based on insider information. He promptly replied, 'Oh, about half.' 'Really?' I asked. He thought a little more. 'Actually, that's a bit on the low side: it's probably more,' he replied. Obviously there are no reliable statistics about the extent of insider trading but every single piece of anecdotal evidence points to its being very high indeed and almost certainly higher in the countries where it is least discussed.

Hong Kong finally got round to making insider trading illegal and in 1998 the SFC actually managed to pull off its most spectacular prosecution of the notorious insider dealer Albert Yeung, whose previous criminal convictions for witness intimidation seemed not to have proved a barrier preventing his stewardship of public companies. It took five years for the SFC to win its battle to bring Mr Yeung to justice for using insider information to buy shares in his company Emperor (China Concept) Investments ahead of an announcement that a consortium was interested in buying the company from Mr Yeung's Emperor International. Not only was Mr Yeung fined a hefty HK$20.69 million ($2.6 million) but he was barred from the directorship of public companies for two years. The conviction of Mr Yeung did nothing to damage his blue-chip political connections, which included the presence of Bob Hawke, the former Australian Prime Minister, on the board of Emperor International (after the insider-trading investigation began) and the appointment of Rita Fan, the President of Hong Kong's legislature, as an adviser to the Emperor Group while she was between jobs before taking up the leadership of the law-making body.

Keeping control

In most major international markets the division between the majority and minority shareholders is less sharp. This is because even listed, family-run companies tend to place the bulk of the equity out to the market. Most Asian markets require a minimum of only 25 per cent of the equity to be in the hands of the general public. Some, including Hong Kong, even allow a company to float shares with less than 25 per cent in so-called 'free float'. In both Europe and North America it is highly unusual for there to be a majority shareholder with a holding exceeding 50 per cent. Indeed, particularly in the United States, some investors are concerned by the fact that so many companies are run by people with practically no equity stake in them.

In Asia it is quite different. As a consequence of the listing rules and the way that large Asian companies are run, it is usual for the bulk of the shares, in most cases over 50 per cent, to be owned by the major shareholder. Many go right up to the minimum limit, meaning that only 25 per cent of the equity is in public hands. After HSBC Holdings, which controls the Hongkong and Midland banks, moved its primary listing from Hong Kong to London, none of the major listed companies domiciled in the territory had a majority of the equity in free float. In Indonesia, just before the 1997 crash, 90 per cent of listed companies kept more than half the equity in the hands of the majority shareholder and two-thirds allowed no more than a third of the equity to remain in circulation. The main motive for limiting the number of shares in public hands is to ensure that the company's founders retain control.

Even in Japan, where ownership of companies has expanded beyond that of the company founders and their families, minority shareholders have little influence and their interests do not loom large in the conflicting mass of management boards' preoccupations.

Japanese shareholders also receive their dividends in a very different way from shareholders in other markets. In Japan dividends are paid as a percentage of the par value of the shares, not, as is usual elsewhere, as a percentage of company earnings. This makes dividend payments comparatively low. Because Japanese companies typically pay only modest dividends they are left with more money for reinvestment, which in theory should increase the company's value to longer-term shareholders.

The bulk of shares in leading Japanese companies are held by related companies through a highly complex system of cross holdings and ownership by companies that form part of the group of the listed entity. A study of three of Japan's leading companies, Mistsui, Mitsubishi and Sumitomo, showed that the biggest shareholder was the company's own mutual life insurance company subsidiary, a privately controlled entity. Next came financial institutions and trading entities tied to the three groups.[28] Where share ownership is not vested in directly related companies it is highly likely to come from companies that have cross holdings in each other. This leaves nonrelated minority shareholders very much out in the cold and powerless and, in many instances, seeing their interests made subservient to those of the interrelated shareholders.

However, it has also been argued that this form of share ownership takes the pressure off company managers to produce ever greater dividends and concentrate on building the underlying foundations of corporate growth.

Minority shareholders fight back

Minority shareholders are not angels: they can be rapacious money grabbers with little interest in longer-term development. Indeed one of the first and most notable Asian minority shareholders' victories was scored back in 1992 when small shareholders in the state-controlled airline Singapore Airlines forced the company to produce a bonus share both to reward existing shareholders and to dilute the price of the shares and so make trading more liquid. There is no evidence that this produced one iota of benefit to the running of the airline but it was something of a triumph for a thirty-eight-year-old engineer called Ng Kim Hoo, who spent three years trying to overrule the board and was not deterred when, on the first attempt, his efforts were ruled out of order at the company's AGM. It seems a pity that his tenacity was not devoted to a more worthy purpose.

Despite the generally shabby treatment dished out to minority shareholders, most of them, like majority shareholders in Asia, do not tend to have a longer-term perspective and share a common interest in instant gratification. This does not, however, mean that minority shareholders do not have perfectly legitimate rights.

In Korea, where the legitimate rights of minorities have a tradition of being overlooked, minority-shareholder activism has been placed on an organised basis and has succeeded in producing results.

A group called Chamyoyondae, or the People's Solidarity for Participatory Democracy (PSPD), has spearheaded the campaign for minority-shareholder rights.[29] The PSPD did not start paying attention to this issue until 1997, and did so to the great surprise of the listed companies who had an unbroken record of having little regard for the rights of their shareholders. The pressure group was sufficiently active to gain wider attention, including that of President Kim Dae-jung, the most senior of the government officials to have met PSPD leaders to discuss corporate reform. Within just a couple of years of PSPD activity five of Korea's leading conglomerates, or *chaebols*, demonstrated just how worried they were. In March 1999 they all decided to hold their AGMs on the same day in the hope of minimising the group's intervention in their meetings.

At Samsung Electronics PSPD shareholders grilled the management over its activities and pressed other shareholders to adopt the so-called 'cumulative voting system' under which minority shareholders would have the right to elect a board member. This move failed but the company's management emerged from the meeting rather bemused by the extent to which they had been held to account.

However, PSPD members had better luck at the meeting of SK Telecom, Korea's leading telecommunications company, where not only was the management forced into accepting the appointment of minority-share-holder-elected directors but they also bowed to demands for the establish-ment of an independent auditing committee. SK Telecom was forced by the PSPD to issue an apology for diverting a chunk of its profits to the majority shareholder's family.

Among the directors appointed to keep an eye on minority-shareholder interests was Nam Sang Koo, an academic from the Korea University who specialises in business studies. Within no time at all he forced the company into disclosing holdings in the commercial paper of connected companies totalling some $250 million. This typical way of supporting associated companies, without telling shareholders how their funds were being used, was unusual at SK Telecom only because Mr Nam's persistence paid off in exposing it. He got the company to divest itself of these holdings and put them on watch that shareholders could not so easily be covertly used to shuffle money from one company to another.

At the Daewoo Corp., the bosses of the troubled conglomerate were sharply told that a suit was to be launched against board members guilty of making illegal internal transactions.

In 1998 the PSPD obtained a court order compelling the Korea First Bank's board of directors to pay fines of 40 billion won ($32.5 million) for managerial irregularities, including illegal funding to the bankrupt Hanbo Steel & Iron company.

Also that year the PSPD managed to keep the directors of Samsung Electronics at their annual meeting for over thirteen hours while they grilled them over secret fund-channelling to the ill-fated Samsung Motors

Inc. The directors were then taken to court and fined for refusing to reveal information about the unlawful assistance given to Samsung Motors. Minority-shareholder pressure also compelled Samsung Electronics to increase the number of independent directors and give minority shareholders preference when issuing convertible bonds.

Such action was remarkable given that there was no sign of pressure groups even focusing on business matters until 1989. Once they did they found allies among foreign investors who were increasingly frustrated by the way that minorities are treated by public companies in Korea. The Koreans have shown what minority shareholders could do elsewhere in Asia if they were prepared to stir themselves for action.

However, it would be a gross exaggeration to say that Korean companies are now in the grip of minority-shareholder control. If any reminder that this is not so were required it came in March 1999 when Chung Ju-yung, the legendary founder of the Hyundai group, engineered the removal of Chung Se-yung, his younger brother, in favour of his eldest son as head of Hyundai Motors. Chung Se-yung had tried to remain in his job by gathering minority-shareholder support but his elder brother was far too wily to allow this to get in his way, especially when he was determined that his son's succession should be ensured.

Elsewhere in Asia minority shareholders are usually galvanised only by specific and outrageous instances of majority-shareholder abuse. In Singapore, under the ever watchful eye of the state, there has been a growing trend towards increased awareness of minority-shareholder rights backed by regulations to safeguard these rights.

Across the causeway in Malaysia, where minority-shareholder abuse is routine, there were also some attempts to address these problems. In 1998 a Malaysian Institute of Corporate Governance (MICG) was founded by six institutions representing lawyers, accountants and corporate entities. Its head, Datuk Megat Najmuddin Khas, said the aim was both to improve corporate governance and also to change the perceptions of corporate malfeasance, which were sullying the whole nation. He believed, however, that bad behaviour was the responsibility of just a few 'black sheep'. In a parallel move the government started work on a 'Malaysian Code on Corporate Governance', designed to codify good practices and require directors of public companies to adhere to a set of minimum standards. Critics view both moves as being more concerned with window dressing than tackling the substance of the problem. However, the very fact that Malaysia saw the need for corporate governance window dressing was a step forward.

In Hong Kong the watchdog Securities and Futures Commission (SFC), born out of the debris of the toothless old Securities Commission, has been making a stab at stamping out some of the more typical minority-shareholder abuses, even though it is under little public pressure to do so. Indeed Chim Pui-chung, the legislator who was elected to represent the financial sector's interests in the legislature, was one of the SFC's main adversaries. This is not unconnected with the fact that he is also a major-league minority-shareholder abuser in his capacity as the major share-holder of listed companies. In 1996 the SFC sought to have Mr Chim's Mandarin Resources wound up to prevent further actions by Mr Chim that would be prejudicial to his minority shareholders. Among them were old favourites like selling assets to related companies at grossly inflated prices. The saga was interrupted when Mr Chim was sent to jail for forging share-transfer documents in another of his companies called Lucky Man but – and this is worrying in what it says about so-called professionals in the financial sector – they re-elected him to the legislature with a big majority after the charges had been laid although before he was convicted. The SFC was widely criticised for its heavy-handed approach towards Mr Chim and few people came to its defence, even after it was vindicated by the courts.

Occasionally some of the overseas funds operating in Hong Kong markets are stirred to raise the issue of minority-shareholder rights, not least because they had been led to imagine that this was a world-class market on a par with other leading financial centres where these rights are much more firmly rooted. The biggest single owner of shares in Hong Kong (aside from the government, which went on a share-buying spree in 1998 – more of which later) is the United States-based Templeton group, which in 1999 owned something like 7 per cent of the local market. Mark Mobius, the high-profile, attention-seeking managing director of Temple-ton Asset Management, launched a mini-offensive in that year to try to get some of the bigger local companies to acknowledge their responsibility to local shareholders. First he kicked up a fuss at Hongkong Electric, part of the Li Ka-shing stable of companies, which had pushed through a proposal to allow directors to issue new shares without offering them first to existing shareholders. Then Templeton turned its attention to the even bigger target of HSBC Holdings, the banking group. In May 1999 it blatantly ignored its shareholders by issuing a $3 billion share placement without even giving existing shareholders a chance to apply for a piece of the action. Templeton reasonably asked why this was so and was told that it was because the law allowed it.

Mr Mobius made it clear that his company would be paying much more attention 'to corporate governance and shareholders' rights'. He said that if Hong Kong companies really wanted to become 'truly global companies . . . they must accept outside ideas and the inclusion of independent outside directors on their board of directors who do not have connections with the majority owners'.[30]

Waking up to the need for better corporate governance

Mr Mobius is not alone in paying closer attention to corporate governance. However, this subject was not much talked about before the crisis. Indeed when it was first raised it tended to be treated as meddlesome interference.

For example, there was an outcry in Singapore, just before the crisis broke, after the government introduced new rules for listed companies requiring them to establish audit committees within boards of directors who would act as an independent voice and be required to report fraud or irregularities to the stock exchange. Stockbrokers and heads of companies expressed alarm. Richard Hu, the finance minister, was forced on to the defensive. He pleaded with investors to understand that good corporate governance was not inimical to their interests and said it was not the government's intention 'to curtail the business discretion of listed companies or create an adversarial relationship between managers and shareholders'.[31]

It is doubtful whether these outraged stirrings would be heard these days. On the contrary, in the post-crisis period the region was awash with born-again corporate reformers.

Among them was Daim Zainuddin, the senior Malaysian finance minister and Minister of Special Functions overseeing post-crisis economic recovery policies. Mr Daim, a former businessman, has been associated with some of Malaysia's most controversial corporate dealings but in March 1999 he told a meeting of the Asian Institute of Management in Manila that 'the weaknesses in East Asia's corporate and financial sectors had been one of the factors contributing to the collapse of the equity and capital markets. When the crisis deepened, investors became worried about the strength and resilience of banks and corporations, which were masked by poor standards of disclosure and accountability.

Shares were dumped with the collapse of investor confidence. The massive outflow of funds that ensued fuelled the contagion nature of the crisis.'

Mr Daim was not alone: practically every finance minister, central banker and leading economic adviser to East Asian governments has now spoken out on the need for better corporate governance, and some, as we shall see, have even put their words into action.

'Few recognised the profoundly corrosive effect poor corporate govern-ance standards could have on seemingly vibrant economies,' wrote the World Bank's Jim Wolfensohn. 'The cost has been enormous. In East Asia two thirds of Indonesian companies and one quarter of Thai companies appear insolvent. Cost estimates of financial sector restructuring range from a low of 18 per cent of GDP in Indonesia to 30 per cent in South Korea and Thailand.'[32]

Good corporate governance, according to the Asian Development Bank, 'has a significant impact on investment and growth'.[33]

Although battles for better corporate governance had been fought with some vigour in the West, no one seemed to draw any conclusions from these struggles when it came to looking at Asian companies. Like other aspects of the so-called Asian Miracle, this aspect was overlooked on various spurious grounds, most of which came under the catch-all heading of 'different cultural practices'.

Yet the four basic principles of good corporate governance are universal and now recognised and endorsed by East Asian governments. They are transparency, accountability, responsibility and predictability. Bodies such as the Asian Development Bank, the World Bank and the Organisa-tion for Economic Co-operation and Development are busy working on plans to codify these principles and are drawing up what may be described as corporate-governance good-behaviour check lists.

In brief, transparency means that disclosure of information is required in a timely manner to provide a comprehensive understanding of the state of affairs in public companies. The requirement to behave in a responsible manner amounts to nothing more outlandish than complying with the law and behaving in a way that accords with the values of the society within which companies operate. As for accountability, this means no more than making those who manage companies accountable to share-holders and ensuring that corporate boards provide something approach-ing independent oversight of the manager's activities.

Investors, who pride themselves on having foresight to predict the not readily predictable, love predictability when it comes to laws and regulations because a well-understood and properly implemented regulatory system creates a level playing field for all. Only those who have benefited from privilege in the interpretation of the regulations have reason not to want a clearly understood framework within which to make their investments.

These principles may not sound too demanding but if implemented in most Asian companies they would cause something of a revolution. Most companies in the region simply do not know how to behave as public companies.

Thus at the very heart of the Asian Miracle, the miracle of the equity markets, there were flaws stretching as far as the eye could see. Most of these flaws remain in place although at least there is increasing discussion of the problem and some tentative steps are being taken to put things right. However, as we shall see in the following chapter, some of the problems were so bad that they either verged close to or crossed the line where criminality began. Moreover, these problems were built into the political systems that had been hailed as providing the leadership that made the Asian Miracle possible.

6

GREED IS GOOD, CORRUPTION'S OK . . .
LET'S MAKE MONEY

The smell of money

'When I first stepped out on the trading floor, I could smell and see the money. Throughout my time at Barings I had been inching closer and closer to it, and in Singapore I was suddenly there.'[1] These are the words of Nick Leeson, the rogue trader whose reckless gambling on Japanese stock-market futures brought down Barings, the blue-blood British investment bank.

Nick Leeson was one of a long line of fortune seekers attracted to Asia when, so it seemed, fortunes were to be made and no one was going to be too fussy about *how* they were made.

The single-minded pursuit of the quick buck was the order of the day during the heady years of the Asian Miracle. There is nothing remarkable about this: booms, bull markets and the sudden discovery of riches always attract a fair gathering of shysters, crooks and other dubious characters. The problem in the Asian high-growth economies was that these characters were often aided, abetted and in some cases led by the people who ran these nations.

Of course greed was not invented in Asia – indeed the now famous phrase 'greed is good' comes from *Wall Street*, the seminal film about financial wheeling and dealing in America. *Wall Street* is set in the modern era but rampant corruption was much more a feature of Western societies during their periods of high growth and transformation from agricultural to industrialised societies.

Corruption: a stage of development or an Asian curse?

It is almost tempting to describe rampant corruption as being no more than a stage of development. Samuel Huntington, the much-quoted American academic, has argued that economic development, especially during its more intense periods, is more than likely to disturb the existing social order and undermine public order as social inequalities are exacerbated and those who lose out in the struggle for economic advancement are frustrated – a frustration heightened by rising expectations.[2] Professor Huntington is basically describing the breeding grounds of a corrupt society.

Asia is far from alone in providing examples of these breeding grounds. However, there is a lurking suspicion that Asian nations may have added some special ingredient to the corruption equation. This suspicion was given sustenance from a highly unlikely quarter when Lee Kwan Yew, one of the founding fathers of the Asian-values concept, addressed the Europe Asia Forum in 1998. He told his listeners that nepotism was a weakness rooted in Confucianism. The Chinese practice of *guanxi*, or using connections, he said, 'is not a good Asian value and is not compatible with the competitive free market'. Deploying *guanxi* led to nepotism.

According to Mr Lee this problem was overcome in Singapore only by using Western concepts of law. 'One of the great benefits that the Western systems of law have provided Singapore', he said, 'is to keep a check through impartial means of recruitment, of tender awards against any such tendency.'[3]

Sunanda Datta-Ray, a well-known Indian journalist who lived for a while in Singapore, was inspired by Mr Lee's comments to add some of his own. He wrote,

> In the West, a mix of institutional religion, moral instruction, parental discipline, laws and administrative structures try to counter weakness and temptation.
>
> In the East, while we have abandoned our own systems of religious and moral instruction, and public life has reinvented the concept of family ties, our laws and administrative structures are not yet firmly enough established. Even tradition can be travestied when projected beyond time and setting.[4]

'It's part of our culture'

The most insulting distortion of so-called Eastern traditions is that which suggests that corruption is part of Asia's local culture and is therefore justified on 'cultural' grounds.

There is a marvellous quote from a Thai army colonel, contained in a study of corruption in Thailand, which makes this point:

> 'In our society we are not so individualistic like westerners', he said. 'Thai people live together like relatives. Favour requires gratitude in return. Today, we help him, in future days he helps us. It may not be proper in the whole process. But it is necessary'.[5]

The Thais tend to be far more open about corruption than most other people in the region. When the notoriously corrupt Chatichai government was on its last legs towards the end of 1990 I found myself with a group of Thai journalists talking to Montri Pongpanit, the transport minister, who was widely rumoured to have accepted a large bribe for awarding a contract for a mass-transit system. 'Was it true?' asked one of the Thai journalists in usually blunt terms. Mr Montri smiled and then simply said, without issuing a denial, 'People say all sorts of things.' He was later investigated for being 'unusually rich'. As for the badly needed mass-transit project, it never materialised.

One of Mr Montri's successors, Pairoj Lohsoonthorn, who served in the equally corrupt pre-crisis Chavalit government as deputy Interior Minister, went so far as to advise staff in the land-sales department to accept any money offered to them. However, he had his standards: the staff were instructed not to solicit bribes or circulate bribe-rate price lists. 'This is part of traditional Thai culture,' Mr Pairoj told the *Matichon* newspaper.[6]

It is estimated that over $800 was spent by politicians in the 1996 election, which brought the Chavalit government to power. Not only did the winners need to find a way of recouping their 'investment' but they wanted to make it pay dividends. They had, after all, invested more money in their election than American political parties invested in campaigns to elect their President.

The malaise

A dangerous coincidence of circumstances lay behind the great Asian Miracle. These circumstances combined to create problems so profound that in the post-crisis period they will prove hard to tackle.

On the one hand there were high levels of economic growth pushing more and more cash into countries unaccustomed to this level of wealth. On the other hand were weak governmental systems with fractured legal systems, making it hard to control malpractices in the economy. Thrown into the mixture was the greed and venality of those running these countries. Many of them were unfettered by the constraint of free elections.

Finally, and perhaps most remarkably, because there was absolutely no need for it, was the endorsement of those outside the Asian systems. It came from people and organisations who were investing in these countries and declared themselves to be satisfied with the way things were being run, mainly because they thought that these lax ways could be used to their advantage.

Some very influential people concluded that because so many of the high-growth economies had managed without the niceties of things like rule of law, these safeguards may not be necessary for economic development. Some went further, as we have seen, and asserted that these nations were actually assisted in their development by cutting legal corners and oiling the wheels of commerce with a few backhanders.

We live in a strange world where views like these are expressed by allegedly respectable and responsible people, such as bankers and even lawyers. The problem of corruption and cronyism in Asia was airily dismissed by Henry Kissinger, the former US Secretary of State who became a consultant to the highest bidders (including such clients as President Suharto of Indonesia). He said that these problems were little more than the 'cost of doing business' in these countries.

There is another strand of argument advanced by the apologists for corruption in Asia. This runs on the lines that paying off politicians directly is no different from, say, the payments made to political parties in the West and therefore is perfectly all right. By focusing on dubious practices in the West to justify dubious practices in the East, those advocating this point of view establish a very low standard for political morality in their own society and blithely ignore the fact that political funding is extremely controversial in the West and would rarely be cited as a good thing in the countries where parties have dubious relationships with those who fund them. Moreover, in most Western countries political funding is transparent and, where it is not, the media are free enough to discover and expose corrupt funding practices. The Asian media are becoming more assertive in performing this role, but in many countries they still operate under constraint.

A cancer of corruption was built into the heart of the Asian economies. The more the development of these economies is examined, the more it becomes clear that this was no side issue but a central fact of life which, in some cases, notably in Indonesia, led to enormous economic distortions, holding back economic development in general and corporate development in particular.

The United Nations World Development Report for 1997 says that 40 per cent of business in Asia is conducted on the basis of bribery. This is a pretty shocking statistic but not as shocking as the estimate of 60 per cent for the countries of the former Soviet Union.

Corruption league tables

So is not surprising to find Asian nations performing notably badly in corruption league tables. Of the eight high-growth economies only two (Hong Kong and Singapore) had systems that could be regarded as generally 'clean', where the rule of law prevailed and where corruption was not a systematic part of doing business. As for the other six nations, Taiwan and Korea had systems originating in government by corrupt oligarchies which left a legacy of malpractice even after the political scenery had changed. Malaysia, with its compromised judiciary, still preserved important aspects of rule of law and had stamped out some of the worst excesses of corruption, but this did not leave it without significant pockets of corrupt practices. This left Indonesia, the Philippines and Thailand at the bottom of the table struggling to keep their systems corruption-free but usually failing. In the Indonesia ruled by President Suharto, corruption was brought right into the heart of government and became an officially sanctioned way of life.

One of the most comprehensive global corruption surveys comes from a joint venture between Goettingen University in Germany and Transparency International, a nongovernmental organisation dedicated to the reduction of corruption as a means of hastening economic development. Because corruption is hard to measure in any precise scientific way this survey measures perceptions.

In the 1997 survey only one of the eight high-growth Asian economies made it into the top ten of 'clean' nations. That was Singapore, which consistently scores well in these league tables.

At the other end of the spectrum Indonesia ranked as forty-sixth out of fifty-two nations surveyed, leaving Nigeria at the bottom of the list. The Philippines slightly improved its ranking but was still ranked at forty in the league. Thailand was down in thirty-ninth place, Malaysia was at thirty-two.

The vulnerable ethnic Chinese

The most corrupt Asian nations have also added a distinctive variant to the corruption equation because of the high levels of wealth in the hands of ethnic Chinese communities. Although it is, in my view, largely obnoxious to say so, this form of ownership is often classified as owner-ship in 'alien' hands. The very term suggests the problems that flow from this concept.

The usual pattern in non-Communist developing countries is for wealth and political power to go hand in hand. However, in circumstances where the wealthy, by virtue of their ethnic origin, are denied political power their relationship with centres of power in authoritarian political systems tends to be less one of 'paymaster and servant', and is more like that of the victim of shakedowns who pays protection money to organised crime gangs.

It is a strange relationship, not quite symbiotic but mutually dependent in complex ways. The big Chinese tycoons are the paymasters. Those they pay are the people controlling authoritarian regimes. This is why, particularly in Indonesia under Suharto, the Philippines under Marcos and Thailand under military leadership, Chinese tycoons were closely associated with those in power. Although they had the leverage to ask for favours, the main reason for their relationships with the rulers was to *prevent* sequestration or other damaging acts which could more easily be perpetrated on 'alien' businesses as opposed to those regarded as being 'indigenous'.

Thus the ethnic Chinese were effectively coerced into paying protection money. Their leverage was not on a par with that of other, 'indigenous', paymasters who also formed close attachments to the ruling elites.

These 'indigenous' paymasters had the option of joining the political elites. The Chinese did not (although once the democratic process was installed they were able to achieve high office). As paymasters they had difficulty switching allegiances in the way that other paymasters were able to do if they became dissatisfied with their political protégés. When, for example, the Marcos family fled from the Philippines, the Chinese-Filipino tycoon Eduardo Cojuangco fled with them. The Cojuangco clan remained on ice during the subsequent Aquino and Ramos governments but were back with a vengeance when Joseph Estrada, another former Marcos crony, became president in 1998.

In Thailand the big-league Chinese businessmen had more difficult choices during the era of money-grabbing military governments that were plagued by factional rivalry. In the 1950s, for example, those who failed to back General Sarit Thanarat, who is generally credited with leading Thailand's economic revival, were left out in the cold when the Sarit government paid back its supporters. The pattern of support and payback was very much a feature of Thai politics for the next four decades.

When Banharn Silpa-archa, Thailand's first ethnic Chinese prime minister, came to power in 1995, after a typically dirty election, the Chinese community were faced with a new set of problems. They might have been expected to swing behind Mr Banharn, but it is to Thailand's credit that he was not seen as a candidate protecting Chinese interests, although some elements in the Democrat Party tried to paint him in this corner. More realistically he was viewed as an old-style regional power broker who was mistrusted by many prominent members of the Chinese community in Bangkok, where the Chinese are most influential and where Mr Banharn's Chart Thai fared singularly badly at the polls. This did not stop some prominent Chinese businessmen from hedging their bets by giving Chart Thai money, not out of conviction, but out of a fear of disfavour should the party win the election. The corrupt Banharn government lasted no more than fourteen months but, fortunately for the Chinese community, its poor performance proved to be a neutral factor in determining their fate.

It is inconceivable that a Chinese could aspire to the highest office in Indonesian politics. Instead Indonesia provides the supreme example of the dependency relationship between the Chinese business community and the ruling order under President Suharto's rule.

Such is the institutionalised nature of the corrupt relationship between the Chinese community and their political masters that there is even a name in Bahasa Indonesia for Chinese businessmen protected by politicians in return for cash. They are known as *Cukong*.

The big difference for Indonesian Chinese is that, despite changing their names, ceasing to use the written Chinese language for communication and generally trying to be as Indonesian as possible, this community is less assimilated than the Chinese communities of either Thailand or the Philippines, where an ethnic Chinese, Corazon Aquino, rose to be President – albeit more on the strength of her assassinated husband's legacy than her own abilities (she is, incidentally, a member of the Cojuangco clan, which says more about the small size of the Philippines elite than it does about her relations with those parts of the clan who were part of the Marcos entourage).

On the other side of the coin, the Indonesian Chinese own an even more disproportionately large share of the nation's wealth than the Chinese community in any other Asian non-Chinese majority nation. This leaves the ethnic Chinese in Indonesia very vulnerable, a vulnerability vividly illustrated in 1965 with the abortive Communist coup which led to the eventual demise of the Sukarno government and the massacre of tens of thousands of Chinese. Again in 1998 when the Suharto government fell, the Chinese community came under siege, this time losing fewer lives but suffering from looting, rape and a general state of terror as the old regime shambled out of office.

Among the looters' prime targets in 1998 were businesses and properties owned by Lim Sioe Liong (whose business empire is described in Chapter 4). Circumstance brought Mr Lim and Mr Suharto together when the former president was a relatively junior army officer in Central Java and Mr Lim had a small business in Semarang. They rose together – Mr Lim made the money and Mr Suharto manoeuvred himself closer and closer to the seat of political power.

Once installed in the Presidential palace, Mr Suharto expanded his circle of Chinese business associates. They were pleased to be connected with the strong man and willingly paid the price for his protection. It remains to be seen how many of them can survive without it.

The relationships of the Chinese businessmen and the political rulers in Asia is not that different from that which characterised the relationship of other wealthy members of vulnerable minority groups with political elites. The Indian business communities in East Africa were in a similar position and, on a larger scale, the European Jewish communities in the pre-Holocaust era often found themselves pushed into the role of being the hapless paymasters of corrupt regimes who exploited their vulnerability and offered only protection in return for cash.

Only in Malaysia and Singapore have the Chinese communities sought to protect themselves by becoming part of the political process and forming political parties designed to protect their interests. In Brunei, Burma, Cambodia, Indonesia, pre-Communist Laos, the Philippines, Thailand and pre-Communist Vietnam the Chinese communities were too small to attempt the political route to protect their interests. In all these countries they were forced to form a patronage-type relationship with the ruling elites.

This built a special form of corruption into Asian societies, one that emboldened the recipients of largesse from the ethnic Chinese to demand rewards from other members of the business community. Had the ethnic Chinese been less important in the business world their unwitting role in fuelling corruption would have been a more peripheral matter.

A little bit of corruption will do no harm

Some individuals and international bodies who turned a blind eye to corruption in Asia simply believed that the problem was not big enough to warrant a lot of fuss. Surprisingly, among those holding this position was Jean-Michel Severino, a World Bank vice-president with responsibility for East Asia. Speaking in the fatal month of September 1997 he said that, although there was evidence of corruption in the region, it was not serious enough to force the Bank to stop lending, as it did in the case of Kenya.

'We are very much aware that the level of corruption in East Asia is high, but the fact is most economies [in the region] are also experiencing high growth rates,' he told a news conference. For this reason, according to Mr Severino, corruption in East Asia was not having a direct impact on economic growth.[7]

A year later the World Bank was telling a very different story. In a report published in 1998 the bank stated:

In the decades of extraordinary growth, corruption coexisted with reasonably effective institutions, from core macroeconomics management bodies to schooling services. Now most observers are concerned that public institutions are largely ineffective and driven more by private gain than public good, especially in Indonesia.[8]

The edifice of lies, cheating and outright robbery was sustained as money was thrown out to cover up the cracks in the surface. While money was pouring in, no one felt inclined to question too closely how it got there. Once the money flow stopped, questions started to be asked but by then it was too late. The fundamentals of good government, good corporate governance and the elementary morality on which good business practices are built were shattered. Rebuilding has been hindered by many of those who still believe that the old days will return and there is no need to make a fuss. Others have retreated into a state of denial and yet others are looking for ways of preserving vested interests that are sustained by corruption.

Corruption and authoritarian government

The correlation between high levels of corruption and authoritarian government is as marked in Asia as elsewhere in the world. Moreover, as in the case of the Philippines, the emergence of democratic government has still left the new order battling with the legacy of corruption institutionalised by the old authoritarian order.

Because of this correlation there has also been a close connection between demands for the removal of authoritarian governments and protests against corruption. In some of Asia's biggest cities demonstrators from all walks of society have taken to the streets to denounce corruption. It is, as we have noted, often forgotten that the rallying cry of China's Tiananmen Square protestors was the demand for less corruption. That same demand was heard when the People's Power movement swept away the Marcos regime in the Philippines in the late 1980s, and again in May 1998 when President Suharto of Indonesia was forced to step down.

Asians reject the apologists

An increasing number of influential Asian personalities are becoming exasperated by the low standards of morality set for their countries by people who should know better. Anand Panyarachun, who served as an interim Prime Minister of Thailand in the early 1990s and is widely regarded as one of the outstanding personalities in his country's political and business world, is a frequent critic of cronyism and corruption masquerading as 'Asian Values'. 'Military figures negotiating business deals, narcotics traffickers serving as parliamentarians, respected business personalities consorting with shady characters, professors offering snake-oil remedies to age old problems, clerics caught under covers – laughable were it not so deplorable,' he said.[9]

Anwar Ibrahim, the former Malaysian deputy Prime Minister, was another leader who spoke a great deal about this matter. In a speech to the Asia-Pacific Roundtable in 1998 he welcomed the 'gale of creative destruction' which 'will cleanse society of collusion, cronyism and nepotism. The result will be a leaner and revitalised market economy, based on fairness and competition on a level playing field, where big corporations, small businesses and all citizens have equal access to capital and resources.'[10]

Fuelling corruption from abroad

Mr Anwar's vision has a long way to go before it is realised. One reason is that corruption in Asia, as in other parts of the world, is fuelled by the connivance of companies and individuals who would not dream of pursuing corrupt practices in their own back yards. In 1996 Meles Zenawi, the Prime Minister of Ethiopia, famously asked the industrialised nations not to encourage corruption in the nonindustrialised world: 'Please do not support bribery by your exporters by giving them tax deductions for bribes,' he pleaded.

In theory most Western companies steer well clear of corrupt practices when they go to Asia. American, British, Canadian and Japanese companies, for example, can be prosecuted back home if they offer bribes abroad.

In February 1999 the Organisation for Economic Co-operation and Development (OECD) promulgated an antibribery treaty. The agreement bans tax write-offs for bribes and other incentives that can be viewed as supporting corruption. All thirty-four OECD member countries hailed this agreement but only twelve nations actually ratified the treaty.

Even so antibribery laws are not taken very seriously by many of the people running Asian subsidiaries of international companies legally bound to eschew corrupt practices. They all know how to get around the law. Usually it means appointing a local agent to pay the bribe, often with another cut-out in place so that knowledge of bribe paying can be denied and the line from recipient to donor is distorted.

It is interesting to speculate what would happen if the ingenuity devoted to bribe paying were devoted to stamping out corruption. To their credit some companies simply take the view that corruption is wrong and that, if the price of doing business means getting involved in corrupt practices, they would prefer not to have the business. I know of one very large German company which operates extensively in Asia and claims never to have paid a bribe anywhere. It concedes that some business has been lost but elsewhere, where it has stood its ground, it has managed to gain greater respect and establish far stronger relations than those that might have been forged by payments into a numbered Swiss bank account.

An acceptable short cut but an unacceptable price

The fact that high levels of corruption did not prevent high levels of economic growth in Asia have led some people to conclude that it really is not much of a problem and in some ways may have provided short cuts to economic development.

Yet for many corruption represents a short cut, which in the view of some people is simply unavoidable. Lowly paid government officials see bribes as part of their remuneration package. Some could not survive without backhander payments; others have got used to a lifestyle that needs constant supplement beyond the modest reaches of government pay.

Moreover, as is evident from the reluctance of OECD member states to ratify the antibribery treaty, there is a great fear of losing business by failing to go along with the bribery game. The United States State Department estimated that American companies lost $30 billion in contracts in the twelve-month period from mid-1997 because they declined to pay bribes. This figure should be treated with some caution because it represents views expressed by American companies about contracts they failed to secure because of not paying bribes. Some may have ascribed corruption as the reason for failure when other factors were at play. Nevertheless, even if the figure is no more than half right, it is hard to ignore a bribery problem of this size.

And what about the costs of these high levels of corruption? There are some fanciful notions that the costs of corruption are minimal because what is described as corruption is merely business by other means. Moreover, it is suggested that corruption is, in effect, a way of making the business cycle more efficient as it cuts away bureaucratic obstruction.

In his study of corruption Robin Theobald argues that it has the effect of dissipating the accumulation of capital because most of the proceeds of corruption are not invested in productive ways but tend to 'be channeled into unproductive and wasteful pursuits.'[11] In Asia we have seen the proceeds of corruption quickly whisked out of the country into Swiss bank accounts. At the time of writing, a decade-long battle was still under way to extricate some of the cash made by the Marcos family from Swiss banks. The money that is not hoarded in overseas bank accounts tends to be spent on imported luxuries such as cars, private aeroplanes and other extravagances which tilt the national balance of payments in an unfavourable direction.

A burden on business activity

Robin Theobald also points out that

rather than encouraging it, corruption stifles entrepreneurial activity in basically two ways: firstly, those with innovative capacities and a risk taking disposition are deflected from a business career into what appears to be the vastly more lucrative opportunities in the public sector . . . Secondly, those actually engaged in commerce and industry must spend a vast amount of time and money simply dealing with a corrupt administration.[12]

As we have seen in Chapter 1, Asia suffered from what has been described as 'runaway bureaucratisation', not least because bureaucracies have expanded precisely to give scope for a greater degree of graft. A United Nations Development Programme (UNDP) and OECD report, published in 1998, collected data from three thousand companies operating in fifty-nine countries which clearly demonstrated that 'in countries with higher incidence of bribery firms tend to spend a higher share of management time with bureaucrats.'[13] The study contains a vivid chart plotting high corruption countries and high levels of management time spent dealing with government officials. There is a direct correlation between the two.

Moreover, these officials are engaged in what can only be described as a flagrant squandering of national resources. If it costs twice as much to build a road, for example, because the graft element adds to the cost, that means that the resources to build another road have disappeared. The additional cost of bribery in infrastructure projects in Indonesia and China, for example, often rose as high as 100 per cent.

In its annual report for 1998 the Asian Development Bank (ADB) stated that rampant corruption adds between 20 to 100 per cent to the costs of procuring goods and services. The report stated that 'corruption exacts a heavy price from developing economies in terms of reducing investment, increasing capital costs, while lowering asset life and hindering the development of a robust and competitive private sector.'[14]

These additional costs are mirrored at the corporate level, according to the UNDP/OECD study cited above, which also looked at fifteen hundred companies in forty-nine countries and found that 'where bribing is more prevalent the costs of capital and investing for firms tend to be higher.'[15] This may seem pretty obvious, but it shows that the burden at the corporate level is probably as great as it is at the state level.

Yet tackling corruption was not a big issue until the Asian crash came. It is interesting to note that it took until 1998 for the ADB to consider the matter of sufficient significance to command a special section of its annual report.

According to the ADB 'losses due to corruption can total more than a country's foreign debt'. Moreover, the bank said, costs of direct corruption are 'dwarfed' by the costs of indirect corruption. 'Scarce resources are squandered on uneconomical projects because of their potential to generate lucrative payoffs, and priority sectors such as education and health suffer disproportionately,' it said.

The bank makes another interesting point that 'legitimate entrepreneurial activity is hindered or suppressed, capital is redirected elsewhere and public safety is endangered by substandard products and construction'. In China this safety problem has become so widespread and notorious that a name has been given to unsafe infrastructure projects that have been developed as a result of the payment of backhanders. They are called 'Tofu Projects', or beancurd projects, because on the outside they are shiny and look OK but inside they are soft and quickly disintegrate.

A corruption 'tax'

Wei Shang-jin, a researcher at Harvard University, has been doing some interesting work on the impact of corruption on foreign investment.[16] He estimates that the difference in costs for foreign investors between doing business in a relatively noncorrupt country, like Singapore, when compared with a corrupt country, like Mexico, is equivalent to raising the tax rate by 21–4 percentage points.

Previous studies have shown that a 1 per cent increase in the marginal tax rate reduces foreign direct investment (FDI) by 5 per cent. Mr Wei cannot fix an exact correlation for how the rising costs of corruption impact on FDI but he concludes that the effect is 'negative and significant'.

He also examines the thesis that East Asia is somehow immune from the deterrent effect of corruption on FDI flows because the region was receiving higher levels of foreign investment than any other part of the world. He points out that the FDI figures are distorted by investment in China, which is larger than anywhere else in the world, but in reality China is an underachiever in attracting investment because some 60 per cent of that investment in fact comes from Hong Kong, some of which is recycled investment from China itself. Hong Kong Chinese are more tolerant of corruption than Western investors. In countries where their presence is not so strongly felt, such as in the rest of East Asia, higher proportions of FDI flows are directed towards countries, like Singapore, where the costs of corruption are low.

In a subsequent study[17] Mr Wei found that corruption tended to discourage foreign investment to a greater extent than high tax regimes. He offers this reason: 'Corruption, unlike tax is not transparent, not preannounced, and carries a much poorer enforcement of an agreement between a briber and a bribee. In other words, corruption embeds arbitrariness and creates uncertainty.' He then proceeded to quantify the effect of uncertainty on investment decisions, concluding that the deterrent effect was equivalent to raising taxes on foreign firms by 32 per cent when comparing a corruption-free society with one where corruption is rampant.

A deterrent of this order is not to be lightly brushed aside. Indeed it explains why FDI flows to East Asia, although high, were not in line with the region's spectacular economic growth.

The main point here is that talk of corruption is not some vague moral issue but a discussion of very real and damaging additions to the costs of doing business. If the corruption malaise were viewed entirely in this perspective, ignoring the moral issues, it would remain a serious matter. However, as we shall see below, the moral issues also impact on how business is conducted.

Those who maintain that corruption is a side issue have seriously missed the plot. It is a key matter and one that will have to be addressed if the Asian Miracle is ever to be revisited.

Tackling corruption – getting results

It can hardly be a coincidence that the two most successful of the eight high-growth economies, namely Hong Kong and Singapore, are the least corrupt. They did not attain this state of affairs easily. Both societies have experienced high levels of corruption and taken the conscious decision to throw resources at combating it.

A Corrupt Practices Investigation Bureau was established in Singapore as early as 1952 and has rapidly expanded. It was part and parcel of the island state's tough policies of zero tolerance for crime and corrupt practices. Not only is policing intensive in Singapore but the administration of justice is swift – too swift, say some. There are no juries in Singaporean courts and no big backlogs of cases waiting to be heard. Sentencing tends to be harsh. There is a downside to the administration of justice, as government opponents quickly discover whenever they are involved in civil or criminal cases. However, as far as the eradication of corruption is concerned, the system works well.

Hong Kong took a little longer to come to grips with the problem but eventually did so with the introduction of fairly draconian antibribery legislation and a sprawling enforcement body known as the Independent Commission Against Corruption (ICAC). Established in 1974, initially to tackle endemic corruption in the police force, it now deals with both private- and public-sector corruption. At the end of 1997 the ICAC employed 884 officers, probably making it the largest anticorruption-dedicated force anywhere in terms of officers per capita of the population.

Any society hoping to eradicate this cancer needs to make an effort of this order. The rather timid anticorruption measures initiated by the Aquino government when it took over from the Marcos regime in the Philippines proved to be ineffective. Indeed the main complaint of the late 1980s was that under President Aquino, who was personally clean, the problem of corruption got worse because it was no longer centralised at the Presidential Palace. The Aquino regime made some pinprick impressions on corrupt practices but stopped short of the drastic measures that would have made a real impact.

An atmosphere of moral laxity

Because corruption was never tackled, and is still not being tackled in many Asian countries, an atmosphere of moral laxity prevailed, which spread into the heart of the business community. Flowing from this came a dangerous disregard for elementary rules of business conduct and a general sense that no rules were needed. Bad business practices proliferated, and continue to proliferate. In some cases this led to the ruin of companies. In other cases it meant that companies were built on precarious foundations and in most cases it led to the creation of businesses that could be sustained only by wholesale flouting of normal business practices. Not all of this is criminal; probably most of these bad practices are within the law, albeit within legal systems that are inadequate to regulate the modern business world.

Nick Leeson, the rogue trader mentioned above, provided some insight into this when he described how his head office in London blithely ignored all the many signs that he was veering way out of control. They did not really want to know how the money was being made. 'I knew', wrote Mr Leeson, 'that people in Barings were more interested in the bottom line than they were in how it had been reached.'[18]

Although Mr Leeson's losses were large they do not compare with the more widespread corruption problems in some Asian companies which, at the end of the day suffered the same fate as Barings.

The Thai morass

The problem with describing this morass lies in knowing where to start. We could, for example, get going in Thailand, where fraudulent loans brought down the Bangkok Bank of Commerce (BBC). Like all Thai banks it had a big following of small savers who supplied cheap money to what turned out to be big borrowers without the means to repay them. At the time of writing the BBC saga has not been sorted out, although it is estimated that the bank was weighed down with debts of some 200 billion baht ($8 billion at conversion rates when the loans were taken out). Of this it is estimated that politicians had outstanding loans of some 75 billion baht. The notorious Indian-Thai financier Rakesh Saxena is believed to have owed 40 billion baht. Mr Saxena and a colleague, Kirkkiat Jalichandra, were officers of the bank, and lent more money to themselves than to any other single borrower. In addition Mr Saxena made illegal donations to the then ruling Chart Thai party run by Banharn Silpa-archa (mentioned above), a politician so immersed in money politics that he was commonly known as 'Khun ATM' or Mister Automated Teller Machine. Chart Thai members were prominent among the bank's unsecured borrowers. The heady mixture of banking, politics, fraud and corruption cost the Thai taxpayer dearly because the central bank had to bail out BBC. There was a time when BBC was considered to be an ordinary mainstream bank. Its political connections were well known but considered unremarkable because everyone was in the market for political patronage.

Mr Banharn, as we have seen, was a singularly unsuccessful Prime Minister but hardly more tainted by money politics than, say, Chatichai Choonhavan, who served as Prime Minister from 1988 to 1991, when the military moved in to take over the government, citing the corruption of the Chatichai administration as justification. This fig leaf of respectability produced some support for the military but provided insufficient cover to gain public endorsement because the military itself was viewed as one of Asia's finest money-making machines. Chavalit Yongchaiyudh, a former army chief who presided over the government at the time of the baht devaluation, provided a good example of the rotten mixture of the military, politics and big business. It is to the credit of the Thai system that after the financial crash he was swiftly removed and replaced by the relatively clean government of Chuan Leekpai, who seems to be personally honest, although, in the bizarre coalition world of Thai politics, he is surrounded by others who would not do well upon close scrutiny of their personal finances. Mr Chuan has a high degree of popular support precisely because he is seen as clean. It is interesting to note that he was not particularly popular in the business community during his first term of office because he was viewed as being indecisive. In the post-crisis period honesty has shot up to the top of the list of priorities and Mr Chuan is being reassessed in this light.

The Indonesian morass

Thai politics may be murky and business ethics could be said to have taken many holidays but Thailand never quite sank to the levels of institutionalised corruption that marked three decades of rule in Indonesia by President Suharto. According to a *Time* magazine investigation, the Suharto clan amassed a fortune estimated at $15 billion during Mr Suharto's thirty-two years in power.[19] To put this figure in some perspective, it is equivalent to over two-thirds of the entire nation's international reserves, including gold, in 1998, the year he was forced out of office. Mr Suharto has denounced this report of his wealth as a 'slander and a lie'. Even if its estimate is not accurate and, say, the figure is half the amount that *Time* reported, that still does not explain how a man earning $1764 per month as president got his hands on even a million dollars.

The Suharto saga is well known, and our interest here is to examine how the institutionalised corruption brought Indonesian business to its knees. It was not only corruption as such that caused the problems but a whole structure of monopolies, anticompetitive practices and privileged access to business opportunities for the Suharto family, which so distorted the economy that when the family were no longer in charge, the house of cards they left behind quickly collapsed.

Before looking at this matter it is worth recalling the extent to which Indonesia was held out as a model of economic development. With a nod and a wink, those doing business in Indonesia told visitors like me that, sure, 'the Family', meaning of course the Suharto family, were a little bit greedy but overall the structure for sound economic development was in place. 'One of the reasons for increasing interest here', said Taizo Watanabe, the Japanese ambassador in Jakarta, 'is a comparatively stable political climate and a much stronger social structure growing.' He made these remarks in 1995.[20] That was the argument of those days – political stability was worth the price of a bit of nepotism, collusion and corruption, the three Ks in Bhasa Indonesia, the language of Indonesia. A less benevolent view of the three Ks was taken by the demonstrators who took to the streets to bring the regime down.

What did all this mean at ground level? In the previous chapter we looked briefly at the Humpuss political hotchpotch conglomerate built up by Mr Suharto's youngest son Tommy. All six Suharto children had mini-empires of their own. None, however, was bigger than that belonging to the second son, Bambang Trihatmodjo.

The Bambang political hotchpotch conglomerate is based around the Bimantara group, which embraced some 150 companies. Whereas Tommy's Humpuss was viewed as foreign-investor-friendly and good at deal making, Bimantara was, unbelievably in the light of what happened, seen as a more serious, better-managed conglomerate.

Bimantara is almost a textbook example of how the three K's worked to sacrifice the nation's economic interests for personal interest.[21] Indonesia's most valuable natural resource is its oil and gas reserves. Bimantara was quickly given the trading rights by the state oil company Pertamina. To put it crudely this was a method of skimming profit off the top as Indonesia's precious natural resources were lifted from the ground. Next came imported plastics and international air-freight monopolies. Under foreign pressure these monopolies were relinquished but not before prices were artificially distorted by the existence of the monopolies, which acted as a leach, in one case, on a building block of basic industries and, in the other, on the portal through which vital imports entered the country.

Bimantara's link with Pertamina quickly extended beyond trading. As the company expanded and needed to build new facilities it soon became evident that no one was going to get a share of the action unless they formed an alliance with one of Bambang's companies. It added to costs, delayed the construction process and involved little or no positive contribution from the Bimantara group.

When Indonesia decided to go hi-tech and get into the satellite business, the two government satellites were transferred to Bimantara-controlled companies. Arriving at the cutting edge of a new industry with tremendous potential, especially in the field of telecommunications, the new owners might have been expected to exploit this potential. Instead of working to develop these assets as a normal company would have done, Satelindo (the Bimantara-controlled company that was given the satellites) did little until it was given more special privileges, such as licences for a mobile-phone business and the right to set up in competition with the state telecommunications company in the lucrative field of international telephone networks. Had the market been thrown open to real competition Indonesia would have stood a chance of following the example of other countries, where the introduction of competition led to the sharp reduction in telecommunications costs and great improvements in service.

Because Bimantara was little more than a creature of political patronage it quickly started unravelling once that patronage was removed. The vast sums of money lent to the company by banks, who had little choice but to advance borrowings to the President's son, were not going to be repaid. The deals that Bimantara promised various investors were not going to materialise; the popular television station owned by the company hardly needed its management expertise to keep going; and so on.

The same applies to the companies run by all the other members of the Suharto family. Yet when the going was good they were the business partners of choice for anyone seriously intent on doing business in Indonesia. Where the President's offspring were not directly involved in big deals, President Suharto's cronies were sure to be found. One of the most prominent of the cronies was Mohammad 'Bob' Hasan, who, incredibly, was appointed to serve in the cabinet of B.J. Habibie, immediately after Mr Suharto's downfall. This appointment did not last long: even the hapless President Habibie had to acknowledge that he was just too tainted. Mr Hasan went rapidly from being a cabinet member to being a suspect in investigations linked to the collapse of his Bank Umum Nasional. Investigations focused on the cheap loans the bank had received from the government, which were funnelled into Mr Hasan's many businesses. Once the investigations began the familiar picture of patronage, casual use of public money and outright dubious dealing quickly emerged.

It would be pleasant to report that the end of the Suharto regime put an end to all these malpractices but this is not the case. One of Mr Habibie's first pledges was to 'stamp out corruption' but it was hard to take seriously.

First, Mr Habibie had been too close to the President and his entourage for too long to want to hurt them. Secondly, the new President was not free from charges of nepotism and corruption. In the same week that he announced the crackdown on corruption he appointed his brother Junus Effendi to run the successful Batam island industrial-development zone. Batam island, close to Singapore, is one of the few places in Indonesia to have emerged from the crisis in relatively good shape. This is Mr Habibie's old fiefdom and a source of cash. Passing it on to his brother was just too much for the increasingly assertive public opinion, which had shown its muscle by forcing Mr Suharto to step down.

The rapid resignation of Mr Junus came as no surprise. However, as he went, another piece of blatant effrontery remained in place. Mr Habibie appointed Hartarto Sastrosunarto, a long-time Suharto crony, to head a new anticorruption task force. Critics suggested that Mr Hartarto could do no better than begin his job by investigating his own family's extensive business affairs. Mr Habibie then established another enquiry into the former president's wealth. It was headed by the former Attorney General Andi Ghalib. According to the pressure group Indonesia Corruption Watch, Mr Ghalib and his wife were recipients of substantial bribes from businessmen who were part of the old Suharto crony network. Some observers believe that Mr Ghalib's singular failure to turn up any information about the Suharto fortune may not be unconnected with the tainted Attorney General's own business affairs. The enquiry ended in late 1999 with a report concluding that there was insufficient evidence to justify any prosecution. The Habibie regime failed to persuade people in Indonesia that it was serious about tackling the endemic corruption problem. Because things in Indonesia are so bad, malpractices in other countries seem pale in comparison.

The Malaysian morass

Generally speaking, much of the malpractice, aside from outright bribery of government officials, centres on the banking sector, which in most countries of the region is heavily controlled by the government or closely tied to the ruling elite.

This is certainly the case in Malaysia and when, in the wake of the crisis, the government in Kuala Lumpur decided to do some spring cleaning it was not surprising that attention focused on the banking system. Perhaps more surprising, to some, was that the most high-profile victim of the government's enthusiasm for a clean-out was Ismail Zakaria, one of Malaysia's best-known bankers, who had been seen as a candidate for the central bank governor's post when it became vacant in 1994.

Mr Ismail can be accurately described as one of the ruling elite's inner-circle members. In 1996 he became the chief executive officer of Sime Bank, an offshoot of the formerly British-controlled Sime Darby group, which rode high during colonial days but was taken over by local interests after its colonial connections ceased to be an advantage (the fate of Sime Darby, incidentally, is a timely reminder of how the colonial regimes employed political favouritism to distort economic development every bit as thoroughly as their successors, and reflects the resulting inherent weakness of the companies developed at this time).

As the crisis swept through Malaysia the once profitable Sime Bank plunged into the red, not least because of dubious loans made during Mr Ismail's stewardship. Nonperforming loans worth some $6 billion were finally taken over by the central bank and Sime Bank was shuttled off into the hands of RHB Bank, where it came under the ownership of Abdul Rashid Hussain, another politically well-connected businessman. Meanwhile, Mr Ismail was pushed to one side and ended up facing a number of charges arising from illegal provision of loans.

Using bank coffers as piggy banks for the politically well connected to buy shares, speculate in property and generally obtain cheap credit secured against questionable assets was a common practice throughout the region. Malaysia signalled its intention to clamp down on these practices but elsewhere they were not exactly illegal.

Indeed much of what went on was not necessarily illegal but reflected the climate of lax moral attitudes concerning business affairs and a general feeling that the rules existed to be ignored and circumvented because they were little more than bothersome obstacles to money making.

Theft without malice

A widely known example of this but one from which few people drew conclusions was the explosion of intellectual-property theft in Asia. American software companies, record companies and film producers from everywhere in the world became increasingly exasperated by the high levels of intellectual-property piracy seen in practically every corner of Asia. Not only was the piracy blatant but the copyright owners had a hard time convincing governments of the need to put an end to it. As for those who bought pirated software programs and the like, they simply saw them as good deals and nothing more.

In Thailand, where anyone could walk down a major thoroughfare in any of the main urban centres and buy copy versions of designer-label fashion goods or compact discs copied in vast numbers, the very first prosecution for selling pirated goods was not made until May 1999, when a trader at Pantip Plaza, one of Bangkok's many pirate-goods centres, was sent to jail for selling pirated computer software.

Hong Kong, which claims to be much more efficient in enforcing intellectual-property laws, frequently announces big raids on pirates, and officials equally frequently announce that they have nipped the problem in the bud. In May 1998, just after the Hong Kong authorities claimed to have won a major battle in the war against pirated software by pulling in the biggest ever seizure of pirated compact discs (CDs) and video compact discs (VCDs), I set out to find how easy it still was to buy pirated CDs and VCDs. I asked some friends to recommend locations where I could see these goods on display. The suggestions came in thick and fast. I ended up visiting a place called Kwun Tong Plaza, located in the heart of the grimy Kwun Tong industrial district, and bordered by sprawling public housing estates. It was awash with pirated software, software that the authorities said they found hard to trace.

Over a year later in the middle of the hype over the launch of the new *Star Wars* film, *Star Wars: Episode 1 – the Phantom Menace*, I went out again in search of pirate copies on VCDs. The word from Hollywood was that all precautions had been taken to ensure that pirate copies would not seep out. The word in the tiny pirate VCD pirate shops was that the film was available for HK$20, almost $3. That was far less than the cost of seeing it in the cinema, besides which it had yet to be released in Hong Kong.

In South Korea a belated recognition of the problem of intellectual-property theft persuaded the government to conduct an audit of its own use of pirated software. According to leaked reports of this study, it turned up very embarrassing conclusions. For example, 99 per cent of the software used by the National Tax Administration office was found to be pirated; 87 per cent of the software in use at the Economy and Finance Ministry came from the same source.[22] As pirated software was so prevalent on government premises it is hardly surprising that there was a deluge everywhere else.

Users of pirated software, even civil servants who should know better, are not hardened criminals. Indeed it is unlikely that they even had criminal intent. Pirated software is bought in vast quantities for no other reason than that it is cheap and the people who buy, assuming they give the matter this much thought, do so in the knowledge that they are buying an illicit product but somehow feel that there is nothing wrong with cheating big software companies.

It seems highly likely that pirated software would also be bought in vast quantities in Western countries were it available. But here's the rub: copyright theft is treated far more seriously in the West, ensuring that it is quite hard to pick up piles of pirated software. In East Asia the reverse is true, even though in recent times governments have been making much more of an effort to tackle the problem.

However, it is arguable that the deluge of pirated software in East Asia is a reflection of a wider malaise that affected the entire business world. It is a malaise seeping into every corner of the business community. In short it reflects a feeling that ends justify the means, even though the means may not be strictly legal or follow laws established to create a level playing field.

There are many examples that illustrate this point but the one that most vividly demonstrates how contempt for the rules brought down one of Asia's most high-profile companies relates to the collapse of the Hong Kong-based Peregrine group in 1997.

The collapse of Peregrine

Peregrine was founded in 1988 with the aim of becoming Asia's first indigenous comprehensive financial-services company. Within a year it looked set to fulfil this objective. John Mulcahy, a journalist turned stockbroker who used to work for Peregrine, has researched his former employer's collapse. He described it as 'an idea whose time has come; the notion that Asia, with all its celebrated entrepreneurial talent, productivity and money sense, was unable to produce its own regional financial-services company was a conundrum requiring a solution.'[23]

The solution came from two men. One was Philip Tose, a stockbroker who arrived in Hong Kong in the early 1970s and shrewdly realised that the real power in the money markets was moving away from the old colonial firms into the hands of the emerging Chinese tycoons. His partner was Francis Leung, an investment banker who became known as the 'Godfather of the Red Chips' because he was responsible for bringing so many Chinese state-owned companies to the Hong Kong market.

Mr Tose was famous for his arrogance and lecturing on the perils of democracy. In 1992 he described the region's most democratic countries, Australia, India and the Philippines, as 'basket cases'. What was needed, he said, was 'strong government, some would call it dictatorship' to produce the necessary economic results.[24]

This kind of talk went down well in those heady days. As for Peregrine itself, it seemed to be riding the crest of a wave. Companies lined up to have Mr Tose and Mr Leung handle their stock-market floatations. It became the market leader in Asian junk bonds and was pioneering business in new areas such as Asian currency notes and securities exchange certificates. By the time the crash came, less than ten years after the company had been established, it had some 2000 staff, branches throughout Asia and a balance sheet of some $1.5 billion, excluding bonds.

The people at the top of Peregrine thought they were invincible. They were beyond silly little rules about capital adequacy ratios; they did not need to go through all the usual rigmarole of credit-risk assessment before handing out massive loans; after all they were Peregrine, the people who really knew Asia.

The downfall was triggered by a $260 million loan to a taxi-operating company in Indonesia named, with wonderful irony, Steady Safe. Irony piled on irony: Steady Safe operated in one of those authoritarian regimes so beloved by Mr Tose. The company's founder, Yopie Widjara, Indonesia's first corporate raider, had managed to form an alliance with Siti Hardiyanti Rukmana, President Suharto's eldest daughter. Thus another prerequisite for creating a big business in Indonesia had been fulfilled. Brandishing lavish expansion plans, Mr Yopie persuaded investors that Steady Safe was a stock going places. Its share price doubled in 1996. But Mr Yopie wanted more and so he turned to Peregrine for a bridging loan that, in theory, should have made a quick and handsome profit for the Hong Kong-based lender and popped another feather in the cap of Andre Lee, the young self-confident Korean head of Peregrine's fixed-income department.

When the Indonesian currency plunged into free fall in July 1997 it should have become clear that there was no hope of this loan being either serviced or repaid. Steady Safe had nothing like the means to make good its borrowings. Nor, so it turned out, did a number of other Indonesian debtors who had been ushered into Peregrine when it was mopping up business with little regard to the usual precautions that banks are supposed to take.

It is not known what exactly was going on at Peregrine but it is clear that there was wholesale neglect of the normal rules of business. Peregine's debt may be as much as $3 billion – the high-priced liquidators were still, at the time of writing, trying to sort through the debris. Many people lost their jobs, many investors lost their money and Peregrine creditors are standing in a long line to get something back.

Astonishingly the Hong Kong government was reluctant to launch an investigation into the Peregrine affair, although eventually it was bullied into embarking on a limited enquiry. Even the Securities and Futures Commission, which does not have a bad record in these matters, washed its hands on the grounds that it was an Indonesian problem. 'The only lesson to be drawn so far', wrote Mr Mulcahy, 'is the fact that size does matter – the bigger the collapse, the less likely there are to be consequences.'[25]

Some people drew a comparison between Andre Lee and the rogue trader Nick Leeson, who opened this chapter. Although they are both young, aggressive and none too fussy about the means as long as the ends turned out all right, there is no suggestion of criminal deceit on Mr Lee's part. Unlike Mr Leeson, sitting out on the periphery of Barings, Mr Lee rose to a very senior position at Peregrine, working hand in hand with Mr Tose. This meant that the trouble at Peregrine came right from the top, not from a distant outpost. Moreover, it is clear that Peregrine deliberately sought to mislead its customers and creditors about its financial affairs because just before the collapse in October 1997, it went so far as to take out large newspaper advertisements denying the rumours of its difficulties.

In many ways this makes the situation at Peregrine worse. Barings was clearly hideously sloppy in allowing Nick Leeson to run out of control in Singapore but Peregrine's bosses were directly complicit in the decisions that led to their own downfall. Unlike the Barings bosses, they knew how deep a hole they were in and then lied about their problems. All the powerful friends Mr Tose and Mr Leung had cultivated over the years quickly slipped away when they sniffed the stench of failure.

They failed because they thought they were above the rules and that success would simply carry on bringing more success. Clearly a business conducted on these lines is likely to be riddled with problems, most of which will come to light as bull markets turn bearish. There does not have to be any degree of outright corruption to fuel the kind of avarice that ruled at Peregrine during the 'good' years but it stemmed from the same kind of attitudes in which corruption thrived.

More and more corruption?

As for corruption itself, there is a lively and no doubt fascinating debate[26] under way about the morality of corruption. There is even an academic journal devoted to the subject called *Corruption and Reform*, but none of this should obscure the bottom-line costs of corruption and the distortions it imposes on the conduct of business.

It may well be that there are Western and Eastern, not to mention African and Latin American, concepts of corruption. However, the corollary sometimes drawn from this suggestion is dubious in the extreme. It is argued that the West is trying to impose its particular version of morality in the corruption debate and that Westerners make far too much fuss about this issue. Those who advocate this point of view have to explain why practically every movement for social and political change in Asia (this may be true for other continents, but is beyond the scope of this study) focuses on the eradication of corruption as a major issue. They do so because it is known that the anticorruption struggle is a popular cause. That is also why practically every coup d'état staged in Asia has been justified by the coup makers on the grounds that they had to make their move to thwart rising corruption. It can even be argued that the fight against corruption is a more popular cause in the East than it is in the West, where people have grown more complacent about corruption-related matters.

In Thailand, where, as we have seen, corruption is sometimes regarded as an immovable force, the government of Chuan Leekpai made it a priority to change this image. 'People thought we could afford it. Now corruption makes them angry,' said Abhisit Vejjajiva, one of Mr Chuan's deputy Prime Ministers.[27]

Laws have been enacted to give greater powers to a revamped anticorruption agency in Thailand. However, as Weng Tochirakarn, the president of the Confederation for Democracy pressure group based in Bangkok, said, 'no red tape organisation is going to root out corruption in this country. It has to be done by people power – that is what politicians and officials really fear.'[28]

7

HALLO – ANYONE AWAKE THERE?

Try doing nothing

Think the unthinkable for just one moment. What would have happened if governments and multinational institutions had done nothing once the Asian financial crisis gathered pace – or for that matter before it began?

For a start there would have been no government decision to devalue the Thai baht, the event that triggered the crisis. There would have been no record-breaking International Monetary Fund (IMF) bail-outs of Indonesia, South Korea and Thailand. Malaysia would not have slapped down exchange controls. The Hong Kong government would not have become the biggest share owner in its domestic market. The World Bank would have shut up shop and provided no emergency funding.

The true believers in laissez-faire economics argue that, if nothing had been done, the markets would have dealt with the problem. They would have allowed the bankrupt to go bust, closed down uncompetitive companies, allowed the financial markets to find their true value and by following the rigorous logic of the market economy equilibrium would have been achieved. As a result greater strength would have emerged from the weaknesses exposed by the crisis.

We shall never know in this, or any other major crisis, whether the laissez-faire theorists are right. Those who dwell in the world of laissez-faire theory have the advantage of rarely seeing their theories put into action, so they cannot be tested against the empirical evidence of their consequences.

The only certainty is that the do-nothing option would have hit the poor hardest. Bankers might have lost bonuses, shareholders might have had to forgo dividends and capital gains but the real pain would have been borne by those far removed from the financial markets who would have slipped below the poverty line. Doing nothing would have meant the denial of even short-term assistance, particularly that which came from the World Bank designed to mitigate some of the worst consequences of the crisis.

The laissez-faire idealists concede that there would have been severe pain in letting the market deal with problems but they maintain that in the longer term the root causes of the pain would be eradicated. I have never heard of a laissez-faire ideologist living on the poverty line, which may account for why the perspective seen from some place well above this level is different from the view from below.

Yet there are sound intellectual arguments for the laissez-faire point of view. The problem is that the short-term consequences would be too severe, certainly too severe to contemplate for any responsible government trying to avoid civil unrest. That is why every crisis produces a post-mortem on how it was handled and every post-mortem starts with the assumption that things needed handling.

The simple fact of the matter is that governments and multinational governmental institutions are incapable of doing nothing. They are not designed to do nothing: they are designed for action, however foolhardy it may prove to be. In many cases, including those that came to light in the wake of the Asian financial crisis, foolhardiness was much in evidence.

Doing something – the historical record

The paradox is this: governments find it hard to do nothing yet in times of crisis, especially economic crisis, they have a poor track record for doing anything well. This sweeping statement is certainly not confined to Asian governments. Take, for example, the Great Depression of the 1930s, which began in 1929 in the United States and spread quickly to Europe. For a decade governments struggled to put an end to the depression, and the debate about the effectiveness of their intervention is endless. However, the facts are that the depression lasted for a full decade and was brought to an end not, as many myth makers would have it, because of President Roosevelt's reflationary and skilfully publicised New Deal policies, but because of a far more dramatic event – the outbreak of World

War Two. No one in their right mind is going to recommend launching a world war as a means of combating economic decline but it was the unintentional by-product of this war that put global economies back on their feet. In the intervening period most government policies aimed at solving the depression were either ineffective or downright counter-productive. President Hoover's confident 1930 prediction that 'prosperity is just around the corner' is among the most famous of the stupid remarks made by senior government officials at the time, reflecting their inability to understand what was happening.

Going both backwards and forwards in history demonstrates a consistent pattern of official incomprehension and limited ability to tackle the great economic crises that have delivered body blows to the world economy. The two-decade-long recession triggered by the property-price bubble that burst in Austria in 1873 proved to be quite resistant to government attempts at economic revival.

Catapulting forward in history to the early 1990s, it seems that Japanese policy makers were as much at sea when confronted with the enormous negative turnaround in their economy as their European and American counterparts had been in previous years. The only big difference in Japan is that its economic woes did not spread like a plague throughout Asia: indeed, as we have seen, Japan's problems were, for a time, actually an advantage to a number of Asian economies.

One big reason why governments, especially democratic governments, are so bad at tackling economic crises is that they find it hard to come to terms with the social consequences of taking action. Remedial action rarely comes without severe social cost. A politician facing re-election does not want to be identified as the initiator of policies that cause people to lose their jobs and suffer a reduced standard of living. It is theoretically easier in authoritarian systems but, as we have seen, the typical trade-off that dictators and dictators *manqué* make, at least in their eyes, is between liberty and economic prosperity. Therefore, in practice the least democratic politicians are often also the politicians most worried about removing the last struts of support for their autocratic regimes, which have been secured by the delivery of the economic goods.

Better than doing nothing?

The evidence of the Asian financial crisis suggests that in many crucial areas of crisis management less action or no action would have been better than the action taken and that, by and large, the best results were achieved by governments and organisations that took action to remove themselves from areas of economic activity where they had once more actively intervened. Moreover in most instances where action was taken it was taken either too soon or too late. Timing is crucial during crises and in the Asian crisis most timing was off beam.

Yet before becoming too sweeping in negative judgements it is worth saying that the evidence of the Asian crisis also suggests that there were some instances and circumstances where government intervention was required and worked to good effect. Not only that but the crisis provoked calls for far higher levels of government intervention, calls rarely heard previously from this region, which prided itself on moving towards a smaller role for government.

The calls were raised not so much because businessmen and others suddenly became believers in big government but because of an enormous backlash against the unfettered free rein given to market forces. Individuals, institutions and governments that had been fully paid-up members of the free-market-works-best school of thought, turned away from these ideas and started looking for ways of restraining the market.

Rethinking globalisation

More than anything else the onset of the Asian crisis brought home the reality of what a global money system really entails. When it did, many people came to realise the extent of the power vested in those at the top of the global money tree. It made those further down the tree feel vulnerable and fearful.

The abrupt reversal of thinking on the subject of globalisation is no better and no more comically illustrated than by looking at the theme for discussion at that great annual business and political talk fest, the World Economic Forum in Davos. In 1996 the great and the good, with the *aspirant* great and good in toe, made their way to Switzerland to discuss 'sustaining globalisation'; a year later they were back with a new topic: 'managing volatility'. Globalisation had been firmly removed from the menu and the new *plats du jour* were given names like 'controlling capital flows', 'limiting capital transfers' and so forth.

Now that the benefits of globalisation are being questioned so are the principles of financial liberalisation that made globalisation possible. The revisionist school of thought has started to question whether the West's big push for financial liberalisation and open markets, aided and abetted by the IMF, was not in itself one of the prime causes of the financial crisis. Forcing open markets in countries with infrastructures that were inadequate to bear the strain of coping with the consequences was, even leading American government figures now admit, a contributory factor in causing these structures to crumble.

Mickey Kantor, who as the US trade representative, was among those most forcibly engaged in pushing open doors in emerging markets, later admitted, 'It would be a legitimate criticism to say that we should have been more nuanced, more frightened that this [the crisis] could happen. But alas, that was not the case.' He also believes that the risks of financial liberalisation in places lacking modern banking and financial systems is akin to 'building a skyscraper with no foundations'.[1]

Why did the Americans push so hard when it was clear that the foundations were none too firm? Jeffrey E. Garten, a former US Commerce Department official who became an academic, provides an answer. He said that Asian markets were seen as a potential gold mine for the US financial-services industry. However, it required government help to make this happen. President Clinton's administration endorsed an emerging-markets plan designed, according to a *New York Times* report, to 'identify rising economic powers and push relentlessly for business for American companies in these countries'.[2] According to this report Ron Brown, the late Commerce Secretary, established a 'war room' in his department where 'computers tracked big contracts and everyone from the CIA to the ambassadors to the President himself was called upon to help land deals'.

Those who warned that the government was pushing too hard were pushed aside in the scramble for new business. In other words the US government was holding high the banner of free markets, primarily to develop markets for its own companies.

None of this would come as a surprise to left-wing thinkers who have always been sceptical of the validity of free-market ideas. Karl Marx long ago warned of the power that international capital would exercise over sovereign nations. He should be having more than a chuckle from his grave in Highgate Cemetery. In a typically vigorous letter to the Russian economist Nikolai Franzevich Danielson, written in 1879, Karl Marx spoke of how the formation of 'joint-stock' companies and banks 'gave, in one word, "impetus", an impetus never before suspected to the new concentration of capital, and also to the accelerated and immensely enlarged cosmopolitan activity of loanable capital, thus embracing the whole world in a network of financial swindling and mutual indebtedness, the capitalist form of "international" brotherhood.'[3]

Seeing the founder of Marxism talking in these terms hardly raises an eyebrow but it is quite another matter to hear words like these coming out of the mouths of fervent anti-Marxists. Mahathir Mohamad, the Malaysian Prime Minister, for example, spoke about the 'rape' of his stock market. It was also Dr Mahathir who talked about the 'unnecessary, unproductive and immoral' business of currency trading and the fact that Malaysians were 'very sacred about foreign capital' and the need for 'society to be protected from unscrupulous profiteers'.[4]

Even his nemesis, the financier George Soros, the fund operator who Dr Mahathir claimed had helped 'rape' his stock market, expressed disquiet over the laissez-faire idea of leaving markets to their own devices, 'I consider it a dangerous idea,' he said. 'The instability of financial markets can cause serious economic and social dislocations.'[5]

In October 1998 Sir Donald Tsang, Hong Kong's financial secretary, describing himself as 'finance minister of one of the world's most free and open economies', gave a speech in the United States outlining the limitations of the free-market economy. 'Free markets need not only sound macroeconomic policies,' he said, 'but also an understanding of how the microstructure of markets work.'[6] Sir Donald is a master of the contradictory statement. He claims to be among the leading advocates of free markets and believes that this is perfectly compatible with control over these markets and the imposition of international rules to monitor 'free' flows between markets.

To be fair, Sir Donald was not alone: the aftermath of the Asian crisis left everyone scratching their heads trying to make sense of what happened. Those who claimed affinity to the God of the Free Market were reluctant to say that they had lost faith so they simply moved the goal posts and said that free did not quite mean free but something close to free. Those who had always advocated market controls were busy saying that they had been vindicated but were having difficulty identifying which controls had actually worked. Only a country that operated genuinely closed and totally controlled markets could claim to have been unaffected by the

Asian storm. Thus the government of North Korea still presided over Asia's poorest and most inadequate economic system, a system completely untouched by the financial turmoil in the region.

Predicting the crisis: business cycles

Now the storm has passed, there is a temptation to examine it with perfect 20/20 vision. Some have such perfect retrospective vision that they can now claim to have predicted the crisis, others have said, with some justification, that it is the nature of markets to be cyclical and so no one should be surprised to find Asian markets moving from a boom-to-bust part of the cycle.

The modern history of big international capital movements suggests that the biggest surges have been caused when the business cycles of the United States and Europe are out of sync. In other words capital got moving when the United States moved from recession to recovery ahead of Europe.[7] As we have seen, until comparatively recently, Asia was too small a part of the world economy to be part of this cycle, but now that it has gained in significance it appears to have had its crisis in a manner that was exacerbated by big capital movements.

However, they did not follow the traditional pattern of recent history inasmuch as Asia's financial crisis was not triggered because of disparities in growth rates between the United States and Asia or between the Asian countries and those in Europe. Well, not quite, because when the crisis hit in 1997 the high-growth Asian economies were indeed slowing down in terms of growth and American economic growth was picking up. Nevertheless, American growth levels lagged way behind those in Asia and, as far as portfolio investment was concerned, the big shift to the United States came only after the bubble burst in July 1997.

It therefore seems questionable to suggest that history, except in the most general sense, might have been useful in pointing to the emergence of the Asian crisis. So there is little use in pointing accusing fingers at those lacking in predictive ability. It was quite one thing to suggest – as, to be fair, both the IMF and World Bank suggested – that there were fundamental problems with macroeconomic policy in Asia and that markets were becoming overheated, but quite another to predict when the consequences of this overheating would be realised.

The joint Asian governmental response

Much attention has been focused on how the so-called Washington Axis of the US government, the World Bank and the IMF responded to the crisis but relatively little has been said about the abysmal record of Asia's own multilateral governmental organisations. That may well be because the three main governmental Asian and Asia-Pacific-based economic multinational bodies were almost entirely overlooked as the crisis gathered pace.

The Asian Development Bank, which may have been expected to play a leading role in co-ordinating a regional response, did nothing of the kind, although it did increase its crisis-related lending from $5.54 billion in 1996 to $9.41 billion in 1998. As we have seen it also took a high-profile stand on the matter of corruption during its annual meeting in Manila in April 1999. However, it remains to be seen what impact this will have.

As for the Association of South East Asian Nations (ASEAN), originally conceived as a bulwark against the advance of Communism in Southeast Asia but more recently self-consciously seeing itself as a body dedicated to economic progress, its response was unbelievably unimpressive. When the ASEAN leaders gathered for their annual meeting in Kuala Lumpur in December 1997, the best they could do was to agree to act as supplicants and argue that the international community, i.e. the West and Japan, had not offered enough aid to their countries. 'Greater national, regional and international efforts by the major economies such as the European Union, Japan and the United States and international financial institutions' were required, said the leaders.[8]

Had the summit host, Mahathir Mohamad, had his way there would have been more said about how the West was to blame for all their troubles but the other leaders realised that there was a bit of a problem with demanding increased assistance from nations while saying how awful they were.

By March 1999, almost two years after the crisis erupted, the ASEAN finance ministers gathered in Hanoi and went beyond merely asking for more aid. They demanded that international credit-rating agencies should display 'more transparency' in their operations, suggesting, by implication, that they had been responsible for capital flight – although, as we have seen, their revised ratings tended to lag behind events rather than trigger them. ASEAN also solemnly called for better monitoring of short-term capital flows, an idea much discussed at the time. Thirdly, they were keen to find ways of regulating the activities of the big market players. It was clear that they were talking here about Western fund managers, not the local big players who were every bit as responsible for capital flight as those from overseas.

So, even well after the dust had settled, it would be hard to argue that ASEAN was bringing much to the table, although it just about got down to thinking about the problems in terms other than those of a supplicant.

As for the Asian-Pacific Economic Co-operation forum (Apec), at the best of times it is little more than an unwieldy talk shop which arranges meetings where national leaders are required to wear funny shirts and pose for large family snapshots. Generally Apec has little of interest to say. During the crisis it moved even further away from the centre of gravity, providing a little sideshow as the Malaysians and Americans snipped at each other while everyone else kept their head down and agreed that a recovery would be a good thing.

Coping with the crisis: the Washington remedies

Little therefore came from joint Asian efforts to combat the crisis. All eyes were on Washington, where officials, in the early stages of the crisis, were looking at what was happening through a cracked glass. It now seems to be generally accepted that the Americans and the International Monetary Fund initially thought they were looking at a rerun of the 1995 peso crisis in Mexico, essentially a crisis caused by massive government deficits. The IMF responded in kneejerk fashion with plans for cuts in public spending, the imposition of high interest rates and various proposals for keeping banks from going under.

I must say that even without the benefit of hindsight this looked rather off the mark at the time because everyone outside Washington seemed to have noticed that the problems were lodged in the corporate, not the state, sector.

The Japanese, who are more often than not painted as the villains of the peace in the Asian crisis, were taking a more sensible view than the IMF but taking it too slowly. Not only were they wary of the IMF austerity programme but they were prepared to put their money behind an Asian rescue.

As the world's financial leaders were gathering in Hong Kong for the annual IMF/World Bank conference in October 1997, the Japanese were proposing an ambitious plan for an Asian Monetary Fund, with resources of $100 billion, half of which would have come from Japan. It was not unrealistic to expect that the other $50 billion could have been raised from places like Hong Kong, Singapore and, indeed, Malaysia. This large sum of money would have been quickly sent into action to help prop up falling currencies and provide governments with a breathing space that should have stemmed the outflow of funds. Most importantly it would have signalled that the US dollar was not the only safe haven for the worried investor.

Why did the Japanese plan never get off the ground? Why did the Americans not want to save themselves a great deal of money? Why did the other Asian nations, which professed themselves to be supportive of a regional response to a regional problem, so meekly back away from the Japanese plan? The answer in two words is: superpower politics.

The Americans, highly conscious of their role as the world's only remaining superpower, were not at all pleased to find Washington being ignored when it came to a matter of this importance. Not only that but the Clinton administration in Washington simply did not understand the urgency of the problem. It believed that a quick fix in Thailand would be enough to get things back on an even keel and that after a bit of tweaking from the IMF, under American guidance, everything would settle down.

The Americans made it clear to their friends in Asia that they were to have nothing to do with the Japanese plan unless they thought they would be better served by tying themselves to the shaky Japanese economy instead of the robust engine of growth chugging away in the United States. Japan was duly left on its own and decided not to fight its corner.

Thus, from the outset of the crisis, the means of putting things right got off to a very bad start. Even at this stage it is still possible to argue that if nothing had been done, particularly by the IMF, the contagion effect might have been less and, although Thailand would have undoubtedly suffered, there is no reason to believe that it would have suffered more than it did.

The Thais, who had more or less emptied the foreign-exchange reserves of the central bank in a futile attempt to prop up the fast devaluing baht, felt they had little choice but to go along with the IMF, because a failure to do so meant that no cash would have come their way. The alternative was to try to persuade the Japanese government to come to the rescue. The bureaucrats in Tokyo took their time responding and as the Thais were desperate they signed on with the IMF.

The fund's austerity programme was pushed into action and quickly exacerbated an already bad situation, causing investors to flee in greater numbers from the Thai market. It also spread panic into the markets of neighbouring countries.

Coping with the crisis: the World Bank record

The World Bank has as its main remit the task of encouraging economic development through judicious lending. It's current buzz words are 'sustainable development', which clearly does not mean that it is supposed to have a role as a firefighter, called out in emergencies. However, it felt that in East Asia, as in other regions, it could hardly stand by while the fire was blazing. In the wake of the crisis it pledged $18 billion to the countries affected, most of it targeted at programmes aimed at keeping crisis victims off the breadline.

The problems it encountered understanding the crisis were largely similar to those of the International Monetary Fund (IMF), stemming, as we shall see below, from the nature of the bureaucracies that run these organisations. In 1998 Joseph Stiglitz, the Bank's chief economist, gave some tacit recognition to this institutional dilemma. He told an UNCTAD conference in Geneva that 'we are now recognising that there are systematic problems not limited to individual countries. We realise that for every borrower there is a lender, and that the lender is as much to blame as the borrower.'[9]

However, when it came to fixing the problem, it seemed that both the IMF and World Bank were paying undue attention to solving the problems of the lenders, mainly large international banks, rather than those of the borrowers.

Moreover, according to a leaked (and not denied) version of an internal World Bank evaluation of its lending policies in Indonesia, the Bank came to realise that its lending policies in the pre-crisis period helped lay the seeds for what followed.[10] The report says that its officers ignored the endemic corruption, growing repression and disintegration of the financial system in the final years of President Suharto's rule because of the 'halo effect' of the Bank's relations with the former

197

President, who was credited with leading a successful battle against poverty in his country.

Open confrontation with the President did not emerge until 1998, the year he resigned, when Bank officials finally acknowledged that he was more interested in saving the skin of himself and his associates rather than saving his nation from economic collapse. Before that the World Bank had poured $24 billion into Indonesia over three decades, some of which contributed to the malaise that ultimately brought the economy to its knees. However, it was also estimated that about 20 per cent of this amount was syphoned off by officials. The report suggests that, if the Bank had pushed harder for reforms and had not been so much in awe of President Suharto, it might have helped tackle some of the institutional faults that led to the crisis.

On the other hand the Bank is faced with the problem that it could trigger investor flight were it to engage publicly in confrontation with its 'clients', i.e. the governments pursuing policies that give rise to concern.

At the beginning of 1998 the World Bank established a special internal audit committee to examine problems of corruption in its lending policies. This looked very much like an attempt to shut the stable door after the horses had bolted but, as is often the case in large bureaucracies, remedial action is taken only when a considerable shock is delivered to the system.

Coping with the crisis: the IMF record

The IMF is still reeling under the shock of the barrage of criticism it received over its handling of the Asian crisis, not least from Milton Friedman, the godfather of monetarist economic theory, who cited the very existence of the IMF as a prime cause of the crisis. He argued that the fund should have been closed down in 1973 when the system of fixed exchange rates ceased to operate. As it continued in being it was there to bail out countries that encountered severe financial difficulties. Thus it was there for the Mexicans during the 1995 peso crisis, and according to Dr Friedman, by bailing out the Mexicans, the fund 'encouraged individuals and financial institutions to make loans to and invest in East Asian countries drawn by high domestic interest rates and returns to investment and reassured about currency risk by the belief that the IMF would bail them out'.[11] He went further and argued that

the IMF has been a destabilising factor in East Asia, not so much because of the conditions it imposed on clients (in the post-crisis period), whether good or bad, as by sheltering private financial institutions from the consequences of unwise investments. It is not too much to say that had there been no IMF, there would have been no East Asia crisis, though countries might have had internal crises as with Japan, whose troubles cannot be blamed on the IMF.[12]

Dr Friedman, who is a leader of the laissez-faire school, goes further than most other observers, particularly in accusing the fund of laying the ground for the crisis. Most other critics focus on how it behaved after the crisis broke and how its response exacerbated the problems. As we have seen in the Introduction to this book, Henry Kissinger, the former US Secretary of State, was quick off the mark in pointing an accusing finger at the Fund, describing it as

'like a doctor who has one pill for every conceivable illness, its nearly inevitable remedies, mandate austerity, high interest rates to prevent capital outflows and major devaluations to discourage imports and encourage exports. The inevitable result is a dramatic drop in the standard of living. Exploding unemployment and growing hardship weakening the political institutions necessary to carry out the IMF programme.'[13]

Among those who expressed similar views was Eisuke Sakakibara, one of Japan's most influential financial policy makers, who served as deputy to the powerful Kiichi Miyazawa, when he was Finance Minister. He accused the IMF of being obsessed with 'free market and sound money' pre-occupations, which led to the 'blind application of the universal model on emerging economies'. Mr Sakakibara freely admitted that he was among those who had devised these policies 'but unlike the [IMF's] managing director Michel Camdessus I can only say that if I am confronted with similar situations I will probably handle them differently.'[14]

There is now a widespread feeling that, as an institution, the IMF is not equipped, nor does it have the right attitude, to tackle crises such as those that emerged in Asia.

Much of the blame is heaped on the ample shoulders of the IMF's boss, the French government banker Michel Camdessus, who is not the most gifted of communicators and often reinforces the IMF's image as an imperialist ogre. There is a picture of Mr Camdessus which sticks in many people's minds. It was taken at the end of 1997 when Indonesia was forced to accept the Fund's conditions for its $23 billion bail-out package. The Indonesians had done little to disguise their view that the terms were onerous and so when President Suharto came to the public signing ceremony for the agreement he did not look a happy man. However, he must have felt a lot unhappier when he later saw the pictures of himself bent over appending his name to the document while Mr Camdessus towered over him, with his arms crossed and a smile of smug satisfaction on his face. No doubt Mr Camdessus had not set out to offend, and quite possibly he had been caught at an unfortunate moment, but this was a picture that really did seem to say more than a thousand words. Here was the bully and here was the supplicant. Could anything have been more humiliating?

No wonder the IMF prefers to do most of its work out of the limelight. From its Washington headquarters, where a small army of economists and varied number crunchers sit huddled over computers, the IMF is supposed to be keeping what can only be described as a predictive eye on global money movements and economic developments. Unlike other analysts, the IMF officials are supposed to move from observation to participation. So, on the one hand the Fund performs a role not dissimilar to that of a management consultant, while on the other it exercises the leverage of a powerful bank manager over a tardy borrower. The combination is far from ideal.

The problem is, as many IMF officials will concede when they are confident that no one will quote them, that reality as seen from the IMF headquarters is a series of spreadsheets, econometric models and other numerical equations which in all likelihood bear only a tenuous relationship to the reality on the ground. The people poring over this data have impressive academic qualifications, mainly in economics. Very few are drawn from other disciplines or other fields where they would have developed a better understanding of the politics of the nations they are studying. The IMF has become such an insular bureaucracy that it is actually resistant to receiving the kind of on-the-spot intelligence that would make officials better informed. Therefore there is an institutionalised problem of dealing with crises, simply because those responsible for responding have no feel for the matter to hand.

Nor, in the wider sense of the word, is the IMF constituted in a manner designed for the problems of today. For a start it is clear that the IMF cannot fulfil its original mandates, which were to supervise the 1944 Bretton Woods agreement on fixed but adjustable exchange rates and to be the lender of last resort. This is fine in theory but in practice the demands on the IMF have grown and it cannot possibly gather enough cash to cover every crisis.

In 1994 the IMF and World Bank organised a conference in Spain to consider the future of these organisations as they passed the fiftieth-anniversary mark. Reading the proceedings of the conference[15] is much like reading the proceedings of any other high-level international talk fest in terms of hot air, highfalutin rhetoric and the like, but this event was characterised by a special poignancy because the participants seemed to be going out of their way to say what a good thing these institutions were and how much they were needed while at the same time forlornly agreeing that they needed to be changed.

Not for the first time it was Paul Volker, the former chairman of the United States Federal Reserve System, who put his finger on a central problem: 'It seems to me', he said, 'that there are inherent difficulties in a public bureaucracy lending to private enterprise. If that is where the action is – and the action clearly is there, much more than in the earlier postwar period.'

More prophetically he added,

in this world of private markets and many more international capital flows, the idea of managing floating exchange rates is more difficult; to some, managing exchange rates today is almost an oxymoron. We are told time and again that the volume of capital flows makes all the old possibilities in that respect nonfunctional.[16]

If nothing else was learned from the Asian crisis, this lesson certainly was. Maybe the challenge was just too great. Maybe the volume of capital flows has reached levels beyond the control of individual governments or transnational institutions.

Moreover, the international community has to resolve the inherent contradiction of how to preserve the freedom of global capital markets – which is generally regarded as a good thing – while keeping them under control. At what point does a free market turn from stimulating economic growth into becoming a speculative leach draining away the lifeblood of economies? There is no simple answer to this question.

Nor is there a simple answer to the question of how much control should be exerted over 'free markets'. We shall examine this further in the coming chapter; meanwhile, we have the evidence of how the IMF responded when it was clear that capital flight had taken hold first in Thailand and then in Indonesia. In both instances it seems that the IMF added to the problem. Even IMF officials concede that this is so.

Testing the IMF prescriptions

In Indonesia, according to a leaked internal report, the fund realised that it had spurred a panic by forcing the closure of sixteen insolvent banks as part of the price for its bail-out. IMF economists thought that they would restore confidence in the banking sector by eliminating 'bad apples' but instead they touched off a panic.

The fund also conceded that it had greatly underestimated its ability to deal with the authoritarian President Suharto, who blithely ignored agreements that it assumed were set in concrete once the terms for the IMF bailout were agreed. However, as the report noted, these agreements on 'economic reform seemed to disappear from the government's agenda' within days of the accord being signed.[17]

In January 1999 the IMF finally released a public document containing its internal evaluation of how the fund had handled the crisis. By and large it saw no reason to question its actions in Indonesia, Korea and Thailand, which collectively received $120 billion for bail-outs. Being true believers, the authors of the report defended the Fund's insistence on bringing in high interest rates and insisting on balanced budgets as a means of getting the economies back on their feet. 'Monetary policy, albeit only after some period, achieved its basic objective of avoiding a depreciation/inflation spiral in both Korea and Thailand,' argued the report.[18]

It went on to say, 'This is not to deny, of course, that monetary tightening had a cost for the economy but the alternative would have been more costly.' The authors conceded that the fund had got its economic-growth estimates wrong and, as a consequence, had insisted on higher-than-necessary spending cuts. There is also an admission that its insistence on the closure of insolvent banks and financial institutions exacerbated the market response to the crisis.

This cautious appraisal falls far short of views of critics, such as Jeffrey

Sachs of Harvard University, who consistently argued that the demise of the banking sector was caused by the IMF and that this in turn deepened the financial crisis.

Although IMF and World Bank bashing is reasonably good fun – and not without justification – it seems to overlook the basic point that the underlying problems that caused the crisis were not created by international bodies but by the countries themselves. Hubert Neiss, the director of the IMF's Asia and Pacific department, made the perfectly reasonable point that 'the three countries which have suffered most – Thailand, Indonesia and South Korea – each got into deep trouble on their own before they were prepared to follow the recommendations of the IMF . . . By the time the Fund was called in to help each country all the low cost options had been foreclosed.'[19] Even more tellingly, as will be seen below, some of the most severe repercussions of the crisis occurred in Hong Kong, where there was no IMF intervention of any kind.

Indonesia's response

In the case of Indonesia not only were low-cost options foreclosed but the floundering government of President Suharto seemed to go out of its way to make things worse. Having agreed to the IMF's conditions in October 1997, the government blithely ignored most of the undertakings it gave when publishing what many observers regarded as an 'Alice in Wonderland' budget in January of the following year. When President Suharto read out the budget a group of bankers were watching it on television in Jakarta. One of them later told me, 'It was just amazing: here was this enormous crisis and he was telling the nation that a bit of tinkering here and a bit of adjustment would put things right. We sat and watched him and just could not believe what we were hearing.' The IMF's demand for a budget surplus was ignored and President Suharto made it clear that he had no stomach for some of the austerity measures that had been part of the deal.

Moreover, he started toying with plans for a currency board, a mechanism that would have pegged the Indonesian currency to the US dollar at a fixed rate in a vain attempt to prop up the constantly sliding rupiah. This voodoo scheme for fixing the currency problem was the brainchild of the American academic Steve Hanke, who for a while looked as though he would be virtually running the Indonesian economy. The days before the collapse of the Suharto regime were indeed very strange.

In some ways they became even more strange when President Suharto was deposed in May 1998 and B. J. Habibie was installed to replace him. President Habibie's great contribution to international economic thought was the idea of 'zigzag' economics, which pivots economic recovery on lowering interest rates to combat rising inflation. Although the squeaky-voiced president talked a great deal about this he spared his country the embarrassment of actually trying to put the theory into practice. To be fair, he was attempting to think creatively about solutions to the over-whelming problems facing Indonesia.

In this he was unlike his predecessor, whose primary concern was, as we have seen, to protect the interests of those nearest and dearest to himself.

The net result of President Suharto's last days in office was to alienate the international community, send international investors scurrying away from Indonesia, persuade domestic investors to get out of the local market and, eventually, encourage his people to rise up in revolt. The IMF's folly was to increase the panic, make unrealistic demands and not recognise that they were dealing with someone whose sell-by date had long passed.

Yet the IMF did not create the fatal conditions for the collapse: they were laid by years of domestic economic mismanagement and all those aspects of policy that are now conveniently grouped under the heading 'moral hazard'. What is most astonishing in retrospect was that anyone seriously believed that Indonesia could indefinitely carry on as before and, equally absurd, that President Suharto would suddenly don the mantle of economic reform and start undermining the business interests of the so called 'First Family'. Those who questioned the President's commitment to reform in the pre-crash days were given little air time.

The Thai response

In Thailand, the first country to be 'rescued' once the crisis broke, the IMF was dealing with a very different set of political circumstances. A $17.2 billion rescue package was rushed over to Bangkok by the IMF in August 1997. The bewildered government, led by Chavalit Yong-chaiyudh, went along with the IMF's austerity demands. However, by

October the Chavalit administration was facing mounting political pressure and the austerity programme had to be relaxed. Nonetheless fifty-eight bankrupt finance companies were forced to close their doors, quite a remarkable achievement in a country that, at the time, had no bankruptcy laws.

By November the largely useless Chavalit government was pushed out of the door and a new administration, led by Chuan Leekpai, was installed in office. Mr Chuan and his investor-friendly, cigar-chomping Finance Minister Tarrin Nimmanahaeminda were seen as the perfect pupils for the IMF's tutelage. All was sweetness and light after they had taken over the reins of office and started negotiations with IMF officials. The fact that the IMF's recipe had not worked in the previous months was put down to the nature of the previous regime.

New measures were introduced, including one that was particularly hard to swallow in fiercely nationalistic Thailand. It allowed foreigners to take a 100 per cent stake in most companies outside the finance sector. Officials from the IMF were then sent along to vet the budget, another blow for Thai self-esteem.

Yet none of the IMF's measures showed any particular sign of being effective, aside from the provision of cash to a severely depleted central bank. There was much talk in Thailand about 'IMF imperialism'. Inevitably this lack of success and the severe social consequences of the austerity policies provoked political infighting, both inside and outside the coalition government. Mr Chuan was jokingly referred to by critics as the captain of the 'Thai-tanic'. Regular demonstrations were held outside his office where protestors held up banners mocking the slogan devised by the Thai tourism authority to encourage visitors to Thailand: 'Amazing Thailand', was the slogan; 'Amazingly Poor' was the reality. The result of the political pressure and protests was some watering down of the IMF's medicine.

Economic growth remained stubbornly in reverse but the outflow of foreign funds was capped, the currency stabilised, foreign exchange reserves were rebuilt, the balance of payments improved and inflation was brought under control. It is hard to say whether this was a product of the IMF's policies or a response to the confidence inspired by the Chuan government, combined with the work of Thai companies and overseas companies in Thailand successfully exploiting the advantages of a more competitive cost base.

However, what is becoming increasingly clear in retrospect is that if the IMF has ended up putting things right it also needed to spend quite a lot of time repairing the damage it inflicted at the early stages of the rescue programme where IMF actions encouraged capital flight and fuelled the economic downturn.

The Malaysian response

Malaysia, on the other hand, took an early decision to avert the prospect of coming under the IMF's tutelage and avoided having to go cap in hand for a bailout. Yet, while Anwar Ibrahim was still Finance Minister, the initial response to the crisis was very much on the lines of the IMF blueprint. Interest rates were raised, government spending was cut and monetary policy considerably tightened.

Money continued to flow out of the country. Prime Minister Mahathir Mohamad grew increasingly frustrated and sacked Mr Anwar, brought back his old friend Daim Zainuddin to mastermind economic policy and turned the IMF formulas on their head. Then he went one big step further, formulating a bold, isolationist policy aimed at cutting Malaysia off from the Asian crisis by removing the nation from the international markets in which capital flows were flooding out of the region.

In September 1998, while other Asian countries were looking at ways of attracting international investors back into the markets, Malaysia abruptly announced that it was slamming the door on them. It imposed severe capital controls, preventing money both leaving and coming into the country. Foreign investors holding Malaysian equities were trapped; Malaysian businesses wanting to invest overseas or indeed transfer funds for buying goods were subject to formidable restrictions. The local currency, the ringgit, was pegged to a fixed exchange rate.

Criticism of the isolationist policy flowed thick and fast. Among the most vitriolic critics was David Roche, the Irish founder and chief strategist of Independent Strategy, a company that, as the name suggests, provides strategic investment advice. 'The Malaysian government is turning a financial crisis into an IQ crisis,' he wrote. 'Imposing capital controls on one of the smallest and most open economies in the world is purblind stupidity. It will bring the Malaysian economy to its knees.'[20]

Fund managers and other finance officers said, with some conviction, that if Malaysia did not want them then they had no wish to be in a country where they were shunned. Let the Malaysians see just how well they would cope by relying on domestically generated capital – or so went the spoken and unspoken challenge made by the foreign investors.

Within months, however, Malaysian officials were declaring victory. They pointed to success in capping off the decline in economic activity, share prices rallied, the foreign reserves were rebuilt, a record trade surplus was achieved.

The isolationist policy, announced with such venom that it scared foreign investors, turned out to be not quite so isolationist as it at first appeared to be. By February 1999 the highly controversial twelve-month freeze on foreign repatriation of sales of Malaysian equities was removed and exit taxes were imposed as a replacement. Dr Mahathir went out of his way to distinguish between longer-term foreign investors, building businesses in his country, and short-term market players. The former were still welcome, he insisted.

A key to his strategy was to provide economic stimulus by lowering interest rates. Had the Malaysian foreign exchange market remained open this might have triggered a flight out of the ringgit but, as the market was closed, interest rates could fall without concern about the impact on the exchange rate. The result was, as planned, that credit was easier to come by and the debt burden on borrowers was reduced.

The old maxim about nothing ever being as bad as it seems appeared to have been realised. Yet, for all the government posturing and the predictable excitability of stockbrokers' analysts – who were as extreme in their condemnation of the government's policies as they were euphoric over their 'success' once the markets started to rise again – it remains less than clear whether the Malaysian recipe was any better than that of the IMF.

The simple fact of the matter is that shutting the doors has done nothing to solve the severe problem of nonperforming loans or heavy indebtedness. In early 1999 it was estimated that Malaysian debts were equivalent to 150–70 per cent of GDP and that 20 per cent of loans were nonperforming.[21]

The large conglomerates, particularly the political hotchpotch conglomerates, have not had to suffer the radical surgery they really require to make them viable businesses and the bad aroma of cronyism still lurks around these companies which occupy a notably large role in the Malaysian economy.

Moreover, some of the 'successes' of the policy look distinctly suspect. For example, it is easy to improve the balance of payments by slashing imports, a consequence of the currency controls, but far harder to do so by increasing exports. Secondly, Malaysian equity markets, made considerably smaller by the diminution of foreign players, are far more volatile because volumes are so much lower. Thus market rises and falls are exaggerated and mean very little. In general the Malaysian 'recovery' has moved more or less in line with that of countries following the IMF recipe, which suggests either that neither of these approaches has made much difference to underlying regional trends or that both work with equal benefit.

However, the big questions remain outstanding. How is Malaysia to recover its previous growth levels, which had been fuelled by foreign investment? If money is to be made, will foreign investors come back, even if they remain unhappy over the new control regime? In global markets where choices are vast and where similar opportunities are quickly judged on grounds of convenience, the likelihood is that Malaysia will lose out because no one can be sure what new penalties might be imposed on foreign investors.

Over and above all this there is considerable political uncertainty overhanging a former high-growth economy still run by an old-style autocrat who is becoming even more autocratic in his ways and less tolerant of criticism. The only other high-growth economy still run in this way is in tiny, easy-to-control Singapore, but, as we shall see, its government is more inclined to open up its system rather than close it down.

The Hong Kong response

It could also be argued that the Hong Kong Special Administrative Region (SAR), since 1997 under the sovereignty of the world's largest Communist regime, is also run by an old-style autocracy and brings to three the number of previously high-growth Asian economies remaining under autocratic government. However, the circumstances of Hong Kong are complex to a point that makes it too glib to simply describe the SAR as an autocratic regime. Even after China resumed sovereignty Hong Kong remained a society with a high degree of personal liberty and freedom, which was certainly far greater than that enjoyed by the citizens of its sovereign power living on the Chinese mainland.

However, and this may explain why the Hong Kong government

handled the crisis far worse than any other government in the region, it remains a nonelected bureaucratic administration, lacking all the instincts and reflex responses required by those subject to the ultimate discipline of an electorate. The great mystery is why there is so little comment on the government's panicky and highly interventionist response to the crisis. Somehow the Hong Kong government propaganda machine has managed to persuade a great many people that not only was the noninterventionist policy not changed but that, had the government acted differently, the problems would have been infinitely worse.

On the face of things Hong Kong should have been among the best placed to avoid the Asian crisis. Not only was there no government debt but in the corporate sector borrowings were at a very manageable level. Nonperforming loans, the scourge of other high-growth economies, were largely restricted to loans to mainland Chinese-based companies advanced by Hong Kong banks. When the crisis broke Hong Kong had the third highest level of foreign reserves in the world and a currency tied firmly to the US dollar through a currency board mechanism which had held the currency firm for a decade and a half.

Looking at these indicators, Hong Kong government officials, led by the new Chief Executive Tung Chee-hwa, watched the baht go west in Thailand and proudly declared that Hong Kong's 'fundamentals' were sound. Others may be in trouble but not the prosperous SAR, they declared. As if to underline how well placed Hong Kong was, the government made a great fuss over its financial contribution to the Thai bailout.

Denial mixed with arrogance was the order of the day. In December 1997 the Financial Secretary Sir Donald Tsang predicted that 'the dust might settle down by Christmas'. He reckoned that the financial turmoil in Asia had 'already done the full circle and I believe we are now at the tail end of that process'.[22] As for Hong Kong, Sir Donald had no doubt that its economy would keep surging forward and grow by 5.5 per cent in 1998.

The reality, signs of which were already emerging when this ridiculous prediction was made, was that the economy *declined* by around 5 per cent. Unemployment shot up to record levels; retail spending registered its biggest fall since figures were kept; the all-important property market slumped by at least 40 per cent. A deflationary spiral, the worst in over two decades, got into its stride. The balance of trade deteriorated sharply as both imports and exports fell. It was, by any standards, an economic nightmare.

Officials, like Sir Donald, simply had no experience of dealing with economic decline of this order. They believed their own propaganda until the second half of 1998, when the truth suddenly hit home and they started panicking. Having exercised stewardship over what the monetarist guru Milton Friedman described as 'the world's most laissez-faire economy', they decided that the rot could be stopped only by enormous government intervention which involved ditching the old rules of nonintervention and plunging into the property market, the stock market, the futures market, the foreign-exchange market and into the equally dangerous area of industrial policy making.

Other governments in the region may have responded with some form of panic but none emulated Hong Kong's terrifying combination of denial, incompetence and arrogance. Having long pledged itself to a policy described as 'positive noninterventionism', the government decided that it could no longer afford not to intervene. So in the very place where government has done best by doing little and where the markets have, in the past, adjusted without the government lifting a finger, the Hong Kong government started lifting many fingers and pointing them in many directions.

In the new order the government was run by Tung Chee-hwa, a former shipping tycoon, chosen in Peking and 'elected' by a small group of pro-Peking 'selectors' hand-picked for the task. Conventional wisdom may well assume that a businessman is less likely to be an economic interventionist than a bureaucrat or run-of-the mill politician but, as the Hong Kong experience showed, businessmen feel they can fix problems. When they are running governments people like Mr Tung believe they should behave as they do when running their companies. In other words they do not rely on others to put things right. Tung Chee-hwa has a special reason to think on these lines because he was involved in one of the biggest corporate bailouts in history when the OCCL shipping line, founded by his father, was about to go belly up in the 1980s and he masterminded the rescue. He also caused the problems that led to its collapse, but that is another story.

What then could be more natural than for Mr Tung and his team of unblooded but supremely self-confident bureaucrats to assume that they could turn around the economy and remove Hong Kong from the financial crisis? First they turned their collective attention to the property market. Much of Hong Kong's collective wealth is invested in this market: stamp duties raised from property transactions are so large that they kept other taxes at a minimum. Some 55 per cent of listed companies on the Hong Kong stock exchange are directly or indirectly dependent on the property market for their livelihood. It therefore takes little imagination to appreciate the sheer panic when property prices began to tumble in 1998. By the end of the year prices in the commercial sector had dropped by as much as 70 per cent and elsewhere by around 40 to 50 per cent from the peaks achieved just a couple of years previously.

Although in theory Hong Kong has a totally free property market, this is far from the case. All land is owned by the state and land prices can be manipulated by the manner and size of land sales (on a leasehold basis) to property developers. The traditional method of land auctions has been designed to favour Hong Kong's six largest property developers both because the lot sizes are usually too large for smaller developers to manage and secondly because the larger developers are given vital information about the land that is not available to other potential bidders. Therefore the system itself introduced a significant element of distortion into the free market for property development.

However, this was nothing compared with the government's decision, taken in June 1998, to suspend all land sales until March of the following year. Hong Kong's golden opportunity to bring down its ludicrously inflated property market was sacrificed to the interests of influential property developers who were sitting on undeveloped land and a mass of property projects which were rapidly falling in value.

High property costs are the key to the problem of Hong Kong's high cost base, which is making the territory increasingly uncompetitive relative to its neighbours. Instead of allowing the developers to the take the full impact of the market fall, they were bailed out by the government, who artificially tightened the market, allowing prices to creep back up.

It might have been thought that this body blow to the free market had wreaked sufficient damage upon Hong Kong's laissez-faire reputation but the panicky people who ran the government were in such a deep state of denial that they brushed these concerns aside and prepared for their next assault on what was left of the laissez-faire illusions.

It came with a vengeance over two months later when the government was caught up in a panic over what it saw as a concerted attack on the Hong Kong dollar coming from a so-called 'double play' on the equity and foreign-exchange markets. It alleged that the double play was designed to force the government to devalue the local currency and make fortunes for those who had gambled on its demise. On 28 August 1998 the Hong Kong administration launched the biggest stock-market raid ever undertaken by a government. By the end of the day it had spent over $15 billion and bought up almost 10 per cent of the blue-chip stocks in the market.[23]

It did so in the middle of a frenzied atmosphere. Many influential market players were confidently forecasting that Hong Kong would have to abandon the currency's fixed link to the United States dollar, which had helped see it through a number of crises in the past two decades. The hedge funds and big investments houses were circling for the kill.

Other Asian governments have either intervened or threatened to intervene in their stock markets but never on the same scale as the Hong Kong government did in a single day. However, in Singapore, government-controlled entities are much bigger players in the local stock market, accounting for some 25 per cent of the local market's capitalisation. This very large holding was not built up in a single day and consists in large part of companies developed by the government.

Most Asian governments, including the Japanese, who previously claimed to eschew such behaviour, have been big players in the forex markets alternately intervening to raise and lower the value of their currencies. In addition the Japanese have been by far the biggest players in their own stock market. It is believed that this has been going on since 1992, although the government declines to confirm it. Japan's motives were somewhat different from those of the Hong Kong administration. It acted to ensure that its banks did not go under because their balance sheets were heavily dependent on equity holdings which, as they slumped, caused the debt-to-equity ratios to collapse and thus threatened the viability of the banks.

Both Malaysia and Taiwan have also threatened to enter the market for the more crude purpose of bringing share prices up to levels deemed by the government to be more realistic. The Taiwan government's intervention, conducted through local banks, was not on a very large scale and quickly fizzled out once it became clear that it was doing little more than exercising a downward pressure on share prices.

However the Hong Kong government self-righteously denied that it was propping up share prices, insisting that its intervention was merely designed to protect the local currency.

On 7 August 1998, a week before the government started intervening in the market, Joseph Yam, the Chief Executive of the Hong Kong Monetary Authority (HKMA), effectively the central bank, alleged that Hong Kong was facing a 'severe conspiracy' by speculators trying to break the Hong Kong dollar peg. Later he said 'speculators launched co-ordinated and well-planned attacks across our markets'. Sir Donald Tsang, Hong Kong's diminutive bow-tie-wearing Financial Secretary, bought the conspiracy theory and was looking for revenge. 'I'm going to hurt them', he warned.

'I'm going to hit them where it hurts and tell them don't come here and make a lot of money.' Instead it was the Hong Kong taxpayer who paid out more money than they had ever paid before on a single day. After a frenzy of market intervention the world's supposedly most laissez-faire government became the world's biggest market player. The speculators were seen off.

The Hong Kong dollar is the only currency in East Asia pegged to the US dollar at a fixed rate and sustained in value by the operation of a currency board (like that which was planned for Indonesia by Dr Hanke). It works by raising overnight interest rates as pressure mounts on the local currency's value. The idea is to squeeze liquidity out of the market so that those involved in currency speculation simply cannot get their hands on the currency.

According to Mr Yam the speculators would have netted some $500 million for every 1000-point fall they could engineer in the Hang Seng Index. If they actually succeeded in forcing a devaluation of the currency their bets on its fall would have produced profits running into the billions.

The authorities had been given a small avalanche of reports about the build-up of short futures-markets contracts in the Hang Seng Index. In other words positions taken by speculators who believed the market would fall. Speculators were also going short in individual stocks, and, of course, going short on the Hong Kong dollar. I was told by an official that 'they were getting more and more worried'. Mr Yam asked the watchdog Securities and Futures Commission (SFC) to provide him with evidence of market manipulation and was not pleased to be told that such evidence did not exist. 'A bunker mentality started to grow,' said this source. 'They could not accept that a confluence of events was under way. And they were taking it personally.'

The problem with Mr Yam's conspiracy theory was that he failed to produce a scrap of evidence to back these allegations. When I was trying to piece together the story of the market intervention, Mr Yam declined to be interviewed. However, I spoke to two of his officials. One of them, Amy Yip, the HKMA director who ran the reserves management department, said, 'The facts are all there. A number of players in the market consistently and repeatedly [were] making the same play to reap a profit.' In Hong Kong this may be viewed as a conspiracy but elsewhere in the world it is known as playing the markets.

Hong Kong's problem was that it had a market designed for plays by well-funded investors looking for spectacularly high returns from leveraged investments, in other words investments requiring only a proportion of the funds to be paid up front. Peter Churchouse, the managing director of the Hong Kong branch of the stock brokers Morgan Stanley Dean Witter, described the process as being 'like an ATM [automated teller machine] machine'. It works like this: speculators take big short positions in the futures market, the stock market and the currency market. Because Hong Kong has a currency board the speculators can put pressure on the Hong Kong dollar by forcing the HKMA to raise interest rates to defend the currency. As interest rates rise, stock prices fall; therefore those who are holding short positions should make a profit.

This does not always happen in practice. When the Hong Kong dollar came under pressure back in October 1997, overnight interest rates rose above 300 per cent. The squeeze hurt but the speculators were beaten off.

'Both sides learned from that experience,' said Peter Pang, the HKMA director responsible for monetary policy and markets. The speculators also learned to get their hands on Hong Kong dollars in advance so as to avoid being caught short and having to borrow at very high rates to cover their short positions. According to Mr Yam they had built up a battle chest of HK$30 billion ($3.8 billion) through an unprecedented number of short-term bond issues denominated in Hong Kong dollars. The government felt that Hong Kong was like a sitting duck. 'Obviously we needed to do something to frustrate those plays,' said Mr Pang.

By 14 August they did the unprecedented and moved into the stock and futures markets and started taking positions that hurt those betting on a market fall. However, the pressure failed to ease. Mr Yam and Sir Donald together with the Chief Executive Tung Chee-hwa decided that something far more dramatic needed to be done. Thus the full-scale stock-market intervention was launched.

'We have frustrated the speculator's plan,' said a triumphant Sir Donald. Others saw things differently. The economist Milton Friedman, once a cheerleader for Hong Kong, simply described the market intervention as 'insane'.

The extraordinary irony of the situation is that had the Hong Kong authorities waited until the following week they would have seen most of the big speculators being forced out of the market because they desperately needed funds to cover the positions they had built up in Russia. After the great Russian default they were all dangerously over-exposed and would have gone to Hong Kong's liquid market to raise cash.

However, it is only with hindsight that this became apparent. Nevertheless believers in market forces, which used to include the Hong Kong government, know full well that markets work in this way and that it is always more than likely that a market that has overshot in one direction will achieve a correction in another. Yet, to be fair, even true believers cannot tell exactly when all this will happen.

Even if the government had lost faith in the idea of free markets it could well have saved itself the consequences of becoming a market player and frustrated the so-called double play by introducing a series of regulatory and trading reforms, which were put in place a week after the market intervention ended. They basically made short selling considerably more difficult and introduced tight rules on the settlement of trades, which further squeezed the speculators' ability to play the market without putting funds up front.

Brian Lippey, the managing director of Hong Kong-based fund managers Tokai Asia, told me that the government had 'legitimate concerns' but they sent a 'real chill through the market' by intervening rather than taking the regulatory action that was introduced after the share-buying spree. He said that market participants would have understood and supported reasonable control measures.

Many participants fully understood what the government had done; some even supported it but they were not prepared to pay the additional risk premium of going back into a market where the state had introduced a new uncertainty of intervention, creating additional risks in an already risky situation.

The government denied that it wanted to be a long-term market player but refused to rule out future interventions. Moreover, once bitten by the intervention bug, it was tempted into more and more behaviour that suggested that it was having trouble keeping out of the business of business.

In March 1999 Sir Donald used his budget speech to triumphantly tell legislators that he had acquired a vision of the future for getting Hong Kong out of its economic malaise. The former colony was to become an international hi-tech communications hub. The plan was breathtaking in its stupidity and instantly criticised, not least because it involved giving away the last piece of prime residential development land on Hong Kong island to a company run by Richard Li, the youngest son of the tycoon Li Ka-shing, who was to build something called a Cyberport. In effect this was nothing more than a couple of office blocks, wired up with telecommunications cables. Most the property development, however, was to be for residential purposes, the idea being that the money raised from building luxury apartments would finance the Cyberport. The plan was criticised from all quarters, not least by other property developers, who would not have minded being given the land. In all other circumstances developers are required to pay upfront for land, not after the development has started to generate revenues. The Cyberport developers were allowed to acquire their land without upfront payment. However, this was not the nub of the matter. Perhaps Hong Kong businesses had become so used to the ways of its new interventionist government that its representatives failed to notice that the government was now setting out its priorities for industrial development rather than letting the market determine how business should develop.

The record of government laying down the priorities is mixed. In South Korea and Japan, where big business and central government worked closely hand in hand to develop new industries, there is little question that successes were achieved. In Malaysia, where the government had its own hi-tech vision and designated a vast area of land in the suburbs of the capital as a 'Multimedia Super Corridor', the plan looks as if it will fall flat on its face. In Hong Kong the government chose to work with a well-connected company but one with no track record of successfully developing a single high-technology product or service. Unlike the Koreans and the Japanese, it will not mobilise its resources behind the project but let Mr Li's company do all the work on its own. This half-hearted course of action is a neither-fish-nor-fowl approach which may well turn out to represent the worst of all worlds.

Having decided it could determine industrial policy by picking a company, giving it special privileges and hoping that it would give rise to a new industrial dawn, the government then proceeded to intervene, yet again, in the financial markets. Just nine months after its buying spree in the equity markets, it turned its attention to the debt market for the second time. Previously it had been keen on opening up this market to make it an international centre of debt trading in Hong Kong dollars. When pressure was on the Hong Kong dollar in 1998 the government leaned on debt issuers to persuade them not to issue new bonds denominated in the local currency. When asked by people like myself whether it had done so, an HKMA spokesman denied that this was the case. Yet there was an abrupt cessation of Hong Kong dollar bond issues. Then, in May 1999 the HKMA grew jittery again and stopped the issue of all bonds with less than a three-year term. Again it did so because it was worried that hedge funds and other investors might try and build up a Hong Kong dollar battle chest by buying in the bond market and selling off the bonds when the time was right to have another go at breaking the Hong Kong dollar peg. That at any rate was the theory.

The reality was that, yet again, the government was intervening to distort the operations of the market, in this case to thwart the development of a market it had once been keen to encourage. 'Sooner or later – and it looks like much later – the HKMA is going to have to learn to trust the foreign exchange market,' wrote David DeRosa, a foreign-exchange market specialist. He continued, 'Hong Kong cannot continue to serve as a financial centre with its authorities peeling back every transaction to see if a black-hearted speculator is ready to pounce.'[24]

Dr DeRosa gets to the nub of the issue here. He correctly notes that the government was so concerned with 'protecting' itself from what it saw as speculative attacks that it had lost sight of the role the Hong Kong markets are supposed to play as hosts to the international community of investors. Of course, if these investors are not welcome, the government could always say so and they would happily depart in search of new homes.

The upshot of the government's gross mismanagement of the crisis, starting with a period of denial, followed by a period of panic, topped off by a total muddle about its role as the steward of a supposedly free economy, helped Hong Kong remain in recession, while all the other former high-growth economies (with the exception of politically unstable Indonesia) were on the road to recovery. Worse, far worse, was the long-term damage inflicted on the SAR's role as an international financial centre and, because none of the fundamental problems of high costs in the Hong Kong economy were tackled, the government has ensured that the SAR enters the new millennium at a distinct competitive disadvantage.

There is, incidentally, no evidence that the government of the People's Republic of China, Hong Kong's new sovereign state, was responsible for the highly interventionist stance employed by the local SAR government. On the contrary, unconfirmed reports reaching Hong Kong suggest that the Chinese central government was rather taken aback by this stance but honoured its pledge of giving autonomy to the SAR, not least because it had originally been persuaded that the people running the territory had a better handle on managing the economy than the leaders in Peking.

Hong Kong stumbled out of the Asian crisis without further damage not because of government action but in spite of it. Corporate balance sheets remained in relatively satisfactory shape; fiscal reserves remained strong, despite the government embarking on the unfamiliar territory of deficit budgets; and there were no more than a handful of big corporate failures. Having entered the crisis with many of the benefits denied to the countries who either had to go to the IMF or suffered serious debt crises,

Hong Kong found that all its other economic weaknesses were painfully exposed, propelling it into a crisis that was unique to the SAR and may prove ultimately more damaging than the crisis that affected the region as a whole.

The Singapore response

While Hong Kong responded to this crisis with an uncharacteristic seizure of the rudder, brutally steering the territory away from its former laissez-faire stance, the Singapore government, which is hardly famous for being hands-off at the best of times, surprised many by using the crisis as an opportunity to lift controls and generally open up the economy. A friend of mine who is a stockbroker in Singapore put it this way: 'Hong Kong is becoming more like Singapore was and Singapore is becoming more like Hong Kong used to be.'

An opinion survey conducted by the Hong Kong-based Political & Economic Risk Consultancy Ltd asked over 400 expatriate businessmen working in Asia how they thought various countries had handled the crisis. This was its conclusion relating to the island state:

> Singapore stands apart from just about every other government in the region in the way it has pursued a largely non-interventionist stance towards market forces while searching for ways in which it can take advantage of the new regional conditions to enhance its own competitive position.'[25]

Like Hong Kong, Singapore entered the crisis with strong corporate and national balance sheets. Unlike Hong Kong it was closer to the countries most affected by the crisis and suffered a contagion effect which quickly caused the value of its currency to drop and its stock market to plummet.

Singapore, as we have seen, is run by an administration still dominated by the former Prime Minister Lee Kuan Yew but an administration that still subjects itself to elections and is still concerned about maintaining popular support and thus legitimacy for government actions, even though it remains intolerant of organised opposition. The political background is important to understanding the government's response to the crisis.

From the start the government made no attempt to minimise the extent of the problem. 'We are in for some very tough times,' said Goh Chok Tong, the Prime Minister, in a post-National Day speech delivered in August 1998. He also did nothing to disguise the sacrifices that would need to be made to get Singapore back on track.

Being honest with the people did no harm. On the one hand, for example, the government decreed that all employees should take a pay cut as part of the effort to sharply reduce Singapore's cost base. On the other it made a considerable and effective effort to ensure that those at the bottom of the scale were not pushed into poverty.

Companies, banks and even government departments were ordered to be more transparent in their operations. The banking sector and other parts of the financial market were opened up to something close to the full blast of foreign competition. Unlike Hong Kong, Singapore has used the strength of its banking sector to promote a more active local bond market.

Of course, old habits are hard to kick, so the government has hardly retreated into a shell and adopted a totally hands-off policy. While Hong Kong is pinning its hi-tech hopes on the dubious Cyberport, Singapore unveiled ambitious plans to produce an 'e-nation' by installing a broadband network for the whole country, effectively meaning that the island is wired up for the latest developments in communications technology. The government has, once again, aggressively gone out into the marketplace to lure international direct investors with attractive tax breaks and related offers. Nor has there been much of a pause in Singapore's perpetual effort to create a superb infrastructure. Although these improvement programmes are far too statist for free-market purists, they clearly work and carry popular support within Singapore.

They were also working at the macroeconomic level, allowing Singapore to be among the first of the crisis-hit countries to pull out of recession and actually benefit from the crisis. The reason being that it emerged as a rock of fiscal and economic stability attracting an inflow of funds as part of the flight to quality which encouraged those with money to look to places like Singapore as a safe haven.

The South Korean response

If Singapore responded to the crisis in a manner that was not expected, the same can be said of South Korea, only more so. Of all the governments in

219

the region it was the Kim Dae-jung administration that has shown itself most determined to learn from the crisis. When President Kim, a long-time dissident and former political prisoner, came to office after Korea plunged into crisis, the people who usually get it wrong, brokers analysts and the like, confidently predicted that he was absolutely not the sort of person to be put in charge of economic recovery. President Kim, they declared, would be soft on the unions because he had been allied to them for many years. He would know little about economics and he would be more concerned with populist political measures than the hard choices required to get the economy back on its feet.

However, President Kim is a thoughtful man and quickly realised that the success of his democratically elected administration would be judged by little other than its ability to cope with the economic crisis. Precisely because he had a popular mandate and precisely because he had the legitimacy of an election behind him he was able to make demands on the workforce, the big corporate bosses and even the international community, which the army generals, who previously occupied the president's seat, could never have contemplated.

Shortly after coming to office in January 1998, President Kim showed Koreans how a democratically elected president might be expected to behave. Years of autocratic government had led the people to expect rule by a clutch of distant bureaucrats who would belt out answers to the nation's problems rather than deign to listen to what the people might have to say. He showed he was in a different mould, starting by holding a town-hall-style meeting shown on television. Taking questions from the floor and answering them in a thoughtful manner, he created a profound impression. He also used the occasion to spell out the hardships to come and to tell his people frankly that some of their previous benefits, such as lifetime employment, would become a thing of the past.

Such was President Kim's charisma that he was successful in spearheading a campaign called 'Let Us Overcome the Economic Crisis', which, in part, persuaded some two million Koreans to boost the value of the local currency by handing in their gold jewellery in exchange for won.

True, President Kim was engaged in little more than effective public relations but he created the right atmosphere against which he could twist arms and get the entrenched forces of big business and labour to shift their positions. Unions were forced to accept new labour legislation that made it easier for employers to make workers redundant. The bosses of the big *chaebols* were told that they had to make the operation of their companies more transparent and, like it or not, they would have to consolidate their activities, in some cases merging units with other companies, in others simply shutting them down. The banking sector also felt the heavy hand of government 'persuasion'. Korea entered the financial crisis with thirty merchant banks, loaded up with bad and dubious loan books; it emerged in 1999 with just thirteen banks still in existence. Shotgun weddings and sharp downsizing became the order of the day.

Meanwhile, Korea extracted the IMF's biggest ever loan of $58 billion and, so it appeared, was following the IMF's prescriptions for fiscal reform. However, the Kim administration was in reality ignoring some of the more extreme demands from Washington, primarily in the area of interest rates, which were pushed way below the levels that the IMF viewed as desirable. By keeping rates at more reasonable levels the Korean administration helped pull companies out of the heavy burden of the borrowing trap. The IMF kept quiet both because they could see that President Kim had such overwhelming support at home and because he was riding the crest of a wave of international support. In other words, as ever, political expediency overrode economic formulas.

Meanwhile, foreign investment came flooding into Korea, much of it from foreign companies buying up trouble-hit Korean entities. We shall consider the upsurge in merger and acquisition activity in Asia in more detail in the following chapter but at this stage the point to note is that although many Korean companies were in bad financial shape they were still engaged in businesses with considerable potential and had a worthwhile basis to build on. They were not like the hotchpotch conglomerates floundering elsewhere in Asia, whose main business consisted of buying and selling assets of various kinds.

Yet critics of the Kim government feel that the President has not been radical enough, nor have the root problems of *chaebol* dominance been sorted out. It is also said that little has really been done to fundamentally change laws or ways of doing business in Korea. This was underlined in the middle of 1999 when President Kim expressed his concern over the way that the *chaebols* were using subsidiary companies to take on loans intended for their parents so as to disguise the level of their indebtedness. At the same time the central bank produced a report showing that the big conglomerates were slipping back into their old ways as soon as they saw signs of an upturn in the financial markets. The bulk of borrowings by the *chaebols* at the beginning of 1999 were devoted to portfolio investments instead of equipment purchases and research and development. Yet again the lure of the quick buck took precedence over longer-term investment.[26]

That Korea has a long way to go in achieving reform was clear, but at least it is proceeding in the right direction. Some of Korea's progress is based on tangible reforms such as moves by the government run Korea Asset Management Corp. to buy up nonperforming loans from distressed financial institutions, thus clearing the books and preparing for a fresh start. However, even more of what is going on in Korea is about creating a new set of atmospherics, leading to new expectations, including, as we have seen, higher expectations among minority shareholders. Changing expectations can be seen as superficial, or may be better viewed as an essential building block laying the foundations for more substantial change.

The Taiwan response

Only one country, among the eight previously high-growth economies, managed to avoid a recession altogether during the crisis and suffered no more than turbulence on its financial markets. It remains a mystery why Taiwan was not given more credit for this achievement. Indeed it is quite surprising not to see a mass migration of analysts heading towards Taiwan in search of the recipe that kept its economy afloat while others were sinking. In these terms Taiwan, just an hour's flight from Hong Kong, is the flip side of the perception coin. In other words while Hong Kong's multiple failures during the crisis were consistently overlooked, Taiwan's somewhat surprising successes were also glossed over.

One reason for this may well be that Taiwan's success is not straightforward, the weaknesses of its economic system are many and, thanks to the much greater transparency that now prevails in Taiwan, these weaknesses are much more clearly visible. I have been a visitor to what is officially called the Republic of China for almost two decades. When I first went I was installed in a room that had been bugged by the authorities, martial law was still in force, government officials were obstructive and mendacious and companies were opaque. The island was awash with pirated products and copyright theft was so blatant that parts of the capital were famous for little else aside from such goods. The transformation, especially in the last decade, has been breathtaking and was triggered by a political achievement seen nowhere else in the world.

Only in Taiwan has an authoritarian, sometimes brutal and often venal ruling party managed to lead its country into fundamental political reform, opening up the political, economic and social system without itself being swept away by the flood of reforms. Taiwan's ruling Kuomintang still bears some of the hallmarks of its former self but it has led a revolution every bit as profound as that led by the Communist Party in China, with the big difference that it has set about demolishing many of the structures and practices that it erected.

The relevance of these profound political and social changes on an economic and political level were explained to me in July 1998 by Prime Minister Vincent Siew, a deceptively low-key and bureaucratic-sounding individual. He said that 'to pursue economic growth, you have to prepare political reform'. Moreover he insisted that 'when you have open economic systems, you have to have transparency'. This means that corruption, mismanagement, political loans and all the other problems that came crawling out of the Asian woodwork could be kept in check.[27]

In 1998 Taiwan's gross domestic product totalled over $280 billion (China's GDP, by comparison is around two times greater but China has a population that is almost sixty times bigger than that of Taiwan). While neighbouring economies were contracting, Taiwan was posting growth of a shade below 5 per cent. Taiwan had the world's third highest foreign-currency reserves of over $88 billion. In the twelve months following the devaluation of the Thai baht, Taiwan's stock market emerged as the best performing in the region. A period of speculation against the New Taiwan dollar caused it to lose some 20 per cent of its value but, if anything, this proved to be an advantage because it reduced the price of exports. A currency backed by massive reserves, a healthy trade surplus and a large current-account surplus, not to mention negligible foreign debts, was unlikely to be in serious trouble.

However, Taiwan has some serious structural problems. First, it is in a hybrid situation where its finance market is half open and half closed to international investors. As it turned out this helped it avoid some of the worst consequences of big capital movements but is not helping the country realise ambitions to become an international financial centre.

Secondly, there is an enormous speculative bubble within the financial and property markets, largely generated by domestic investors who have proved every bit as volatile as the foreign investors who are usually blamed for shifting around funds in an irresponsible manner.

Of more immediate concern are indications that Taiwan, despite its conservative banking policies, shares some of its neighbours' problems of bad debt and high debt-to-equity ratios. In 1997 Taiwan's debt-to-equity ratio was estimated to stand at just over 45 per cent, well below that of the countries hit hardest by the crisis in its initial stages but significantly above Hong Kong, at 25 per cent, and Singapore, at 27 per cent.[28] Nonperforming loans, which have dragged down finance companies elsewhere in the region, were however not so much of a problem in Taiwan, where they accounted for no more than 4 per cent of the loan portfolio.

A run on two banks in 1998 triggered fears that Taiwan was going to join the other 'Miracle' economies in succumbing to a wave of bad debt. However, this failed to materialise and in February 1999 the government introduced reforms to inch open the finance sector to overseas competition, allowing foreigners to own a bigger share in listed companies and reduced taxation on banks. A more radical opening had been planned but it was held back by what the government viewed as the globalisation lessons of the Asian crisis. Shea Jia-dong, the deputy governor of Taiwan's central bank, explained the situation in these terms: 'The massive capital flows on the international capital markets have done much damage to international society,' he said but promised that the government would reconsider 'full capital account liberalisation by the end of 2000'.[29]

Although radical in many ways, the Taiwan government is instinctively conservative. Under the pressure of a developing parliamentary system and the demands of a highly sophisticated society it has learned to swallow some of its conservative instincts and become more imaginative in formulating policies.

This leaves it in a curious position of following some of the old ways, which produced an economy riddled with monopolies and restrictive practices, while making a genuine attempt to break out of this mould. While doing so it remains loath to remove the hand of the state entirely.

In the industrial sector much of what the government has done has been positive. It has encouraged the upgrading of production processes and channelled funds, incentives and backup for the development of a large high-technology sector. As a result some 40 per cent of Taiwan's industrial sector is now devoted to science- and technology-based companies. This has transformed the pattern of Taiwan's export trade, which used to be characterised by shipments of cheap footwear, transistors and other assembly-line items. Now these labour-intensive products account for no more than 20 per cent of exports while capital- and technology-intensive products account for over 40 per cent.

Taiwan's formidable presence in the global high-technology market is most evident in the computer industry, where Taiwanese companies have become the world's leading producers of scanners, keyboards and notebook computers. Indeed, throughout the computer hardware market, there are few products not made by Taiwanese companies, even if much of the routine assembly work has been shipped off to China.

Taiwanese companies have been major investors throughout Asia. Like the Japanese they have shifted labour-intensive production to lower-cost centres. Unlike many Japanese companies and those from places like Hong Kong, they did not pour large sums of money into speculative portfolio investments for the simple reason that the government imposed controls preventing the export of funds for these purposes.

The net result has been to create a far more solid and productive corporate base in Taiwan, which was far better equipped to withstand the storms stirred up by the Asian crisis. To put it simply Taiwan generated better companies with better products combined with more sound, albeit far from perfect, balance sheets. If, as is being argued here, the heart of the Asian crisis is a *corporate* crisis, Taiwan demonstrated the simple truth that better companies are unlikely to be swept away during financial storms. They may get battered but are rarely flattened.

Because Taiwan has become a very open society, criticism of the government and severe self-criticism are the order of the day in the Taiwanese media, often to an extent of obscuring the nation's very real achievements. However, it is because Taiwan has become an open society that it has managed to emerge from the crisis in far better shape than any other country in East Asia.

A great deal could be learned from Taiwan but may well be ignored because it remains in diplomatic deep freeze, shunned by those who want to do business with China.

The Philippines response

In theory the Philippines was best placed to avoid the consequences of the crisis, but that assumes that the theory was emerging from Washington, where the IMF is located. When the baht devalued and the contagion of its fall spread through the region, the Philippines was already under IMF tutelage because of a past crisis which it had managed all on its own. That meant that the Philippine economy was under the constraint of IMF prescriptions and that macroeconomic policy was derived from the so-called Washington model.

Yet the IMF's tutelage was not sufficient to keep the Philippines out of the crisis, although it should be noted that it suffered far less than all the other former high-growth economies (excepting Taiwan). Economic growth was largely sustained during the crisis period, although GDP registered a 0.5 per cent fall in 1998. However, most of that fall was accounted for by the El Niño climatic problems which pushed down agricultural production. Even the Philippine peso managed more or less to sustain its exchange rate against the US dollar.

The administration of President Fidel Ramos imposed a tight monetary policy, much loved in Washington. It also made sure that the problems of bad debts, which plagued other Asian nations, would not be as acute in the Philippines because strict reserve positions and high-capital adequacy ratios were imposed on banks. Nonperforming loans were on the rise in the post-crash period but, at around 13 per cent of the loan portfolio in early 1999, they were far less of a problem than elsewhere in the region.[30]

President Ramos did much to eliminate the cronyism that has plagued the Philippines and started to creep back under his successor. Mr Ramos used his military background and love of order to get things done but unlike some former generals did not lose his respect for the democratic system upon gaining power.

The incoming President, Joseph Estrada, elected in 1998, was fortunate to inherit a remarkably stable economy. He swept to office with promises to pursue a 'pro-poor' policy and to make rural development a priority. Most of his election pledges have remained stronger in the realm of rhetoric than in terms of implementation. However, President Estrada is the sort of president who believes that he can spend his way out of economic problems and this may well involve incurring levels of public debt that will put the Philippines on the path of national debt problems rather than the corporate debt problems that caused so much trouble elsewhere in the region. He does not inspire much investor confidence, which is reflected in the relatively poor performance of Philippine shares since Mr Estrada's election. The main hope is that the Estrada administration, led by a president with little grasp of economics, will opt for noninterventionism, allowing the economy to get on with business. Moreover, were the president more inclined to meddle, he faces impressive institutional hurdles erected to make the bureaucracy, especially the generally well-regarded central bank, surprisingly independent of the executive power.

It may seem churlish to say so but much of the good fortune that blessed the Philippine economy had nothing to do with government policy. First, it was boosted by the poverty of the past, which has driven a small army of Filipinos to work overseas and pour foreign exchange back home. Secondly, improving weather came to the rescue to boost the agricultural sector just as the industrial sector was experiencing a downturn. Thirdly, the Philippines was always the most shaky of the eight high-growth economies, starting with a lower base line and having less far to fall when times got tough.

The IMF may well hail its 'achievements' in the Philippines but much of the credit for economic stability belongs to President Ramos and much belongs to that unpredictable force of nature called serendipity.

Remaining in a state of denial

A great many more lessons could be learned from more or less every aspect of the crisis but, as the initial signs of recovery emerged, it looked as though many companies, governments and international organisations were resolutely determined to remain in a state of denial. Yet, as history shows and this crisis also demonstrated, it is difficult for governments and international organisations to make an impact on large economic crises. They may make some impression on the margins but when they try to tackle the substance of the crisis the record shows scant achievement. Real change – real movement towards recovery – comes from the people and companies and primary producers who are the component parts of the economy.

Because Asia is well stocked with good 'components', or at least with components with a potential to be good, there is hope for recovery. As we shall see in the following chapter, all is far from lost. Some lessons have been learned and in many ways, from the political level to the economic level and back down to the factory floor, the crisis has challenged dangerous assumptions, giving rise to new opportunities.

8

PREPARING FOR THE NEXT CRISIS

Happy days are here again

George Soros, the Hungarian-born, American-based, international financier, can be a bit of a mischief maker. His critics in Asia see him in a far worse light, believing that, almost single-handedly, he was responsible for triggering the Asian financial crisis. This is absurd but maybe he is equally unpopular because of a habit of saying things as they are – in other words spelling out unpalatable truths that others consider best unsaid. At a conference in 1999 he cheerfully told his audience, 'The global financial crisis is now officially over. So now we can look for the next one.'

History tells us that Mr Soros must be right but in 1999 most people in financial markets were too busy patting themselves on the back for having got over the worst of the crisis. They were not interested in hearing talk of another crisis, albeit in the distant future.

The consensus view, which had few dissenters, was that, within less than two years of the onset of the crisis, things were getting back to normal and recovery was in sight. In fact, by the end of 1998 no less a figure than Michel Camdessus, the managing director of the International Monetary Fund (IMF), a sober man at the best of times, was confident enough to say, 'I think the worst is past.'[1]

The year 1999 was deemed to be the year of recovery. It was a year, to paraphrase Charles Dickens, that should have been the best of times, looked like being the worst of times, and, as the great Victorian writer said of the French Revolution,

' . . . it was the epoch of incredulity, it was the season of Light, it was the season of Darkness, it was the spring of hope, it was the winter of despair, we had everything before us, we had nothing before us, we were all going direct to Heaven, we were all going direct the other way . . .'

Dickens was writing this almost a century and a half before the Asian crisis erupted but I looked over these words again once the pundits started declaring the crisis to be over and found it hard to believe that he had not somehow catapulted himself into the tail end of the twentieth century and studied the mood enveloping the financial markets of Asia.

There is cause to be hesitant about taking this analogy too far: after all Charles Dickens was discussing an event that transformed both France and, ultimately, most of Western Europe. Can such a sweeping claim be made for the fallout of the crisis that began in Thailand and spread infinitely faster than the consequences of the French Revolution to neighbouring countries? Probably not, but anyone who fails to understand that the crisis was a seminal event will not understand why its consequences are likely to be far-reaching.

From the beginning of 1999 onwards the mood turned increasingly bullish. Asian stock markets surged and currencies not only stopped devaluing against the US dollar, but started showing signs of strength. Economies that had slumped into recession were crawling back and showing signs of growth. Indeed, as 1999 ended only Hong Kong and Indonesia, among the former high-growth economies, remained in negative territory.

It was, as Dickens put it, 'the spring of hope'. Most Asian stockmarkets surged back from the crash of mid-1997 and doubled in value, at one point, the Malaysian market almost rose three fold.

The bulls, forced back into the corral, sniffed the air and prepared to charge again. The mood in the finance houses around Asia was not exactly euphoric – the word 'relief' might be more accurate to describe the sentiment of the time. Many of those employed in these companies were surrounded by empty desks previously occupied by colleagues who had been laid off. Those who remained felt a bit like survivors, happy to have been saved, fearful of further turbulence but enthusiastic in talking up the markets because as long as they were rising their jobs were safe and the glorious days of big bonuses loomed back into sight.

However, markets were merely doing what they do after big falls – they tend to turn around and bounce back up. When the bounce is fuelled by a market given a healthy infusion of cash, it is likely to have more spring to it. This was certainly the case in 1999 when the big investment funds who had made a packet in the American market took some of their profits and declared that the time had come for another gamble on Asia. As their money made its way back to Asia cash flowed in from local punters who did not want to lose out on the new opportunities.

Notes of caution

Inevitably the market surge excited many stockbrokers' analysts to push out bullish reports. However, they seem to have learned something from the crash, and were therefore careful to qualify their enthusiasm. In June 1999 Lee Hsien Loong, Singapore's deputy Prime Minister, succinctly reflected some of this caution. 'The rise in share prices', he said, 'reflects easier domestic liquidity, lower interest rates and returning confidence, more than an improvement in underlying fundamentals.' More tellingly he went on to say, 'The pick-up has encouraged some perhaps to hope the problems are permanently over; and there is no need for more painful reforms.'[2]

However, as Lawrence Summers pointed out before he became the United States Treasury Secretary, the very solutions to the Asian crisis contained elements of the problems that caused the debacle:

Economies will not recover without a resumed flow of lending to the corporate sector. Yet lending activity will not resume unless banks are recapitalised and the debt burdens of corporations are assessed and then reduced. Yet merely restarting credit flows without a fundamental change in the practices of banks, corporations and regulators runs the risk of the same past mistakes being repeated, and corporate debt/equity ratios and non-performing loans continuing to rise.[3]

The need for reform was the flavour-of-the-month discussion topic in 1998. By the following year the topic remained on the agenda but had lost some of its urgency and, as Mr Lee pointed out, was viewed by some as a less than pressing matter.

'Robust incrementalism'

One of the good things about the crisis is that it stimulated the debate about where the world economy was heading and the role of the financial infrastructure in making the economy perform better. Debates of this kind rarely get under way when times are good.

Once things turn bad the situation changes rapidly and there is much grandiose talk about solutions. The new buzz words, much heard in the wake of the Asian crisis, were all about 'reform of the global financial architecture' – the old architecture having been the 1944 Bretton Woods agreement, which clearly has not stood the test of time.

Nor were the world's finance leaders too sure about the future of the so-called Hong Kong Declaration on the liberalisation of capital movements, which had been agreed by the Interim Committee of the IMF during its annual conference in 1997. As the Declaration was being drafted the crisis was starting to take hold and was throwing into doubt some of its basic assumptions. The Declaration was a statement of intent in favour of more open capital markets, devised just as the moment when the operation of these markets was causing chaos.

In 1999 Michel Camdessus told a conference in New York that a new consensus had been reached which amounted to something far less than constructing a new architecture. 'Where are we heading to now?' he asked rhetorically. Answering himself he said, 'If I had to capture in one sentence the basic thrust of all this work, I would say: no new machinery, no new heavy public intervention, but for all players, both public and private, better behaviour and practices based on transparency, account-ability, and co-operation.'[4] In other words, it took months, rather than years to shift the consensus away from the more radical proposals that were on the table after the Asia crisis broke in 1997, and then the Russian crisis kicked in, followed by fears that Brazil may trigger yet another wave of debt problems.

The dilemma, as Mr Camdessus admitted, is that the new consensus is based on a desire to maintain a system of open global capital markets and to prise open those markets that remain closed, yet – this he did not say – to do so without having to face the consequences of really open markets. Moreover, how was the international community to solve this conun-drum? How were creditors, primarily the big banking institutions to be saved from the consequences of debts turning sour while at the same time not forcing the debtors into an ever-increasing circle of indebtedness

THE YEARS OF LIVING DANGEROUSLY

which would end up killing off their ability to repay their loans? There were other questions of a similar nature.

That is why a consensus formed around the more modest approach outlined by Mr Camdessus. This approach has been given a name by Barry Eichengreen, an economist at the University of California at Berkeley. It is 'robust incrementalism', a term, as the name suggests, that stands for more modest steps to control the excesses of global market volatility.

Yet those adopting the incrementalist approach felt in their heart of hearts that more needed to be done. Policy makers generally believe that doing more is better than doing less.

Taming capital flows

What they wanted to do more about was to prevent a repeated outbreak of financial turmoil by finding a way of taming capital flows. This was because most of those peering into the wreckage of the crisis concluded that it has been caused by sudden and vast capital movements. These problems, they felt, could have been avoided if there was some control on these movements.

Speaking at an IMF forum in October 1998, Michael Mussa, the IMF's research director, said,

> World capital markets were pushing a large flood of capital into emerging markets. In terms of gross flows, that reached an annual rate of $400 billion in the summer of 1997. After the middle of August of this year, those gross flows reached zero, just died completely. No country, no matter how soundly managed are its economic policies, no matter how solid is its banking system, can maintain an open attitude towards international capital flows in the face of that type of systemic disturbance, and the international community has some responsibility to face up to that fact, and to not simply say that all of the responsibility for dealing with that type of systemic-level problem rests with the emerging-market countries.[5]

Thus, even from the heart of the IMF, where capital-market liberalisation had been part of the gospel, the call for capital controls swung on to the agenda.

Paul Krugman stated the problem bluntly:

A growing number of reasonable people now agree that the demands the financial markets place on countries in crisis are impossible to meet, but still believe that imposing currency or capital controls is unthinkable. They are therefore looking for some palatable middle ground. Unfortunately, that middle ground does not exist.[6]

Nevertheless the debate centred not on the desirability of some kind of control or regulation but on the extent to which it was desirable.

The taboo subject of domestic-capital flight

However, nearly all discussion focused on capital movements made by international funds. The capital flight involving domestic investors went largely ignored, yet it is clear that domestic investors in Asia were at least as active as international investors in moving their funds out of the region or in liquidating local currency holdings in favour of US dollars because they had dollar liabilities that threatened to grow as their currencies devalued.

It is difficult to pin down the distinction between domestically generated capital flight and flight emanating from foreign investors; moreover, the whole phenomenon of capital outflows is difficult to measure, not least because some very big movements of cash are not reported to the authorities.

However, some evidence can be extrapolated from the figures to hand. According to the World Bank, net external finance to the East Asia Crisis-5 countries (Indonesia, Korea, Malaysia, the Philippines and Thailand) fell from a positive $40.8 billion in 1996 to minus $16.2 billion in 1997 and minus $19.9 billion the following year. However, in the same three years net capital outflows were as follows: minus $42.5 billion, minus $65.1 billion and minus $52.7 billion.[7] It therefore seems reasonable to assume that some or all of the difference in these figures is accounted for by domestically generated capital outflows. Even if in 1997, the first crisis year, only half the capital outflows came from domestic investors that would amount to over $32 billion, or more than double the decline in external financing.

A small note of caution needs to be added here because the World Bank's capital-outflow figures also include errors and omissions, but these account for a small percentage of the total.

Even with this minor qualification it is likely that the level of domestic-capital flight was at least as large as, if not larger than, foreign-capital flight. This problem was implicitly acknowledged by the Malaysian government, which, as we have seen, slammed down foreign-exchange controls, effectively freezing the movement of domestic capital out of the country. Malaysia was not alone in realising that domestic-capital flight was as important as foreign-capital flight.

Maybe others ignored the domestic side of the capital-flight equation because it was more politically correct to speak of the disruption brought to the markets by foreigners.

However, as Paul Krugman has pointed out, the subject may also have been ignored because the only means of tackling the problem of domestic-capital flight is to employ the taboo means of capital and exchange controls.

A new global financial architecture?

This was too drastic a step for some policy makers, who were looking for reform but hesitated over the prospect of severe market-control mechanisms. Most favoured an incremental approach but there were strong voices arguing for more drastic action.

At the extreme end of the argument was the Malaysian government, which, as we have seen, decided to virtually close its door to foreign capital on the grounds that it was a force for instability in the economy. However, as we have also seen, even the Malaysians appear to have second thoughts about whether this is so because as one door slammed shut another remained open to so-called long-term investors who were deemed to be playing a role in economic development.

In the early 1990s the Chilean government dabbled in capital-flow controls by imposing taxes on inflows of short-term capital. This move was something of a forerunner to the Malaysian government's actions, albeit less extreme.

There is a body of opinion that is sympathetic to the idea of regulating capital flows, although hesitant about erecting barriers to prevent those flows. Advocates of this school of thought are nevertheless radical in their ideas and looking at ways to overhaul the financial system and to create new international bodies to supervise the movement of capital on a global scale.

The German government, which has more than a little experience of interventionism in its own back yard, was keen on a scheme to establish target zones for major currencies, such as the US dollar, the Japanese yen and the euro, which would ensure global currency stability by setting target zones for each currency and intervening to ensure that these targets were met.

Meanwhile, the government of Tony Blair in Britain, which was busy overhauling the financial regulatory system at home, mainly by increasing regulators' powers and concentrating regulatory work in a single agency, came up with similar plans for the international arena. It advocated the idea of creating a global super-regulator which would incorporate the work of all the main international institutions, including the IMF and the World Bank, so as to make them more effective.

The Americans in particular – but many other countries in general – were sceptical about the creation of big new global regulatory bodies and were suspicious of large-scale plans to control market fluctuations. At the 1999 World Economic Forum annual meeting in Davos, Robert Rubin, who was then the US Secretary of the Treasury, embarked on an exercise of lowering expectations. He said that the goal was not to eliminate crises, an impossible task, but to 'reduce the susceptibility of the market-based economic system to financial instability and to respond better if crises occur' by taking some of the risk out of the system. The Americans did not want to see a reduction in global capital flows but set the ambitious goal of improving the quality of these flows.

Some of those present at the meeting seemed to think that if crises were more predictable they could be nipped in the bud. This was Mr Rubin's now famous response: 'Nothing in my twenty six years on Wall Street or my six years in government suggests that there is any predictive capability even remotely reliable enough for such a system.'[8]

Before joining the Clinton administration in 1993 he had been a senior partner at Goldman Sachs and even in government still gave the impression of being more deeply rooted in Wall Street than Washington.

The Group of Seven pronounce

In February 1999 the Group of Seven (G-7) finance ministers and central bankers met in Bonn and came up with a plan to make robust incrementalism a new form of international policy. Their plan was endorsed by the heads of government four months later. As usual it contains rather more rhetoric than substance but careful reading of the proposals suggests that there was more of value in the package than was widely appreciated at the time.

'We have agreed', they said 'to take a number of actions to enhance transparency in our own economies and to strengthen the global financial system.'[9] What did it mean?

Among other things it meant establishing something called a Financial Stability Forum to get national and international bodies together to 'more effectively foster and coordinate their respective responsibilities to promote international financial stability, improve the functioning of the markets and reduce systemic risk'. In other words it is a kind of super liaison group charged both with identifying problems and coming up with solutions. The Forum has its own bureaucracy but is not a shadow IMF or anything of the kind. If it works it may provide a more nimble way of identifying (but not resolving) problems before they swing too far out of control, as they did in Asia.

Alongside the creation of the forum the G-7 set up a series of meetings to look at issues relating to the regulation and supervision of markets, exchange-rate regimes and other crisis-avoidance mechanisms.

There is also a mixture of stick-and-carrot incentives to improve the transparency of markets. Countries not meeting new disclosure standards would, for example, be burdened with high-risk ratings making loans more expensive.

The G-7 encouraged countries to avoid fixed-exchange-rate regimes (with the exception of currency-board arrangements such as those operating in Hong Kong). Those who remain wedded to fixed exchange rates will find it harder to get IMF loans.

But what of those who recklessly poured international commercial loans into emerging markets and expected the IMF to make sure these loans were repaid? Basically the G-7 told these lenders that they are on their own. However, many of them are powerful in the countries that made this declaration and they have ways of ensuring that their interests are looked after. Their trump card, which is hard to trump, is the argument that, if there is not some underwriting of loans to more risky emerging markets, the supply of credit will be curtailed and the scope for economic development will decline.

These proposals could all dissolve into hot air as is the way of proposals handed down by grandiose international bodies. However, they have been given substance by getting bodies such as the IMF and the OECD to devise codes of good practice for lending, for creating best practices for monetary and financial policy, for sound corporate governance, for internationally agreed accounting standards and to examine transparency and disclosure standards for the flow of private-sector funds.

If any of this comes to anything it will represent something less than the claimed new global financial architecture, but something that will influence financial trends. It will demonstrate the inadequacy of the simplistic presumption that the opening up of financial markets will automatically lead to greater benefits. Moreover, if the institutions proposed by the G-7 work they will have created a mechanism that helps markets perform in a more objective and thus more competitive manner.

Regulation for all or some?

It seems that the G-7 is moving down a road already travelled by the global trade policy regime, where a system for regulating world trade is well entrenched, albeit not without problems. Most, if not all, the world's nations have accepted the basic principle that world trade requires a degree of regulation and, in the context of the World Trade Organisation (WTO), and its predecessor, have sacrificed a degree of national autonomy in determining trade policy to abide by WTO rules, even to the extent of allowing the international body to rule on trade disputes and make its rulings binding.

The WTO has also turned its attention to knocking down barriers to competition in the international financial-services industry. The IMF and World Bank, on the other hand, are theoretically in a position to perform a wider task in the area of global capital-flow management, global lending policy and the like, but in terms of exercising control they do so only in relation to debtor countries in receipt of their funding. In practice nondebtor countries lose no autonomy to these international financial institutions.

However, the G-7 proposals, if they are realised, will change this unequal state of affairs and place international regulation on a more equitable footing.

The irony here is that free trade, more highly regulated through the WTO, produces fewer of the harmful consequences that arise from the free flow of capital. There has never been, for example, a free-trade panic, nor have traders demonstrated the terrifying herd instinct seen among fund managers. The international community is now implicitly, if not explicitly, recognising that it has to do something about this irony. In trade terms markets are kept open by means of regulation; in the financial market there are the same pressures for open markets but growing fears over the consequences.

The consensus view, as we have seen, is not to tolerate controls on the movement of capital, which would be the antithesis of open markets, but sentiment is moving towards means of monitoring those flows, perhaps making them less extreme and certainly making them more transparent.

Given the political will to impose a new regime on capital markets, it will happen. However, as we have also seen, the majority of the world's nations remain preoccupied by the fear that international agreements will curtail whatever commercial advantages they happen to enjoy in the global marketplace. This is why most nations cannot even bring themselves to ratify an international treaty on corruption because of fears that they will lose competitive advantage. And this is despite the fact that not a single government will stand up in public and say that corruption is a good thing.

Fixing the heart of the problem

While discussions proceed on how to fix financial problems at a global level, only minimal attention is being given to the heart of the problem, namely the inadequacies of private-sector companies that in Asia simultaneously combusted and created the fireball known as the Asian financial crisis.

The central argument of this book is that the underlying cause of the crisis was the state of bad management in Asian companies. As long as these companies were encased in an asset-inflation bubble they were safe from repercussions, but, as soon as it burst, all their shortcomings were laid bare. Had the companies been better managed they would still have been in trouble when the bubble burst but it is questionable whether they would have been so vulnerable and it is unlikely that capital flight would have been either so large or so devastating in effect. Well-managed companies simply do not operate on knife-edge financing for an indefinite period.

Although a great many people are uncomfortably aware of this problem, they are equally aware that there are no nice, easy, comprehensive solutions. So that when remedies are discussed there is usually mention of the need for the private sector to play a role but rarely are there any suggestions as to what that role may be.

By definition, however, the private sector, in societies operating free markets, cannot be controlled by government. But countries as different as Japan, Taiwan and Singapore have shown that the state can play a considerable role in controlling and directing the private sector. The evidence considered earlier in this book suggests that state intervention cannot be regarded in principle as a bad thing. Its results are mixed but on balance have not been negative.

This raises the question of whether governments in Asian countries should be playing a more central role in private-sector restructuring or whether market pressures alone will be sufficient to do the job. It is generally accepted that governments will anyway be playing a major role in financial-sector restructuring by, for example, re-examining capital-adequacy ratios for banks, imposing new borrowing limits, making the financial-sector report to government institutions in more detail and generally making its operations more transparent. The argument goes that, if the financial sector has to work with this level of government intervention, may there not be a case for governments to be more proactive generally in the corporate world?

This discussion tends to be rather fuzzy on the one hand and emotional on the other, because laissez-faire advocates tend to take an absolutist position on questions of government intervention. Secondly, there is a great deal of confusion over what can be considered to be government intervention. For example, changes to the taxation regimes are clearly a method of intervention because they have a direct impact on the cost of doing business. However, taxation matters are rarely discussed in the context of government intervention. The focus of these discussions is usually state intervention in the running of companies.

Even in circumstances where governments are inclined to play this role there are very real practical problems of finding ways to work with the small and medium-sized enterprises that constitute the overwhelming bulk of Asian companies. Not only do these companies tend to be fundamentally averse to dealing with official bodies but they are so diverse as to make it hard for the government to reach them.

A worm's-eye view

As I happen to be a director of a fairly typically small-sized company it occurred to me that a useful way of examining this issue would be to draw up a wish list of what the government could do for my businesses, identifying issues that are currently troublesome and, in an ideal world, could be fixed. In other words this is a way of looking at how governments could help business at the ground level rather than from above, where policy often has minimal impact on businesses. The assumption being made here is that if governments were to strengthen the small and medium-sized business sector, the backbone of all Asian free-market economies, they would be underpinning the economy as a whole and making it less vulnerable to shocks such as those produced by the Asian financial crisis.

Having established what the government might do to help, it seems sensible to set this wish list against an assessment of what would be feasible and/or desirable. There may be more scientific ways to approach these questions but the perspective of someone actually involved in running a business seems to me to be as good as any other.

So what would I like the government to do?

- Establish a funding mechanism for small businesses with less stringent security-backing requirements than those normally required by banks and at interest rates that are closer to those paid by bigger borrowers.
- Streamline the bureaucracy for regulating business. Ideally creating a one-stop shop for (in my case) food-sale licensing (we currently deal with three separate bureaucracies – in other Asian countries it is more). Things get even more tricky for those in the import/export business, partly because of the requirements of third countries and partly because practically all customs regimes are horrendous.
- Introduce fair contract legislation to prevent larger companies from imposing onerous conditions on transactions with smaller companies over matters such as rentals etc.

- Create a simple low-tax regime that is consistent.

There is always a temptation to ask for more and take a wish list into the realms of fantasy. After all, is that not what wish lists are all about? However, there are limits and the above should be seen more as a sample than a comprehensive list.

If all these items were to be implemented they would hardly provide a guarantee of increased profitability – that remains the essential task of the business operator. However, they would address problems of cost and convenience. But are these items realistic?

One item is entirely feasible and, as a result of having businesses based in Hong Kong, I can confidently describe it as a major plus. The Hong Kong SAR operates a low-cost and simple tax regime. It still requires a small army of accountants to help businesses make their tax returns, but the overall tax liability of any company can more or less be worked out on the back of an envelope without too much trouble. The same cannot be said of most other Asian countries, where taxation rules are complex and collection procedures arcane. In places like the Philippines and Thailand the government deprives itself of vast amounts of revenue because of the inefficiency and complexity of their tax regimes. Other countries, like Malaysia, keep moving the goal posts so that businesses feel insecure about the tax regime. Generally speaking taxes are low in Asia but dealing with taxation authorities occupies significant amounts of time, which, in itself, represents a cost to business.

So much for taxes. What about the nice idea of having special arrangements for loans to small and medium-sized companies who are typically strapped for both capital and credit when contemplating expansion? To my surprise I discovered that not only was there such a scheme in Hong Kong but in many of the other Asian countries. The Hong Kong scheme, the only one I seriously examined, looked pretty good on paper but in reality it is little short of a bureaucratic nightmare involving dealing with both government and banking bureaucracies because the execution of the scheme is carried out by licensed financial institutions. Not only is this scheme poorly publicised – none of my business associates had ever heard of it – but it looked far too complex for the average business to bother with. Fortunately I did not need to raise any money at the time I looked at the scheme but I rather wonder whether I would have bothered if the reverse had been the case.

There is a more basic financing problem that has emerged since the end of this crisis and is typical of post-crisis situations. In these circumstances interest rates almost always rise and inflict a heavier cost of borrowing on business. Secondly, the fear of bad debt makes bankers and other sources of finance even more conservative in their lending policies. This makes it more expensive and more difficult to borrow even for companies with good businesses. Crises make financiers more risk-averse. This means that they impose rigid lending conditions at precisely the time when a freer flow of credit is required to get business back on its feet.

This creates a problem for large businesses but is an even more serious headache for expanding small businesses because borrowers are typically more concerned about security for loans than ability to service loans out of earnings. Bigger companies tend to have more security to offer while smaller companies usually need to resort to personal guarantees by their directors, which put their homes and other personal assets at risk. Government-backed finance schemes, like that operating in Hong Kong, can help by guaranteeing loans but they will never be big enough or sufficiently bureaucracy-free to be attractive to the number of borrowers who need financing.

Some companies, often those in the hi-tech industries, solve these problems either by seeking help from venture capitalists or by floating shares on the stock market. In Asia second-tier Nasdaq-type markets are thin on the ground and venture-capital funds are not generally well developed. Outside Japan, Korea has the biggest exchange, called Kosdaq; Taiwan has a more slowly growing over-the-counter exchange; and Singapore, which was first into the fray with second-tier exchanges, has a small market called Sesdaq. Aside from these markets, which suffer from illiquidity, there is little second-tier activity. Hong Kong, for example, was still talking about launching an exchange in 1999. Thailand got around to it in June of that year with the launch of its Market for Alternative Investment, a vehicle for smaller companies. The only snag, at the time of the launch, was that not a single company had applied for a listing.

Moreover, many owners of Asian businesses are more reluctant than their Western counterparts to cede control of part of their enterprise to outside investors. This attitude is changing but the feeling persists that, if there is a choice between handing over equity and limiting expansion of businesses to the extent of a company's borrowing ability, many enterprises will go for the latter option.

It is questionable whether the government should step in at this point and offer direct funding, not least because in practice most state bureaucracies would not be the best judge of what to fund and would establish horrendously complex institutions to administer loan-giving schemes.

Yet it does seem possible for governments simply to provide incentives to banks and other lending institutions who are giving loans to businesses. Many governments already do this but it is not a common practice in Asia.

This brings us to the second item on the wish list: streamlining bureaucracy. It is an item on business wish lists practically everywhere in the world. 'Get government off our backs,' scream businessmen in a babel of languages. No one likes bureaucrats crawling over their businesses telling them what they can and cannot do. Yet as the civil authority the government really cannot adopt a totally hands-off approach. In my main line of business I can quite understand why the authorities take an interest in food hygiene to protect the health of the public. I also understand why they need to have the right to inspect new premises to ensure that safety and health standards are met. All this is quite reasonable. However it becomes less reasonable when businesses are faced with a small army of officials sent to implement these regulations. They usually demonstrate a staggering lack of initiative and almost always incline towards the side of restriction, thus covering their own backsides, even when the restrictions they impose are quite illogical and almost always expensive to implement.

Asking governments to streamline bureaucracy does not just mean changing rules: it means changing the culture of those implementing the rules. This is an infinitely more difficult task. I would therefore rate this wish as a middling to ambitious one with only slight hopes of fulfilment.

There is no hope at all of fulfilling the third wish. In truth I am not even sure how it could be done. Fair contract legislation is the dream of many smaller businesses who have an unequal relationship with larger ones; however, that relationship is derived from the law of the marketplace where sometimes the smaller companies get bigger and can then alter the terms of their relations and sometimes bigger companies get smaller with the same result. However, it is nice to dream about a magic wand being waved that would mitigate this inequality.

Broader issues

Notably absent from this wish list is any mention of government incentives for particular industries or even government direction for industrial development. In most places governments are not good at this. Although in countries like Japan and Korea, where national and social cohesion is high and traditions of state intervention deeply embedded, the state has been successful in nurturing new industries or helping existing industries become more productive. Elsewhere the world is littered with examples of the failure of government direction. In East Asia we can cite the ill-conceived Multimedia Super Corridor in Malaysia and the Taiwan government's feeble efforts at making the island an international financial centre.

The big changes in industrial development and the big reforms in companies have to come from the companies themselves. The advantage of the Asian crisis is to have propelled some companies to think seriously about this matter while others are taking some action.

More substantially, the wish list does not include items that relate to the bigger role of government in creating an environment of business growth based on a soundly performing economy.

Nor does the list include what has been shown to be an essential prerequisite for a successful business environment. I refer, of course, to the rule of law and the existence of laws that are relevant to meeting modern-day business needs. Hong Kong and Singapore have enjoyed an immense competitive advantage as business centres in Asia precisely because the rule of law is well entrenched and business contracts can be implemented without fear that the courts are not up to the task.

When the crash came there was much scrambling around to seek the recovery of bad debt. In places like Indonesia, Thailand and the Philippines, creditors were well aware that recourse to the legal system was largely futile, although litigation in the Philippines seems to be one of the country's biggest industries.

In Thailand the government is acutely aware of the shortcomings of its legal system and as a result of the crisis it was finally propelled into action over the introduction of viable bankruptcy laws, providing a proper framework for companies to go under and giving creditors a chance to recover some of the money they are owed. Even the Indonesians managed to get a new bankruptcy law on the books; however, its value was swiftly tested when the World Bank's International Finance Corp. (IFC) brought an action against Dharmala Agrifood (part of the Dharmala hotchpotch conglomerate). The action got nowhere because the court found that the debtor had defaulted only on interest payments, not on the principle sum. The new law makes it clear that bankruptcy action can be taken against debtors defaulting on interest payments; however, the courts appear to have another view.

It is only when you have experience of doing business without a legal safety net in place that the reality of its consequences hits home. That is why, for example, I have never been tempted to venture across the border to do business in mainland China. More brave souls have done so, some have made money, some have even made a great deal of money. However, most people who do business in China have a chronicle of tales about what happens when things go wrong and they are left holding contracts that are not worth the paper they are printed on. In the worst cases, and there are many, businessmen, particularly from Hong Kong, find that their Chinese partners have arranged to get them arrested as a means of settling contractual disputes.

The worst and most highly publicised case of this nature concerns James Peng, an Australian citizen, born in Hong Kong. He was abducted from a hotel in Macau in 1993, dragged back to the Chinese mainland with the co-operation of the authorities and then given a sixteen-year jail sentence for corruption at the instigation of his politically well-connected business partners. A flavour of how the rule of law was operating in this case came when Mr Peng appealed against his sentence. 'I'm innocent, I'm not guilty,' he said. Judge Xing Tong, cut him off: 'This is not the place to defend yourself,' he admonished.[10]

Understandably there are many people who are less than keen to voluntarily enter a jurisdiction in which business disputes are dealt with in this manner.

Even in China the government is turning its attention not only to improving the rule of law but to creating new laws which will regulate business life. However, the rule of law is closely tied to wider questions about political change which go way beyond the boundaries of this work.

Drawing lessons – getting results

More relevant to our current purpose is a glance at what some companies in the Asia region have been doing to draw lessons from the financial crisis and better prepare themselves for the future.

It cannot be repeated too often that real change has to come from within the companies that drive the economies of Asia. Some are perfectly solid and did not require fundamental reform, merely a strategy for surviving the downturn. For some this meant forging strategic alliances;

for others it meant streamlining; for the brave it meant investing in new products and services to provide a competitive edge at a time when others were unable to do more than carry on with what they had before the crisis broke.

Even some of the companies written off as creatures of the era killed by the crisis showed tenacity in proving their critics wrong. Take, for example, Samsung Electronics, part of the Samsung *chaebol*. In 1999 it announced a $1.2 billion investment in upgrading its line in computer memory chips. The company claims to be the world's largest maker of memory chips but realised that sheer volume and competition on price alone was unlikely to be a recipe for continuing success. Therefore it decided to go for technological innovation.

Other companies are in no position to boost investment without selling assets. Because, as we have seen, many large Asian companies mushroomed into being hotchpotch conglomerates, they have plenty to sell in order to rationalise their businesses and regain some focus. In Thailand Siam Cement used to have a perfectly good building-materials supply business but the boom years led its management into a host of other activities, which it decided to sell after the crisis when it was shackled by high levels of debt, including debts of some $1.4 billion in the noncore businesses. Selling off the noncore business provided the means to refocus on the main business and make it grow.

It was the same story in the Philippines, where the San Miguel Corp., one of the only Philippine companies to have developed a genuinely successful international brand, got carried away with property dabbling and overseas investment. The management's eye wandered so far off the ball that in 1997 it sold its controlling stake in the local Coca-Cola franchise to the Australian Coca-Cola Amatil company, in exchange for Amatil shares. The Coca-Cola franchise, alongside the San Miguel beer brand, had secured the company's position as the Philippines drinks-market leader. Now the company has decided to bring its activities back on its home base and get back to what it does best. The results have been spectacularly successful.

While private companies have no choice but to sell off assets to reduce their debt burden, state-controlled entities can theoretically call on the taxpayer to bail them out. In places like China, whole industries, including the banking industry, are technically insolvent but kept afloat because the state simply deems them to be going concerns which will be supported by the national coffers. Where economies are more mixed and state companies have been privatised, albeit with the state retaining a controlling interest, the situation is more complex. Nowhere more so than in Malaysia, which used the days of buoyant stock markets to privatise a number of state enterprises. These privatisations were intensely political and controversial, including that of Tenaga Nasional, the national electricity corporation. Like other major utilities, Tenaga had to make heavy capital investments which left it with considerable liabilities in foreign currencies at a time when demand was falling and the local currency was weakening against the currencies in which the loans were made. Its solution to this problem is ingenious. The power-generating activities, which also generate the highest levels of debt, have been hived off to another company and Tenaga laid plans to sell up to 40 per cent of each power plant to partners. This transforms Tenaga into an electricity-distribution company which can buy power supplies from competing entities. It is, in other words, a form of double privatisation, introducing a new element of competition into the electricity business that should, in turn, produce price-reduction benefits for consumers.

Even in Hong Kong, and in the property sector no less, there are signs that at least some of the leading players in the development market have learned lessons. Li Ka-shing, the head of the Cheung Kong group, declared that the party was over for the old days of very high profit margins. He said that the new game in town was volume. More property needed to be developed and, although margins would be cut, some of the loss would be made up by a higher volume of sales. This may sound unremarkable as a proposition but it is nothing less than a revolutionary statement by the market's most important player. He was simply saying that the rules have changed.

Most typically, however, companies have looked to cost savings to keep the profit-and-loss account in the black. Even more successful companies have used the recession as an opportunity to thoroughly re-examine their cost structure and make economies. Lamentably, this usually resulted in job losses rather than redeployment of employees, but the companies argued, with some justification, that corporate survival depended on rationalisation.

An interesting survey was carried out among fifty-eight senior executives across Asia in April 1999. They were asked, by Grassroots Research, a division of Dresdner RCM Global Investors, what strategies they favoured for tackling the business downturn.[11] Admittedly this is a small sample and may be influenced by answers that the executives thought were most acceptable rather than reflecting what they were actually doing. Nonetheless, restructuring and streamlining ranked only second among their strategies for coping. Ranking first were the 36 per cent who said they were looking to develop new markets; another 12 per cent were hoping to develop new products and the same percentage were seeking diversification.

In other words the overwhelming majority saw the downturn as an opportunity to develop new business. True, companies always say this is what they are doing but usually it remains in the realm of rhetoric until something forces them to act. Clearly the events of the latter part of the 1990s fell into this category.

It is still too early to say how much has really been done by Asian companies to seek new markets and develop new products. The high cost and paucity of credit for companies makes it difficult. Meanwhile, the temptation to compete more actively on price is encouraged by currency devaluations, which automatically reduce prices in export markets.

The debt conundrum

Some companies are just too overwhelmed by problems of debt rescheduling to be paying sufficient attention to the remoulding of the underlying businesses. The problem here is that the loan-giving institutions are demonstrating a singular lack of imagination in their approach. They remain obsessed by the desire not to have bad debt on the books yet are showing such inflexibility in rescheduling arrangements as to make it very hard for companies to meet repayment targets. The problem is exacerbated because the collateral against which these loans were secured has devalued, leaving the loans, in theory, dangerously exposed. The easy solution is simply to demand repayment up to the level of existing collateral values; however, this in turn may simply force the borrower into default. More generally, borrowing costs increase as credit ratings fall. Therefore, badly needed financing may not be sought because of the difficulty of servicing the debt.

It was the financial side of the equation that triggered the crisis and, as matters stand, threatens to prolong it. There is much macho talk around about letting insolvent or shaky financial institutions go under and thus face the consequences of their allegedly reckless lending. This is all well and good but it provides no clue as to how to solve the underlying debt problem, which, in current circumstances, will go away only if there are even more widespread corporate closures.

The most obvious way of extricating companies from these problems is to seek recapitalisation, which means taking in new equity partners or, as we have seen, selling off bits of the business to keep the core business in tact. We have also seen that, in general, Asian businessmen are reluctant to cede control to outsiders and see equity sales as a very last resort. Moreover, in many Asian countries bankruptcy laws are ineffective, allowing technically insolvent businesses to carry on trading instead of having to seek refinancing in the form of capital.

The M&A solution

Nevertheless, there has been an upsurge in merger and acquisition activity and all the countries of Asia which had controls on foreign ownership have significantly relaxed them. Singapore has slashed limitations on overseas ownership in a whole range of financial institutions. Thailand has gone even further and South Korea, which managed extraordinary levels of growth with minimal foreign investment, has now thrown the doors open to foreign investment.

The result, according to an UNCTAD survey,[12] was to increase cross-border mergers and acquisitions (M&As) in Asia by 28 per cent in 1998, compared with the previous year. The total sum involved was $12.5 billion, with the bulk of the activity concentrated in the crisis-hit countries of Indonesia. Korea, Malaysia, the Philippines and Thailand. However, as UNCTAD pointed out, M&As in Asia accounted for a far lower percentage of foreign direct-investment (FDI) flows than in Latin America. In Asia they accounted for 16 per cent of FDI flows, compared with 46 per cent in Latin America. In 1996, they represented only 3 per cent of Asia's FDI flows. In other words, despite the crisis and all the talk of restructuring, Asian companies remained averse to merger activity, even though signs have emerged that the resistance is weakening.

This is even true in Malaysia, where Prime Minister Mahathir's rhetoric suggested that foreigners were not welcome when he talked about being 'colonised again' by the West through the economic rather than the political door. The reality is that foreign M&A activity surged in Malaysia following the crisis, and here's the real irony: the acquisition charge was led by companies from Malaysia's former colonial power, Britain. British Telecom swooped in to acquire a third of the Binariang media and telecoms conglomerate. Blue Circle, the building-supplies company, made an even bigger acquisition of Kedah Cement, owned by the Hicom political hotchpotch conglomerate, and also bought a half-share in the Pan-Malaysian cement works, while the British Prudential insurance group brought its stake in Berjaya Prudential up to 50 per cent by acquiring another 21 per cent from the Berjaya group, yet another of Malaysia's political hotchpotch conglomerates.[13]

The infusion of foreign capital and management skills into Asian companies at a time when they have reached a level of some maturity could well alter the way these companies are run, almost certainly for the better.

This suggestion will not be well received in some circles, which share the Mahathir view about Western 'recolonisation', but the simple fact of the matter is that Western corporations have managed to obtain access to these companies only because they have been run into the ground or severely weakened under the stewardship of their current owners. Any new blood is likely to give a fresh start. If, as is the case of the major acquisitions in Asia, the new blood happens to be foreign and happens to come from generally well-run companies, so be it. If there were well-run Asian companies around with lots of spare cash no doubt they too would have supplied an infusion of new blood.

However, the number of intra-Asian M&As was very small, involving mainly companies from Taiwan and Hong Kong. Whereas the Western companies tended to look for either controlling equity stakes or a sufficiently large share of the equity to give them a substantial say in management, the Taiwanese and Hong Kong companies were often prepared to settle for minority stakes representing more of a strategic investment than a role in management. This too suggests that the Asian companies are likely to have little impact on the way their new acquisitions are run.

However, it cannot be overemphasised that M&A activity in Asia is largely peripheral. Not only are Asian owners reluctant to relinquish control of companies but companies interested in M&As have found it difficult to identify quality assets that are up for sale. When the Asia crisis broke there was a rush to the region by foreign companies hoping to pick up good assets at bargain-basement prices. What they found, by and large, was that the good assets were not for sale but that there were a number of undervalued assets of more variable quality on offer.

This is quite understandable. There was no reason for basically sound companies to put themselves on the market at bargain-basement prices, even though they may have been struggling to stay afloat as the crisis took its toll.

The strong always survive

Companies with a distinctive market presence or a strong brand or a raft of good products, or a combination of all three, may well have been languishing in the ratings bestowed on them by share markets but there was every reason for their owners to cling on to control, wait for the storm to pass and make money again.

Even in Indonesia, which appeared to have reached rock bottom, there are decent companies that fall into this category, such as Asia Pulp and Paper and Indah Kiat. Korea's *chaebols* may well, with reason, have gone out of fashion, but a company like Samsung Electronics retained a perfectly good business with lots of upside. Even the much-battered Korean Air showed that it could make something of a comeback. Some of Asia's real quality companies such as Singapore Airlines, Taiwan Semiconductor and, on a much smaller scale, the retailer Giordano in Hong Kong, suffered temporary setbacks as investors flooded out of the exit doors. However, quality has a habit of reasserting itself.

The problem is that most companies in Asia are not quality companies and the Asian crisis did very little to dislodge poor managements or change management practices. In extreme cases the crisis brought the worst companies to their knees and they went out of business but in most cases a small amount of sticking plaster was applied to cover the cracks without any fundamental repair work being undertaken. Family control of businesses remains the norm in most Asian companies. Restructuring of hotchpotch conglomerates, the biggest business enterprises in Asia, has timidly begun but is barely sufficiently widespread to have achieved the necessary results.

Therefore, as the fundamentals of good management remain weak it is reasonable to assume that the financial crisis of the late 1990s will prove to be no more than a prelude to another crisis, a continuing crisis which is eating at the foundations of Asian economies.

As George Soros said, let's all look forward to the next crisis.

9

IS THAT IT, THEN?

The end of the beginning

In 1942 British troops scored a notable victory over the German forces in North Africa. Hopes were raised that this marked the turning point in World War Two. Britain's wartime leader Winston Churchill took another view: 'This is not the end,' he cautioned. 'It is not even the beginning of the end. But it is, perhaps, the end of the beginning.'

This seems to be a sensible way of viewing the end of the Asian Miracle. Much of what was created during the boom period has not been obliterated by the financial crisis, so it is unwise to say simply that the Miracle has come to an end. Yet the foolhardy optimism that characterised some thinking at the end of the 1990s was also misguided. The boom phase of the Miracle had been brought to a sudden halt, yet some people hoped that the crash could be dismissed as an aberration. Those who cherished this hope pointed to the fact that in 1999 financial markets started turning round and economic growth was reasserting itself.

However, there are sound reasons to believe that the next phase of development in East Asia, the post-crash phase, will be more problematic than even the phase that included the crash.

The former Miracle economies are poised to face the far greater challenge of moving to a more sophisticated stage of production and service-industry provision, which will test their systems at every level.

The Asian way or the global way

Trying to understand what is happening in Asian economies and Asian businesses has been obscured by desperate attempts to ascribe special Asian characteristics to the whole process. This is why so much time was taken up by the largely fatuous debate on 'Asian Values' and another mysterious concept called 'The Asian Way of Doing Business'. All nations and all regions demonstrate distinctive characteristics; a failure to acknowledge this causes its own set of problems. But the bigger failure is a failure to learn the lessons of global history and a failure to see that trends that have emerged in one part of the globe are also taking place in another part, albeit within a different time frame.

Thus the failure to recognise that the Asian Miracle was a phase in development, much like the Industrial Revolution in Europe, was a failure to understand the so-called Miracle's place in history and to understand it as a part of a development cycle.

Asian businessmen were said to be especially entrepreneurial, for example. Yet the truth of the matter is that there is no special entrepreneurial gene pool in Asia but that Asian economies had reached a stage of development where the conditions were right for a great deal of entrepreneurial activity.

The veracity of this assertion can be seen by viewing the upsurge of entrepreneurship in the new high-technology industries in the West. Precisely because the industries are relatively new and precisely because they require quick thinking, risk-taking people to get them off the ground, they are turning out large numbers of entrepreneurs. No one seriously suggests that a special entrepreneurial gene pool is to be found in Silicon Valley in California or heading west out of London, where hi-tech industries are gathering. Yet this suggestion is made about entrepreneurs in Asia who have emerged to lead new industries, some of which, like the automotive industry, for example, are far from new in other parts of the world.

The problem, as we have seen, is that conditions in Asia now require new skills of management, which are not the same as those of entrepreneurship. This too may turn out to be a problem located at a particular stage of development. In the meantime it is worrying and doing much to undermine the strength of Asian economies.

What was new and exciting about the Asian Miracle was the speed with which it took root and the pace of economic development that turned largely agricultural societies into competitors in the world market for manufactured goods. In the process living standards were raised at a rate never seen before in history.

However, the speed of developments caused problems of their own, making it difficult for government structures and corporate management structures to catch up with the reality of the new economies. This meant that structural weaknesses were built into the new system and, as we have seen, they proved fatal.

Better government – better economies

In the aftermath of the collapse government structures started improving at a faster pace than corporate structures. Contrary to the assumption that economic development could not occur when representative government was allowed to flourish, the crisis demonstrated that economic solutions could best be obtained from elected governments who also carried the legitimacy required to demand sacrifices from their electors.

Rotten, nondemocratic governments were kicked out of office and replaced by reform-minded regimes which knew that they would survive only if they did something to improve the structure. That is why the governments of Thailand and Korea, for example, were compelled to tackle basic problems such as the lack of adequate bankruptcy laws, restrictive competition policies and the poor organisation of financial institutions. Even the ill-fated Habibie regime, which succeeded the Suharto dictatorship in Indonesia, tried to make 'reformasi', the slogan of the streets, its own.

Good companies survive better than their owners

The guiding hand of reform was less evident in the corporate sector. Not least because the financial markets, the very markets that triggered the crisis, quickly regained strength and gave the impression of revived prosperity leading to the dangerous assumption that corporate reform was not really necessary.

However, there is a simple lesson of modern-day corporate history. It is so simple that repeating it yet again seems almost facile. The lesson is that well-run companies do not go bust and that companies that produce good-quality, competitive products and services will always find a market for their business. Good companies, with sound management structures, can even survive the worst financial crises and the excesses of their owners when they go off the rails.

A vivid example of this comes from Australia, where the Fairfax publishing group looked as though it would be destroyed by the antics of Warwick Fairfax, the scion of the family that created the company. Armed with business-administration qualifications gained in America, he sped back to Australia after his father died and cooked up an ambitious plan to seize back control of the listed company and privatise it with proceeds raised through American junk bonds. When the 1987 market crash came, the plan, which was already faltering, was blown apart. Young Warwick eventually shuttled back to the United States leaving behind a company that many parties were trying to control but nonetheless had such a good business and sufficiently good line management to ensure that it survived these boardroom shenanigans and continued making good money.

The Japanese economy has lost momentum for more than a decade yet Japan's best companies retain world leadership in the automotive and electronic-goods industries. Corporations such as Honda, Sony and Toyota have not had an easy time but they own some of the world's most valuable brands and remain formidable competitors in global markets. Even the Nissan Motor Corp., which has had more financial trouble than its local competitors, has not only survived but bitten the hard-to-digest bullet of inviting French managers from Renault to come in and help fix its problems.

The big problem in Asia is that so few companies are making efforts to fix problems. They are preoccupied with reshuffling their assets, selling some of them off and buying in others at low prices. The effort required to turn these assets into world-class companies is simply too much for the families who own some of Asia's biggest corporations. Their focus remains firmly fixed on control of their organisations rather than on measures to make them better companies.

Small can be beautiful

While the big corporations flounder, the small and medium enterprises, which are the real backbone of Asian business, continue to flourish. They do so on the basis of extraordinarily hard work, a sharp eye for costs and by developing market niches that are best filled by smaller, more nimble companies. Family ownership and control, as opposed to professional management, is less of a problem for smaller companies – indeed it is generally a benefit, because people who have a stake in a business are far more likely to be diligent in its management than those who merely receive a salary.

However, the limitations are there for all to see. Because most of these smaller businesses rarely engage in strategic planning and eschew more professional management practices, they have few prospects of becoming really large organisations. Many are content to be smaller-sized enterprises and do a perfectly good job within this context.

As we have seen, however, they are not immune from the consequences of the financial crisis, especially when it comes to obtaining credit. The supply of credit goes in cycles and they have become accustomed to weathering the difficult parts of the cycle.

Although rarely discussed when Asian management structures come under review, it is the small and medium-sized enterprises that will provide the real engine for renewed economic growth, while the larger companies sow the seeds for a new crisis as they refuse to change their ways.

Surviving, merging, doing what it takes

Of course some of the bigger companies are changing and introducing structural reforms because the crisis gave them a glimpse of a bleak future and forced them to rethink their way of doing business.

Other companies were forced into the arms of new owners or new partners, mainly from overseas. These overseas investors were hardly buying into these companies to ensure a continuation of business as usual.

Traditionally foreign merger and acquisition activity in Asia has been at a very low level but, as we have seen, there was a surge of activity in 1998,[1] which yielded deals worth $12.5 billion, an increase of 28 per cent over the previous year but a shadow of the $32.6 billion worth of deals transacted in the first months of 1999, according to estimates from Securities Data.[2]

Like it or not the crisis opened the door to foreign corporate takeovers, which, as sure as night follows day, means the importation of Western management practices. However, as has been argued earlier, what it really means is the implementation of global management practices, which are, because of the current stage of development, more prevalent in the West although by no means entirely derived from Western countries. Only those who feel that so-called 'Asian management styles' are inadequate need worry about this development. The really smart companies that have invested in Asian takeovers will learn from the companies they have absorbed while at the same time bringing in their own expertise. This will help give new life to global management practices and make the line between Eastern and Western ways of doing things more blurred.

My experience of managers in this region, as opposed to company owners, is that they would welcome a more professional style of management with open arms and are not greatly bothered whether it is labelled Western or Eastern.

While more overseas companies are entering Asian markets via the merger-and-acquisition route, the level of direct investment from companies who have started their own businesses in Asia remained remarkably stable.

UNCTAD's annual survey of fixed direct investment (FDI) showed a decline of only 7 per cent for East, South and Southeast Asia between 1997 and 1998.[3] Indeed had it not been for a sharp bout of disinvestment from Indonesia, the flows would have been about the same for these two years. At a level of $78 billion, the FDI flow to Asia in 1998 was well above the annual average level of $44 billion for 1991–5.

Companies are not investing in these Asian countries as a matter of charity. They have made a hard-headed appraisal of the prospects for profitability and acted accordingly. As far as direct investors are concerned the financial crisis was something of a sideshow with as much upside as downside. The upside for exporters was a lower cost base as currencies devalued. The downside for foreign companies serving Asian domestic markets was the big drop in local demand. However, most foreign investors were using Asia as a base for export markets.

The expanding presence of international companies, given most force in the manufacturing sector by Japanese companies, has had the general effect of raising standards. Even where technology has not been transferred, in the way that governments hoped it would be, the incoming companies have set new benchmarks, which are quickly followed by local companies.

The learning-and-development process will propel some companies into world-standard levels of production. We have seen this already happening in the electronics sector in Taiwan, in the quality of some Asian airlines, including in small countries like Brunei. In Korea we have seen companies developing domestic market brands that have global impact.

Where corporate standards have been raised it has almost always been as a result of some form of collaboration with more advanced overseas companies. It is a great mystery why this perfectly natural process has become a subject of value judgement by some nationalistically sensitive observers.

Moving on

East Asia, outside Japan and China, is now poised to move to the next stage of economic development, leaving behind basic assembly manufacturing, elementary service provision and all the other characteristics of so-called emerging economies. The region may still be held back by the inadequacies of corporate structures in Asian companies, which in turn make them vulnerable to the turbulence of financial crises.

However, as someone who has lived and worked in the parts of Asia that were once regarded as the home of the Asian Miracle, I am cautiously confident that these inadequacies will be overcome. The overwhelming logic of market forces will simply force companies to change and fortunately Asia contains more than enough intelligent, hard-working and adaptable people to make it happen. As ever, the key to success lies in the quality of human beings.

As I sit in my office finishing off the writing of this book I am perpetually distracted by the demands of my business. There are so many small things to be done, accounts to be scrutinised, plans to be made, staff matters to deal with and so on. Of course it is irritating but it is also a salutary reminder that out there in the real world, where global issues float into the ether and grand strategies pass most people by, the business world is the composite product of vast amounts of minutiae which keep companies afloat.

Naturally the most careful attention to detail cannot prevent companies being pushed off course by events entirely beyond their control. If, for example, your costs of borrowing are suddenly raised or a typhoon comes and destroys your premises, there is little you can do but go back to the drawing board.

Yet most events are predictable, and much of what is unexpected *should* come within the category. So, for example, if a recession destroys one kind of market, the best kind of businesses will search for another more suitable market to meet the new conditions.

The ability to respond to events really means that you have built an organisation that is intrinsically strong. It is like a motor car, basically designed to glide down roads but occasionally called upon to swerve, to brake suddenly or get out of a skid. If the car cannot do these things, it matters little how good it is when road conditions are 'normal'. Companies and other organisations are like that: if they are designed to cope with only the good times they will quickly fade when the bad times come. Designing them for the long-term haul is a mundane process, basically involving a great deal of slog.

If you merely write about these things it is easy to overlook the slog, which is far from glamorous, or interesting. If you are involved in the slogging, it is imprinted on the mind.

That is why I am suspicious of grand visions for the future. I am suspicious about plans to control global capital flows, suspicious about all this talk of a new global financial architecture and above all suspicious of political leaders who blame all their woes on external forces.

Yet no country and few companies are immune from global pressures which swoop down and affect economies and businesses. If the Mexican peso crisis of a previous decade did not prove it, the Asian financial crisis of the 1990s made the reality of global financial contagion an established fact. Everyone loves open markets and the free flow of capital across borders while they are making money. When there is no more money to be made and losses occur the same people blithely turn around, wag their fingers and pontificate on the dangers of unrestricted flows of capital.

The simple fact of the matter is that the globalisation of capital is here to stay – it is pointless to argue about this. Given this reality it is inevitable that some of the players in the global market will be stronger than others and that they will have more influence than the smaller players. My goodness! This is all very basic, is it not? Why then are so many people, who are otherwise quite intelligent, spending so much time trying to alter unalterable realities.

How can the mighty be made weak in a global financial system? Is it desirable for this to happen? How can you stop fund managers from displaying herdlike characteristics when markets move? The answers are that you cannot, it is not, and you have to be joking! This leaves the grand global visionaries with a problem. There is no viable international mechanism for controlling global capital flows. There may be some means of monitoring them and there may be ways of injecting greater transparency into the whole business but that is about as much as can be done.

Real control can be exercised only in very blunt ways. The Malaysian example could be followed, which involves taking the local currency out of international markets and slamming the door down on free flows of portfolio investments. The North Korean example might be more satisfactory for purists as it involves never opening the door in the first place. Of course, what you get as a result is a North Korean economy. I see no line of volunteers preparing to join it. Reality needs to be faced, when it comes to controlling global capital flows. Half-measures will not work. It is like a semi-pregnancy, a phenomenon yet to be witnessed.

There is no point bleating about the consequences of sudden shifts in funds, unless you are serious about challenging the basis of the global capitalist system. There is even less to be said for moaning about the terrible things investors are doing to economies once they decide to pitch their tents elsewhere.

The only sensible response to the inevitable cycles of investor senti-ment, followed by big fund movements, is to strengthen domestic institutions and build better companies. Good banks, good companies and the like are quite likely to be shaken by financial turmoil but they will survive. It is the banks loaded up with dubious loan books who go under. It is companies who have borrowed to the hilt for speculative purposes who get caught in the maelstrom and it is governments who are fundamentally corrupt and unaccountable who cannot cope with the consequences of financial crisis because they have built a disease into the system that quickly gets to work once the system comes under strain.

Big events, like the Asian financial crisis, punctuate the lives of everyone but they do not fundamentally change them. Survivors are people who have learned to cope with crisis and benefit from it.

The Chinese characters that spell crisis contain the meaning of danger *and* opportunity. It has become something of a cliché to point this out, but this is the great value of Chinese ideographs, which express whole concepts in a couple of characters.

The people who can produce opportunity out of danger will flourish. Fortunately there are many of them in Asia. So, in the wake of the Asian crisis when the question was asked, 'Is that it, then?', the answer is obvious.

NOTES

Preface

1. Report by the Deutsche Presse-Agentur, Bangkok, 29 July 1999.

Introduction

1. *South China Morning Post*, 16 November 1997, Hong Kong.
2. Korean Dynasty: Hyundai and Chung Ju Yung by Donald Kirk, *Asia 2000*, Hong Kong, 1994.
3. Agence France Presse, 28 June 1998.
4. World Bank, 'East Asia: The Road to Recovery', September 1998, New York.
5. OUP for World Bank, 'Private Capital Flows to Developing Countries', April 1997.
6. Jeffrey Sachs, speech at Credit Suisse First Boston Asian Investment Conference, 24 March 1999, Hong Kong.
7. ILO, Bangkok, 'The Social Impact of the Asian Financial Crisis', April 1998.
8. ILO, World Unemployment Report 1998–9, September 1998, Geneva.
9. Paul Krugman, 'What Happened to Asia?', a paper to be found on his website: web.mit.edu/krugman/www, 1998.
10. Dr Sachs's views are stated in a number of places, perhaps most succinctly in 'The Onset of the East Asian Financial Crisis', a paper published by the Harvard Institute for International Development, March 1998.
11. Mahathir Mohamad, 'Asian Economies: Challenges and Opportunities', speech made at the annual seminar of the World Bank, Hong Kong, 20 September 1997.
12. Joseph Yam, 'Causes of and Solutions to Financial Turmoil in the Asian Region', speech made in Manila, 5 January 1999.
13. Stephen Brown, William Goetzmann and James Park, 'Hedge Funds and the Asian Currency Crisis of 1997', *SSRN Journal*, 6 May 1998.

14. Henry Kissinger, 'The IMF's Remedies Are Doing More Harm Than Good', *International Herald Tribune*, 5 October 1998, Paris.
15. Ravi Arvind Palat, *Miracles of the Day Before? The Great Asian Meltdown and the Changing World Economy*, abstract from a forthcoming book.
16. Merton Miller, speech given in Hong Kong, 1998.
17. George Soros, speech given at the World Bank conference, Hong Kong, 21 September 1997.
18. *South China Morning Post*, 22 December 1997, Hong Kong.
19. Peter Bernstein, *Against the Gods*, John Wiley, 1996, New York, pp. 294–5.
20. Palat, op. cit.

1 What They Said Before

1. John Phelan in Jim Mann, *Beijing Jeep*, Simon & Schuster, 1989, New York, p. 247.
2. Ibid., p. 284.
3. Reuters, 26.12.96.
4. William Overholt, *China: The Next Economic Superpower*, Weidenfeld & Nicolson, 1993, London, p. 91.
5. Ibid., p. 40.
6. Ibid., p. 42.
7. Ibid., p. 58.
8. Jim Rohwer, *Asia Rising*, Simon & Schuster, 1995, New York, p. 324.
9. Ibid., p. 325.
10. Ibid., p. 329.
11. IMF, 'World Economic Outlook', May 1997, Washington.
12. Muhathir Mohamad in Jon Woronoff, *Asia's 'Miracle' Economies*, M.E. Sharpe Inc., 1992, New York.
13. *The Economist*, 'Asia's Precarious Miracle', 1 March 1997, London.
14. Jonathan Marshall, 'No More Prospects of Easy Fortunes', *San Francisco Chronicle*, 24 September 1996.
15. John Naisbitt, *Megatrends Asia*, Simon & Schuster, 1996, New York, p. 10.
16. Ibid. p. 11.
17. Ibid. p. 230.
18. Rohwer, op. cit., p. 345.
19. Rohwer, op. cit., p. 345–6.
20. Hans Dieter Evers, 'The Bureaucratisation of South East Asia', in *Comparative Studies in Society and History*, No. 29.
21. World Bank, 'The East Asian Economic Miracle', Research Report, New York, April 1996, p. 6.
22. Ibid., p. 7.

23. Michael Backman, *Asian Eclipse*, John Wiley, 1999, Singapore (see Chapter 14 for a full account of this 'kleptocracy').

24. Frank Tipton, *The Rise of Asia*, University of Hawai'i Press, Honolulu, 1998.

25. Peter Mandelson, 'Lessons for Labour from Asia', *The Times*, 22 April 1996, London.

26. World Bank, 'The East Asian Economic Miracle', Research Report, New York, April 1996, p. 29.

27. World Bank, 'Private Capital Flows to Developing Countries', Research Report, Washington, 1997, p. 306.

28. Stock Exchange Fact Book 1995, SEHK, Hong Kong, p. 66

29. James Montier, quoted by Justin Fox, 'The Great Emerging Markets Rip Off', *Fortune*, New York, 11 May 1998.

30. Morgan Stanley Dean Witter, 'The Macro Navigator', Multi-Asset Research, New York, 3 June 1999 p. 3.

31. *South China Morning Post*, 'Foreign funds leave Asia', Hong Kong, 5 March 1998.

32. Quoted in Bernstein, op. cit. p. 178.

33. Jake Lloyd-Smith, 'Worst over for region but way up still bumpy', *South China Morning Post*, Hong Kong, 1 April 1998.

34. This was the conclusion of a survey conducted for the World Bank by Daniel Kaufman, Gil Mehrez and Sergio Schmukler, called 'The East Asia Crisis: Was It Expected?', World Bank, 1998.

35. Edward Luce, 'Credit Agency Accepts Criticisms Over Asia', *Financial Times*, London, 14 January 1998.

36. Figures in this section were supplied from various parts of 'East Asia: The Road to Recovery', World Bank, Washington D.C. September 1998, particularly Chapters 1 and 4.

2 Was It All a Mirage?

1. All the following figures are taken from *Preparing for the Twenty-First Century* by Paul Kennedy, HarperCollins, London, 1993, Chapter 10.

2. *Asiaweek*, 'Trends That Shaped the New Asia', Hong Kong, 15 December 1995.

3. World Bank 'World Development Indicators', Washington, 1997, pp. 116–17.

4. *Asiaweek*, Hong Kong, 15 December 1995.

5. Ibid.

6. Chris Patten, *East and West*, Macmillan, London, 1998, p. 130.

7. World Bank, 'The East Asian Economic Miracle', Research Report, New York, April 1996, pp. 194–6.

8. These examples are to be found in ibid., Chapter 5.

9. Ibid., p. 43.

10. Kennedy, op. cit. p. 340.

11. Morgan Stanley Dean Witter, 'The Asian Edge', Research Report, May 1998, p. 25.
12. Eiichi Matsumoto, 'Japanese Investment: Capital Flows and Priorities', speech to Asia Society Conference, Bali, 4 March 1991.
13. Morgan Stanley Dean Witter, 'The Asian Edge', Research Report, May 1998, p. 10.
14. By far the best book on this subject is Lynn Pann's *Sons of the Yellow Emperor*, Martin Secker & Warburg, London, 1990.
15. Naisbitt, op. cit. p. 19.
16. Naisbitt, op. cit. p. 20, quoting Bustanil Ariffin, a former Indonesian minister whose estimate may be coloured by the particularly high degree of Chinese economic influence in his own country.
17. Deng Xiaoping, *Selected Works of Deng Xiaoping*, Vol. III, Foreign Languages Press, Peking, 1994, p. 97.
18. All figures come from Table 5.3 in 'World Development Indicators 1997', World Bank, Washington.
19. World Bank, 'Choices for Efficient Private Provision of Infrastructure in East Asia', Washington, 1997, pp. 13–15.

3 Asian Values and Confusion about Confucius

1. Anwar Ibrahim, address to the School of Advanced International Studies, John Hopkins University, Washington, DC, 10 October 1995.
2. Fareed Zakaria, 'Culture is Destiny – A Conversation with Lee Kuan Yew', *Foreign Affairs*, New York, March/April 1994.
3. Naisbitt, op. cit., p. 53.
4. Anwar, op. cit.
5. Kishore Mahbubani, 'The Pacific Way', *Foreign Affairs*, New York, January/February 1995.
6. Zakaria, op. cit.
7. *South China Morning Post*, 'Holbrooke Rejects Asian Values', Hong Kong, 28 February 1998.
8. Zakaria, op. cit.
9. Anwar, op. cit.
10. Anwar, op. cit.
11. *Singapore Bulletin*, 'Why we need a National Ideology', Singapore, February 1989.
12. Of the very many books on Confucian thought that fill the shelves of Asian libraries, the one I found most helpful and concise is the slightly old-fashioned work edited by Lin Yutang, called *The Wisdom of Confucius*, The Modern Library, New York, 1966. However, I still failed to understand much

of the argument and was put on the right track by Chad Hansen (see Preface).

13. Ibid., p. 234.

14. Ibid., p. 190.

15. Anwar, op. cit.

16. Donald Wilhelm, *Emerging Indonesia*, Quiller Press, London, 1985, p. 109.

17. Ibid., p. 114.

18. *Mirror*, 'Sharing Singaporean Values', Singapore, 15 March 1991.

19. Tung Chee-hwa, speech to joint chambers of commerce luncheon, Hong Kong, 17 December 1996.

20. Kim Dae Jung, 'Is Culture Destiny?', 'Foreign Affairs', New York, November/December 1994.

21. Ibid.

22. Frank Tipton, *The Rise of Asia*, University of Hawai'i Press, Honolulu, 1998, pp. 110–11.

4 Asian Corporate Myths

1. Morgan Stanley Dean Witter, 'The Asian Edge', Equity Research, May 1998, p. 1.

2. Wang, Jiann-Chyuan, and Tsai, Kuen-Hung, 'The impact of research and development promotion schemes in the Taiwanese electronic component industry', *R&D Management*, UK, April 1998.

3. Tim Studt and Jules Duga, 'Strong US Economy Drives Continued R&D Growth', *R&D*, 1 January 1999, USA.

4. *Business Times*, 'R and D spending still way too low', Kuala Lumpur, 27 October 1998.

5. Alex Lo, 'Steps on hi-tech route', *Sunday Morning Post*, Hong Kong, 14 March 1999.

6. Raju Chellam, 'S'pore attracted $1.1b fresh R&D investments last year', *Business Times*, Singapore, 14 April 1998.

7. Diane Coyle, 'UK research spending dips to lowest recorded', the *Independent*, London, 20 March 1999.

8. John Vinocur, 'Asians are seeking new competitiveness', *International Herald Tribune*, Paris, 13 April 1999.

9. Vladimir Lopez-Bassols, 'How R&D is changing; research and development', *OECD Observer*, Paris, 1 August 1998.

10. *Reader's Digest* 'Asia's Super Brands Survey', *Adweek Asia*, Hong Kong, 7 May 1999.

11. Peter Tasker, *Inside Japan*, Sidgwick & Jackson, London, 1987, p. 248.

12. Ibid., p. 54.

13. William J. Baumol, 'Productivity Growth, Convergence and Welfare: What the Long-Run Data Show', *American Economic Review*, December 1986.

14. Malcolm Dowling and Peter Summers, 'Total factor productivity and economic growth – issues for Asia', *Economic Record*, Economic Society of Australia, June 1998.

15. World Bank, 'The East Asian Economic Miracle', Research Report, New York, April 1996, p. 48.

16. Morgan Stanley Dean Witter, 'The Competitive Edge 1999', Equity Research, New York, 8 February 1999.

17. *Asia Inc*, 'Aiming High', Hong Kong, June 1997.

18. Andrew Chetham, 'Sunday Founder Sizes Up Mobile Market Openings', *South China Morning Post*, Hong Kong, 8 February 1999.

19. For fuller details of how Hong Kong businessmen set about acquiring political insurance see Chapter 9 of *Hong Kong: China's New Colony* by Stephen Vines, Aurum Press, London, 1998.

20. Michael Backman, *Asian Eclipse*, John Wiley, Singapore, 1999, p. 265.

21. *South East Asia, The Economist* Business Traveller's Guides, Prentice Hall Press, New York, 1988, p. 296.

22. Min Chen, *Asian Management Systems*, by Routledge, London, 1995, p. 54.

23. Allen Cheng and William Mellor, 'Saying No to Yes Men', *Asia Inc*, Hong Kong, February 1999.

24. Stijn Claesssens, Simeon Djankov and Larry Lang, 'Who Controls East Asian Corporations?', World Bank Research Paper No. 2054, Washington, February 1999.

25. Lee Hsien Loong, 'Strategies for Recovery: Building Real Capabilities in the Economy', speech given at FEER conference, Hong Kong, 16 June 1999.

26. Agence France Presse, report of ASEAN business, 16 December 1997.

27. E.F. Schumacher, *'Small is Beautiful'*, Harper & Row, New York, 1989, p. 259.

28. Ibid., p. 267.

29. John A. Quelch and Helen Bloom, 'The Return of the Country Manager', *McKinsey Quarterly*, 1996, No. 2, New York.

5 *Other People's Money*

1. Catherine Roc, 'Emerging Asian equity market development', in *'The Changing Capital Markets of East Asia'*, ed. Ky Cao, Routledge, London, 1995, p. 67.

2. Ibid., p. 66

3. World Bank, 'The Emerging Asian Bond Market', Washington, June 1995, Table 1.3.

4. Ibid., p. 75.

5. Ibid., Table 1.4.

6. Finance Asia Research and Thomson Business Intelligence, 'Bank loans favoured way to raise funds', report on a survey, *South China Morning Post*, Hong Kong, 4 March 1999.

7. See pp. 71–3 and tables on pp. 110–20 in Roc, op. cit., for supporting figures.

8. Jim Wolfensohn, 'A battle for corporate honesty', in 'The World in 1999', *The Economist*, London, 1998.

9. Ibid.

10. Cheung Kong Infrastructure Holdings Placing and New Issue document, Hong Kong, 4 July 1996.

11. Lai Fung Holdings Placing and New Issue document, Hong Kong, 18 November 1996.

12. Shougang Concord International Enterprises Co. Ltd, Proposed Very Substantial Acquisition and Connected Transactions and Proposed Rights Issue document, Hong Kong, 5 June 1993.

13. UNCTAD, press release, 27 April 1999, Geneva.

14. Andrew Chetham, 'SCMP sets aside $256m for share falls', *South China Morning Post*, Hong Kong, 12 September 1998.

15. Chinese Estates Holdings – Final Results, Hong Kong, 29 April 1999.

16. Walter Woon, 'Let buyer beware', *Business Times*, Singapore, 15 July 1992.

17. David Ibison, 'Vote ends fight for control at Sing Tao', *South China Morning Post*, Hong Kong, 30 April 1999.

18. Major and Connected Transaction and Conditional Partial Cash Offer, documents issued on behalf of Dickson Concepts (International) Ltd, Hong Kong, 7 May 1999.

19. Reuters, Singapore, 3 May 1999.

20. *Straits Times*, Singapore, 2 July 1999, articles on pp. 74 and 76.

21. Agence France Presse, Kuala Lumpur, 5 May 1999.

22. Stephen Seawright, 'Herd mentality blunts analyst's edge', *South China Morning Post*, Hong Kong, 20 May 1999.

23. Jake van der Kamp, 'Gitic creditors have only themselves to blame', *South China Morning Post*, Hong Kong, 23 April 1999.

24. Lana Wong, 'Deloitte defends Gaungnan audit withdrawal', *South China Morning Post*, Hong Kong, 8 May 1999.

25. Michael Backman, *Asian Eclipse*, John Wiley, Singapore, 1999, pp. 45–6.

26. Stock Exchange of Hong Kong, Press release, 10 May 1999.

27. Denise Tang, 'SFC takes deal advisers to task on rights abuses', *South China Morning Post*, Hong Kong, 6 August 1998.

28. Biggart and Gary G. Hamilton, Marco Orru, Nicole Woolsley, 'Organizational Isomorphism in East Asia', in *The Economic Organization of Capitalism in East Asia*, Sage Publications, California, 1997, p. 166.

29. A good outline of these activities is contained in 'NGO activists fight to protect rights of minority shareholders', Yoo Cheong-mo, the *Korea Herald*, Seoul, 19 March 1999.

30. *Sunday Morning Post*, 'Mobius fuels flames of corporate governance debate', Hong Kong, 23 May 1999.

31. Catherine Ong, 'Call for minimal corporate governance is misguided, Dr Hu', *Business Times*, Singapore, 26 July 1997.

32. Wolfensohn, op. cit.

33. Asian Development Bank Annual Report, Manila, April 1999.

6 *Greed is Good, Corruption's OK . . . Let's Make Money*

1. Nick Leeson, *Rogue Trader*, Little Brown, New York, 1996, p. 33.

2. Samuel Huntington, 'The Challenge to Change: Modernisation Development and Politics', *Comparative Politics*, New York, March 1971.

3. Sunanda K. Datta-Ray, 'Only clear laws can stem the tide', *Straits Times*, Singapore, 1 March 1998.

4. Ibid.

5. In Victor Mallet, *The Trouble with Tigers*, HarperCollins, London, 1999, pp. 38–9.

6. In Wei Shang-jin, 'How Taxing is Corruption on International Investors?' National Bureau of Economic Research Working Paper, Cambridge, MA, May 1997.

7. *Business World*, 'Graft won't cause halt to World Bank Asian loans', Manila, 17 September 1997.

8. World Bank, 'East Asia: The Road to Recovery', Washington, September 1998, p. 92.

9. Also quoted in Mallet, op. cit. p. 39.

10. Anwar Ibrahim, 'A Wave of Creative Destruction is Sweeping Asia', *International Herald Tribune*, Paris, 2 June 1998.

11. Robin Theobold, *Corruption, Development and Underdevelopment*, Duke University Press, Durham, NC 1990, p. 125.

12. Ibid. p. 126.

13. United Nations Development Programme (UNDP), 'Corruption & Integrity Improvement Initiatives in Developing Countries', New York, 1998, p. 69.

14. Asian Development Bank Annual Report, April 1999, Manila.

15. UNDP, op. cit. pp. 69–70.

16. Wei, op. cit.

17. Wei Shang-jin, 'Why is Corruption So Much More Taxing Than Tax? Arbitrariness Kills', National Bureau of Economic Research Working Paper, Cambridge MA, November 1997.

18. Leeson, op. cit., p. 60.

19. *Time*, 'Suharto Inc', New York, 14 May 1999.

20. John McBeth, 'A matter of confidence', *Far East Economic Review*, Hong Kong, 18 May 1995.

21. Information for this description of Bimantara is largely drawn from 'Things Fall Apart' by Dan Murphy, *Far East Economic Review*, Hong Kong, 13 May 1999.

22. San Hun Choe, 'Anti-piracy drive starts at backyard', *Hong Kong Standard*, Hong Kong, 26 May, 1999.

23. John Mulcahy, 'Questions unanswered over Peregrine crash', *South China Morning Post*, Hong Kong, 12 January 1999.

24. Gren Manuel, 'Tose: strongman who went for broke', *South China Morning Post*, Hong Kong, 10 January 1998.

25. Mulcahy, op. cit.

26. For a useful overview of this debate see *Corruption, Capitalism and Greed* by John Girling, Routledge, London, 1997.

27. William Barnes, 'Public underpins Thailand's battle against corruption', *South China Morning Post*, Hong Kong, 5 November 1998.

28. Ibid.

7 Hallo – Anyone Awake There?

1. Nicholas Kristof and David Sanger, 'How US Wooed Asia To Let Cash Flow In', *New York Times*, New York, 16 February 1999.

2. Ibid.

3. Karl Marx, *Marx and Engels – Selected Correspondence*, Lawrence & Wishart, London, 1943, p. 358.

4. Mahathir bin Mohamad, 'Asian Economies: Challenges and Opportunities', speech at the annual seminar of the World Bank, Hong Kong, 20 September 1997.

5. George Soros, 'Towards a Global Open Society', speech at the annual seminar of the World Bank, Hong Kong, 21 September 1997.

6. Donald Tsang, 'Globalisation, capital flows and free markets: lessons from Hong Kong', speech at Harvard University, 14 October 1998.

7. See Brendan Brown, *The Flight of International Capital – a Contemporary History*, Croom Helm, Kent, 1987, for details of this correlation.

8. *Hong Kong Standard*, 'Asean appeal for global rescue', Hong Kong, 16 December 1997.

9. Sheel Kohl, 'Chief economist admits mistakes', *South China Morning Post*, Hong Kong, 27 November 1998.

10. David Sanger, 'World Bank Admits Failings in Indonesia's Collapse', *International Herald Tribune*, Paris, 12 March 1999.

11. Milton Friedman, 'Friedman cites IMF as past its use-by date', article reprinted from *The Times* of London in *South China Morning Post*, Hong Kong, 13 October 1998.

12. Ibid.

13. Henry Kissinger, 'The IMF's Remedies Are Doing More Harm Than Good', *International Herald Tribune*, 5 October 1998.

14. Agence France Presse, Tokyo, 24 January 1999.

15. IMF/World Bank, 'Fifty Years After Bretton Woods – The Future of the IMF and World Bank', Washington, 1995.

16. Paul Volker in ibid., p. 260.

17. *Hong Kong Standard*, 'Strategy on Indonesia backfired: IMF report', Hong Kong, 15 January 1998.

18. *Hong Kong Standard*, 'IMF erred in judgement over Asian turmoil', Hong Kong, 20 January 1999.

19. Hubert Neiss, 'In Defense of the IMF's Emergency Role in East Asia', *International Herald Tribune*, Paris, 9 October 1998.

20. David Roche, 'Financial crisis turns to tragedy of ineptitude', *South China Morning Post*, Hong Kong, 3 September 1998.

21. Brian Mertens, 'Shuffling forward', *Asian Business*, Hong Kong, April 1999.

22. Stephen Vines, 'Lassitude rules as economy sinks', *Independent*, London, 12 December 1997.

23. A fuller account of the August market intervention is contained in an article I wrote for the *Independent on Sunday*, London, 'The day Hong Kong panicked', 7 February 1999. The account that appears here is drawn from this article.

24. David DeRosa, 'HKMA ban seen as a subtle form of capital control', a reprint from *Bloomberg News* in *Sunday Morning Post*, Hong Kong, 16 May 1999.

25. Political & Economic Risk Consultancy Ltd, 'Asian Intelligence', Hong Kong, 7 April 1999.

26. Agence France Presse, Seoul, 28 June 1999.

27. Stephen Vines, 'Why Taiwan has weathered Asia's financial storm', *Independent*, London, 11 July 1998.

28. Morgan Stanley Dean Witter, 'Focusing on Restructuring', Asia/Pacific Research, Hong Kong, 9 June 1999.

29. Laura Tyson, 'Firm rein on forex proves its worth', *Financial Times*, London, 12 October 1998.

30. *Barclays Asian Monthly*, 'Out of Trouble or Asset Bubble?', June 1999, p. 29.

8 Preparing for the Next Crisis

1. Sheel Kohl, 'Asian storm passes as nations rebuild, says IMF chief', *South China Morning Post*, Hong Kong, 24 September 1998.
2. Lee Hsien Loong, 'Strategies for Recovery: Building Real Capabilities in the Economy', speech at FEER conference, Hong Kong, 16 June 1999.
3. Lawrence Summers, address to conference: 'Repairing and Rebuilding Emerging Market Financial Systems', 9 September, 1998 from US Treasury Home page, www.ustres.gov/treasury/browse.
4. Michel Camdessus, 'Looking Beyond Today's Financial Crisis – Moving forward with international financial reform', speech to the Foreign Policy Association, New York, February 24 1999.
5. Michael Mussa speaking at an IMF Economic Forum entitled 'Capital Account Liberalisation: What's the Best Stance?', 2 October 1998; details on IMF web page.
6. Paul Krugman, 'Curfews on capital flight: what are options?', a paper to be found on his website: web.mit.edu/krugman/www, 1999.
7. World Bank, table 2.3, 'Balance of payments of East Asia Crisis-5, 1996–98', Global Development Finance, Washington, April 1999.
8. *Toronto Star*, 'Learning to live with global volatility', Toronto, 6 February, 1999.
9. Communiqué of G-7 Finance Ministers and Central Bank Governors, 20 February 1999, Petersberg Bonn, from US Treasury Home page, www.ustres.gov/treasury/browse.
10. Stephen Hutcheon, 'Australians to continue Peng fight', *South China Morning Post*, Hong Kong, 29 November 1995.
11. *Asian Wall Street Journal*, 'Executives Take the Offensive in Asia', Hong Kong, 27 April 1999.
12. UNCTAD, 'Foreign direct investment into developing Asia has weathered the storm', press release, Geneva, 27 April 1999.
13. Murray Hiebert, 'Eyes Wide Open,' *Far East Economic Review*, Hong Kong, 13 May 1999.

9 Is That It, then?

1. UNCTAD, 'Foreign direct investment into developing Asia has weathered the storm', press release, Geneva, 27 April 1999.
2. Rodney Diola, 'Asia explodes with M&A deals', *Hong Kong Standard*, Hong Kong, 6 July 1999.
3. UNCTAD, op. cit.

INDEX

investment capital 130–2

Jack Chia-MPH 143
Japan
blamed for 1997 crisis 14
bubble investment 15
domestic market 30
investment in Southeast Asia 60–1
Japanese management style 119–20
patents 100
R&D 95–6, 99–100
response to crisis 195–6, 255
shares ownership 151
junk bonds 184

Kim Dae Jung 86, 87, 220–1
Kishore Mahubabani 75
Kissinger, Henry 13, 199
Krugman, Paul 10, 59, 233
Kuala Lumpur, Petronas Towers 47–8
Kuok, Robert 139
Kwong Sang Hong International 143

labour conditions 37–8
Lai Fung 135
Lai Sun group 134
Lazard Asia 142
Lee Kwan Yew 27, 29–30, 86, 218
Asian values 74–8, 160
Leeson, Nick 159, 175–6, 185
Leung, Francis 184–5
Li Hongzhang 88
Li Ka-Shing 105, 134, 215, 247
Liem Sioe Liong 105–6, 166
Lim Por-yen 135
literacy 56
loans 10, 241–2

macroeconomic policies 59
Mahathir Mohamad, Dr 192, 194, 206
Asian values 74, 86, 145–6
currency fall 5, 11
Eastern supremacy 29–30
Malaysia
1997 currency fall 5
business owners 116
Chinese communities 167
corruption 163, 180–1
education expenditure 55
minority shareholders 154
national ideology 83–4
R&D investment 95–6
response to crisis 206–8
management 93–4, 110, 117–18, 253–8
Asian style 119–21, 257
cultural misunderstandings 112
face 113–14

Japanese style 119–20
multinational style 122
Western style 118–20
Mandelson, Peter 36–7
Marcos family corruption 35, 53, 171
merger and acquisition 249–50, 256–7
Mid-Continent Equipment Group 135
middle class, growth of 51–2
Moody's 43
morality of corruption 186
Morgan Stanley Dean Witter 41, 91, 103, 214
MSCI Emerging Markets 41

nepotism 160
Nissan 100, 255

Organisation for Economic Co-Operation 157, 170
Overholt, William 25
overproduction blamed for 1997 crisis 21
own-account trading 19

Patten, Chris 54
Peregrine group 143, 183–6
Phelan, John 24
Philippines
business owners 116
corruption 35
and IMF 225–7
Marcos regime 35, 53
prostitution 51
price earning ratios 38
privatisation of state companies 246–7
professional advisers 146–8
property market 46, 91
protection money 165
Proton cars 61

R&D investment 95–7
Ramos, Fidel 226
rating agenceis 43
Renong Group 108, 141
research see R & D
rights issues 136–7
risk, psychology of 18–20
robust incrementalism 231–2
Rohwer, Jim 26, 33

Salim group 105–6
Samart Corp 118–19
Samsung 103, 119, 153–4, 246, 251
San Miguel beer 99, 246
savings 56–7
share ownership 150–2
shareholders
independent directors 148–9